[2] **Alfred Tritschler,** *Airship Hindenburg: View Inside the Engine,* c. 1936

[3] **Jacques-Henri Lartigue,** *The Crystal Ball,* 1931

[4] **Nikolai Kubeev,** *May Day in the Red Capital,* 1932

[5] **Edmund Kesting,** *Dancer Dean Goodelle,* 1930

Tom E. Hinson, Ian Walker, and Lisa Kurzner

FORBIDDEN GAMES

SURREALIST AND MODERNIST PHOTOGRAPHY

THE DAVID RAYMOND COLLECTION

IN THE CLEVELAND MUSEUM OF ART

Distributed for the Cleveland Museum of Art by Yale University Press, New Haven and London

**THE CLEVELAND
MUSEUM OF ART**

Published on the occasion of the exhibition
*Forbidden Games: Surrealist and Modernist
Photography, the David Raymond Collection
in the Cleveland Museum of Art,*
October 19, 2014 to January 11, 2015,
at the Cleveland Museum of Art.

This project is supported in part by
Mark Schwartz + Bettina Katz.

The exhibition is sponsored in part by
the Robert Mapplethorpe Foundation.

The Cleveland Museum of Art is generously funded
by Cuyahoga County residents through Cuyahoga
Arts and Culture. The Ohio Arts Council helps fund
the museum with state dollars to encourage eco-
nomic growth, educational excellence, and cultural
enrichment for all Ohioans.

ISBN 978-0-300-20861-0 (casebound)
ISBN 978-1-935294-25-2 (paperback)

Library of Congress Control Number: 2014935068

Front cover: [30] Anton Stankowski, *Photo Eye,*
1927. © Stankowski-Stiftung Ltd.

Back cover: [12] Dora Maar, *Forbidden Games,* 1935.
© 2014 Artists Rights Society (ARS), New York /
ADAGP, Paris

Prepared by the Publications department of the
Cleveland Museum of Art, Barbara J. Bradley,
editor-in-chief

Edited by Amy Sparks, Jane Takac Panza, and
Kathleen Mills

Designed by Thomas Barnard III

Printed and bound by SYL Creaciones Graficas, Spain

Distributed by
Yale University Press, New Haven and London
302 Temple Street
P.O. Box 209040
New Haven, CT 06520-9040
yalebooks.com/art

The Cleveland Museum of Art
11150 East Boulevard
Cleveland, OH 44106-1797
www.ClevelandArt.org

Contents

[6] **Erwin Blumenfeld,** *Profile Study,* c. 1944

Foreword

This book introduces a fascinatingly varied group of 178 surrealist and modernist photographs assembled by art collector and filmmaker David Raymond. These extraordinary vintage prints from the 1920s through the 1940s were acquired by the museum in 2007 from Raymond's collection, one of the finest still in private hands. We are proud to celebrate this important acquisition with this first in-depth examination of a segment of our increasingly important collection of photography.

David Raymond assembled the collection with astute judgment and connoisseurship, seeking out works that reflect the eye in its wild state (*l'oeil à l'état sauvage*), a tenet of surrealism supplied by André Breton, founder of the first surrealist group in Paris. Raymond assembled works of both surrealism and modernism, two usually opposing movements that share a desire to bypass conventions about composition and content to experiment with new processes, materials, and subject matter.

This collection of work from fourteen countries in the Americas and Europe reflects an international movement to reimagine the photographic image. Acquisition of the Raymond collection was transformative for the Cleveland Museum of Art's photography collection, which lacked examples from this key period in the medium's history. Works by notable artists such as Hans Bellmer, Ilse Bing, Bill Brandt, Manuel Álvarez Bravo, Brassaï, Marcel Duchamp, Germaine Krull, László Moholy-Nagy, René Magritte, Man Ray, and Alexander Rodchenko were added as well as numerous rare examples of equally provocative but less well-known photographers. Special highlights are bodies of work by Georges Hugnet, Marcel G. Lefrancq, Roger Parry, and twenty-three photographs by Dora Maar, one of the largest holdings of her work in a public collection.

This book and accompanying exhibition mark the collection's first appearance in print or in a gallery. Tom E. Hinson, the museum's founding curator of photography, now emeritus, spearheaded the acquisition. He tells the story of how it came to the museum and discusses the philosophy and the psychology behind Raymond's collecting style. Photo historian Ian Walker of the University of South Wales sets the photographs into historical and historiographic contexts. Independent curator Lisa Kurzner delves into topics of special interest ranging from examinations of techniques such as photograms and photo collage to explications of the symbolism of the mannequin and biographical studies of Maar and Hugnet. While the essays are aimed at a general audience, information for scholars in the field is contained in the back matter, including artist biographies, full cataloguing information, and bibliographies.

Collection catalogues like this, along with the presentation of the collection on the museum's web site, provide an ongoing presence for art that is hidden from view most of the time due to its sensitivity to light and concern for its preservation for future generations. This volume serves as a virtual twenty-four-hour gallery and shines a perpetual light on work that stretches the formal limits of the photograph while delving into the dark recesses of the subconscious.

William M. Griswold
Sarah S. and Alexander M. Cutler Director

Acknowledgments

David Raymond's perspicacity, perseverance, and patience in assembling a remarkable collection of surrealist and modernist photography are the seeds from which this project arose. When it was acquired by the Cleveland Museum of Art through purchase and gift in 2007, he recognized the institution's role in preserving, displaying, and disseminating the collection and also gave generously of his time and information, all key to the successful cataloguing of the works.

Tom E. Hinson, the now emeritus founding curator of the museum's Department of Photography, discerned the Raymond collection's importance for this institution and set about acquiring it. The enthusiastic support of Timothy F. Rub, former director and chief executive officer of the museum, and C. Griffith Mann, former chief curator, encouraged the collections committee and board of trustees to agree to the purchase using monies from the John L. Severance Fund. David Raymond also generously donated several key works. Charles Isaacs of Charles Isaacs Photographs, Inc., New York, served as agent for the collection and was integral to the acquisition. The museum's commitment to researching the material and producing a book and exhibition continued under the leadership of David Franklin, former director, and Fred Bidwell, interim director.

Researching the collection, a lengthy and complex process, was accomplished by Tom Hinson and Lisa Kurzner, whose dedication, diligence, and scholarly acumen merits special recognition. The fruits of their considerable efforts are contained in this catalogue and will appear in educational and interpretive materials for the Raymond collection exhibition and whenever works from the collection are shown or published. Paul Messier, consulting photography conservator, was an important partner in this research and in preparing the photographs for exhibition, generously sharing his unique knowledge of the photographers' working methods. Guest essayist Ian Walker's essay brilliantly sets the works in the Raymond collection into their historical and historiographic contexts.

Numerous departments and staff within the museum have made essential and greatly appreciated contributions to the acquisition, research, documentation, and conservation of the art works and the preparation of the book and exhibition. Heidi Strean, director of exhibitions and publications shepherded the exhibition and book through staff transitions, and exhibitions specialist Sheri Walter was the organizational force behind the project. The exhibition was designed by Jeffrey Strean, director of design and architecture, and Jim Engelmann, exhibition designer. This elegant catalogue design is the work of senior graphic designer Thomas Barnard III. Others deeply involved include: Per Knutås, Joan Neubecker, and Moyna Stanton of Conservation; Kimberly Cook, Elizabeth Saluk, Gretchen Shie Miller, Tracy Sisson, and Mary Suzor of Collections Management; Robin Koch of Curatorial; Rachel Beamer, Barbara Bradley, Jane Takac Panza, and Amy Bracken Sparks of Exhibitions and Publications; Louis Adrean, Christine Edmonson, Beverly Essinger, Matthew Gengler, Betsy Lantz, and Marsha Morrow from Ingalls Library and Museum Archives; and Howard Agriesti and David Brichford of Photographic and Digital Imaging Services. Constantine Petridis, curator of African art, and Abram Shneyder of Protection Services provided translation assistance.

The international, diverse nature of the Raymond collection led to requests for information and assistance from experts around the world. Lisa Kurzner wishes to extend special thanks to Julian Cox for collegial support and to Virginia Zabriskie; Adam Boxer, Ubu Gallery; and Rodica Sibleyras and Messieurs Fleiss of Galerie 1900–2000. Heartfelt thanks are also due to the individuals and institutions below, all of whom generously shared information and expertise.

SCHOLARS
Dr. Helen Adkins, Patricia Almer, Damarice Amao, Christian Bouqueret and Eric Rémy, Aube Breton-Elléouët, Victoria Combalía, Magdalena Dabrowski, Larissa Dryansky, Jennifer Edwards, Lloyd C. Engelbrecht, Roxane Haméry, Dr. Gottfried Jaeger, Lewis Kachur, Stuart Klawans, Christiane Krauss, Dr. Ellen Landau, Steven Manford, Neil Matheson, Sarah McFadden, Dr. Christine Mehring, Hattula Moholy-Nagy, Francis Naumann, Rolf Sachsse, Kim Sichel, Dr. C. Zoe Smith, Adrian Sudhalter, Julia Van Haaften, and Bonnie Yochelson

MUSEUMS
Peter Zimmermann, Akademie der Künste, Berlin; Natasha Derrickson, Department of Photographs, Art Institute of Chicago; Dominique Versavel, Department of Prints and Photographs, Bibliothèque Nationale de France; Marguerite Vigliante, Department of Prints and Photographs, Brooklyn Museum; Leslie Calmes and David Benjamin, Center for Creative Photography, University of Arizona; Christian Clément, Director, and Annyck Graton, Cabinet de la Photographie, Centre Pompidou; Jochen Wierich, Cheekwood Museum of Art; Wim Van Sinderen, Fotomuseum, Den Haag; Virginia Heckert, Karen Hellman, and Paul Martineau, Department of Photographs, J. Paul Getty Museum; Claartje Van Dijk, International Center for Photography; Jean Drusedow, Director, and Edith Serkowrek, Kent State University Museum; Meredith Friedman, Department of Photographs, Metropolitan Museum of Art; Ulrich Pohlmann, Sammlungsleiter Fotomuseum, Münchner Stadtmuseum; Xavier Canonne, Director, Musée de la Photographie, Charleroi; Sonia Dinglian, Museum at Fashion Institute of Technology; Robert Knodt, Fotografische Sammlung, Museum Folkwang; Roser Cambray Cambray, Colleció de Fotografia, Museu Nacional d'Art de Catalunya; Del Zogg, Works on Paper and Photography Collections and Study Center, Museum of Fine Arts Houston; Sarah Meister, Roxana Marcoci, Mitra Abbaspour, Megan Feingold, and Tasha Lutek, Department of Photography, Museum of Modern Art; Rainer Stamm, Director, Niedersächsische Landesmuseen Oldenburg; Simone Foerster, Pinakothek der Moderne, Munich; Larissa Ivanova Ostrovskaya, Russian State Archive of Literature and Art; Peter Higdon and Valerie Matteau, Ryerson Image Center, Ryerson University; Sandra S. Phillips, Senior Curator of Photography, San Francisco Museum of Modern Art; Dr. Ludger Derenthal, Sammlung Fotografie, Kunstbibliothek, Staatliche Museen zu Berlin

ARCHIVES AND ESTATES
Aurelia Álvarez; Brigitte Berg, Jean Painlevé Archive; Yorick Blumenfeld; Agnès de Gouvion Saint-Cyr, Brassaï Archive; Robert Gurbo, André Kertész Archive; Peter C. Jones, Josef Breitenbach Estate; Sarah La Moy, Condé Nast; Jörg Lampertius, Ullstein Bild Picture Service; Peer-Olaf

Richter, Herbert List Estate; Katharina Roller, Anton Stankowski Archive; Thomas Sommer, Dr. Paul Wolff + Tritschler Historical Archive; Bruno van Moerkerken; and Pierre Zuber

AUCTION HOUSES
Judith Eurich, Bonhams and Butterfields, San Francisco; Stuart Alexander, Christie's, New York; Sarah Krueger, Phillips de Pury, New York; Denise Bethel and Emily Bierman, Sotheby's, New York; and Susanne Schmid, Villa Grisebach Auctionen, Berlin

GALLERIES
Nailya Alexander, Nailya Alexander Gallery, New York; Hendrik Berinson, Galerie Berinson, Berlin; Jan Ceuleers, Antwerp; Jane Corkin, Corkin Gallery, Toronto; Keith de Lellis, Keith de Lellis Gallery, New York; Hubert de Wangen, Galerie Kowasa, Barcelona; Barry Friedman, Barry Friedman, Ltd., New York; Christophe Gaillard, Galerie Christophe Gaillard, Paris; Howard Garfinkel, Productive Arts, Cleveland; Tom Gitterman, Gitterman Gallery, New York; Marion Grčić-Ziersch, Marion Grčić-Ziersch Kunsthandel, Munich; G. Ray Hawkins, G. Ray Hawkins Gallery, Los Angeles; Paul Hertzmann and Susan Herzig, Paul M. Hertzmann, Inc., San Francisco; Michael Hoppen and Tristan Lund, Michael Hoppen Gallery, London; Edwynn Houk, Edwynn Houk Gallery, New York; Paul Kopeiken, Kopeiken Gallery, Los Angeles; Jorge Mara, Galerie Jorge Mara–La Ruche, Buenos Aires; James Mayor, the Mayor Gallery, London; Priska Pasquer, Cologne; Serge Plantureux, Paris; Howard Read, Cheim & Read, New York; Andrew Roth, New York; Howard Schickler, Howard Schickler Fine Art, New York; and Leon Wilnitzky, Leon Wilnitzky Alte Kunst, Vienna

COLLECTORS
Foster Goldstrom, Robert Hamburger, Mark Kelman, Michael P. Mattis, and Dr. Barry S. Ramer

Barbara Tannenbaum
Curator of Photography

David Raymond: Inquisitive Collector

Serendipity and good fortune are frequently an art museum curator's silent partners. These benefactors were very much present, along with guiding advice by then director Timothy F. Rub, when on the lookout for a defined group of photographs. In late 2006 the Cleveland Museum of Art learned of the availability of one of the finest private collections of rare images created primarily by European photographers during the 1920s through the 1940s. It was assembled with energy and passion, insight and knowledge, skill and opportunity by David Raymond, an avid art collector, independent filmmaker, and producer from New York, now residing at the age of fifty-one in Asheville, North Carolina (fig. 1). The focus of the Raymond collection is primarily surrealist photography, showcasing the height of this important photographic movement, along with a strong interest in modernist photography. In 2007, through purchase and gift, the museum acquired 178 photographs—140 individual prints, two books, and a portfolio—from the larger Raymond holdings.

Raymond's journey shows how a private individual following a thread of interest can, over time, build a magnificently cogent collection by gaining knowledge about a period of art history and culture, developing personal taste to the point of trusting it, and then with skill and savvy traversing an ever-expanding and competitive art market. The development of Raymond's connoisseurship began in childhood. After the divorce of his parents, both immigrants from Iran, Raymond grew up with his mother in Huntington, Long Island, during the 1970s. His mother, who collected antiques and some art, had "an amazing sense of aesthetics."[1] Her brother, a fashion designer living in Palm Beach, Florida, was another early influence, bringing a diverse range of stimulating guests—filmmakers, painters, and art dealers—to his sister's home.

Raymond's lifelong interest in the medium of photography commenced at age eight, when he began taking photographs with a small Kodak camera with a flash cube while at a summer camp in New Hampshire. Later, in high school, he took classes in photography, becoming the darkroom attendant in order to have access to the lab and to follow his creative muse. Raymond enjoyed recording the world around him, finding, as he stated, "beauty everywhere" by searching out minute details in the visually ordinary.

In 1978, while still in high school, Raymond had another defining art experience, which he later identified as "a pinnacle moment in my appreciation of the arts." At the Whitney Museum of American Art in Manhattan, he saw the first traveling retrospective exhibition in the United States of the sculptor Duane Hanson's captivating yet unnerving life-sized sculptures of Americans from many walks of life. Raymond never forgot the impact of inhabiting the same space as these nearly lifelike figures. This was the first of many museum shows that made a deep impression on him.

After high school, Raymond spent the next four years majoring in international business at New York University; required courses were augmented by some photography art classes. After graduating in 1985, he moved to San Francisco, unsure what he would do, but fulfilling a desire to be close to his sister, Doris, nine years his senior. Raymond failed to find a job in

fig. 1 David Raymond

marketing, his concentration in college. Declining to accept proffered positions in sales, he turned to the classifieds and secured part-time employment in an art gallery on Union Street that specialized in selling the twentieth-century French artist Louis Icart's prints that epitomized the depiction of women during the art deco period. Raymond took away two lessons from his first job experience: "I was very good at selling art, and I was very interested in learning about connoisseurship." While working at the gallery, he began devouring art journals and spending hours in the art section of the San Francisco Public Library. Recalling the excitement of discovery, he stated, "It was just a moment of becoming a sponge." During this period of intense self-education, he happened to come across a catalogue by Rosalind Krauss and Jane Livingston, *L'Amour fou: Photography and Surrealism,* published to accompany a 1985 exhibition at the Corcoran Gallery of Art in Washington, DC. As Raymond colorfully put it, this introduction to surrealist photography "rocked my world." He traces the source of his determination to create a model collection of surrealistic photography to the catalogue's revelatory contents.

Raymond lived in California from 1985 to 2000, a period in which San Francisco enjoyed a vibrant, diverse photography community of practitioners, museum professionals, college educators, and collectors whose interests were nurtured by the region's art museums, non-

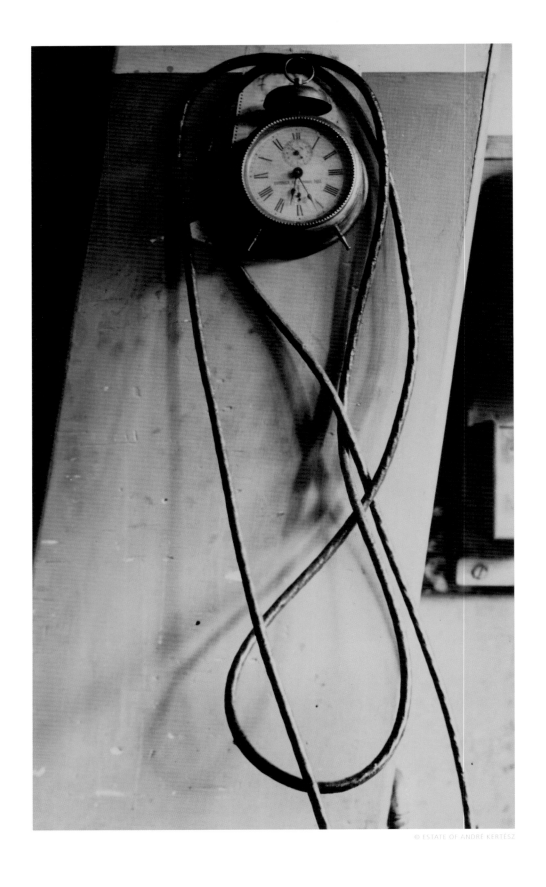

fig. 2 [7] **André Kertész,** *Clock and Rope,* 1928

profit spaces, and commercial galleries. Raymond's steady process of self-education greatly benefited from this pool of rich resources. He particularly credits the San Francisco Museum of Modern Art's photography collection, its photography curators (especially Sandra Phillips), and the photography department's support group, Foto Forum, for helping to develop his eye and exposing him to inherent subtleties of the medium produced by such factors as printing technique, paper, age, and rarity. "It was a wonderful opportunity to really dive in and learn in a deep way," Raymond remembered. "I also thought it was important not to just look at images but to look at as many original prints as possible. To touch them, to smell them, to look at the different watermarks on the backs of papers, to really feel the thickness, textures and to understand why a lot of photographers would print the same image on different papers." Raymond also gained a practical appreciation of how the saturation in the silver in different vintage papers affected the quality, and thus the price, of photographs.

After about a year and a half, Raymond left his gallery job, making the perilous decision to try his hand at private dealing and brokering. Ultimately, he met a Silicon Valley entrepreneur with the financial means and desire to start a painting collection. Initially interested in Norman Rockwell paintings, the collector later voiced a desire to assemble a group of photographs of California. "I started calling dealers and looking at what was coming up at auction," Raymond said. "Before I knew it, I acquired for him one of the best examples of Dorothea Lange's iconic *Migrant Mother* in 1992." This purchase soon made David Raymond's name known to the photography world. (The J. Paul Getty Museum in Los Angeles, for example, later sought his advice and assistance in assembling stellar holdings of images by Lange and the pioneering Mexican photographer Manuel Álvarez Bravo, who was featured in a 1939 issue of the surrealist magazine *Minotaure*.) Beginning in 1999, the relationship with the Getty lasted until 2005. In fact, Raymond maintains a comprehensive library to support his ongoing collecting, although with an emphasis on contemporary work. As part of his personal search for worthy purchases, Raymond was drawn back to the publication *L'Amour fou.* Although familiar with such important photographers as Man Ray and Hans Bellmer, Raymond did not yet know most of the principal photographers connected to surrealism, he admitted. Going through the catalogue again was an epiphany: "I felt like I had found my family." As Raymond began to research the artists and read the publications cited in this catalogue, he was struck by the relative accessibility of surrealist material. One could acquire reasonably priced works of major historical importance without stiff competition from other collectors. When his client declined to acquire the surrealist photographs being offered to him, Raymond, out of frustration, decided to personally take advantage of the enticing material being presented by dealers and auction houses.

Raymond purchased his first surrealist piece in October 1996 at a Sotheby's auction in New York City. He felt a strong visceral attraction to André Kertész's enigmatic *Clock and Rope* (1928) (fig. 2 [7]). "It was so purely surreal, that it was a recontextualization of objects that existed." Raymond soon found that he was "always drawn to works of art that challenge the way that we see the world. Whether it was dreamscapes, distortions, or skewed angles, I searched for works that gave me pause and revealed themselves to me over time."[2] This became a guiding principle for building his collection. The Kertész purchase also established a number of other criteria that would distinguish his holdings: rarity, print condition, and provenance.[3] In the end, however, it was the visually, intellectually, and emotionally charged nature of surrealist photographs that made them so innately appealing to Raymond.

Surrealism, as the budding collector grasped, provided a conceptual framework for photography to escape its traditional role as the literal depicter of nature, to abandon Renaissance perspective, and to introduce chance and irrationality. Surrealist photographers distorted time, space, and scale to create images that appeared to emerge from dreams. The medium was especially suited for expressing intuitive states of being and spontaneous effects. During the period between the two World Wars, photography with its arsenal of historic and new techniques provided artists with a seemingly infinite range of opportunities for manipulation of images as they were being taken or later processed in the darkroom.

Raymond responded emotionally to this flowering of experimentation and astounding juxtapositions quickly made permanent. "I love the fact that there are no limits. . . . It's just magical to me, so it was very important to represent all those types of creativity, in the realm of surrealism and modernism . . . in the collection." Indeed, his holdings evolved into a showcase of the surrealists' innovative use of such processes and techniques as photograms, solarization, montage, multiple exposure, collage, and hand manipulation by scratching, drawing, and painting.

With the bibliography in *L'Amour fou* as his springboard of inspiration, Raymond soon was actively searching for exhibition catalogues, monographs, and publications just on surrealism. He deemed it "absolutely essential" to build a personal library to support his collecting activities. "I was hungry for knowledge about the period," he said, "and would purchase every book I could get my hands on about surrealism and experimental photography."[4] Concurrently, he was also building an extensive group of auction catalogues, allowing him to track provenance and ferret out historical and other pertinent information on objects of interest that were new to the market or had previously been at a public sale. Armed with this often-spare data, Raymond was able to make remarkable purchases, often acquiring a unique or rare print.

A praiseworthy example of his hunt for iconic photography is *Georgette at the Table* (c. 1928–30) (fig. 3 [8]) by the Belgian René Magritte, one of the few surrealist painters actively involved in photography. Raymond easily recalled his reaction to first seeing this enigmatic scene of Magritte's wife and muse seated at a table arrayed with food with a blank canvas on an easel at her back. It was "so romantic and filled with love."

Although Raymond collected in other areas, photography became his passion. Financial resources played a role in determining his focus. "I had a limited budget so I would have to be careful where I spent what little there was," he explained. Asked if he had an annual limit for acquisitions, Raymond responded, "No, I didn't. I think if I had I would not have acquired as much if I had set a budget. I did what it would take to make it happen, and I would worry about it later."

Once focused on photography, Raymond made a fundamental decision to acquire vintage images—those made on or around the time the negative was created—whenever possible.[5] This choice was a key factor in the CMA's interest in the Raymond collection. Photographic papers used between the wars are extremely desirable because of the stunning variety of textures and levels of silver saturation they provided. Another defining characteristic of the Raymond collection was rarity, a CMA prerequisite. Before making a purchase, Raymond always did the necessary research to determine the number of extant prints, despite the unreliability of historic documentation and the fact that there was little financial incentive for surrealist photographers to make more than a handful of prints. If he consented to buy a later print, it was to fill in an artist missing from his collection or because of the image's historical importance, scarcity, or print quality. Raymond benefited from being in the right place at the right time. But he also sagely recognized that the opportunity to acquire stunning images in outstanding condition by historically significant photographers at fair prices would not last forever.

Counterbalancing the necessity of being strategic about the allocation of his limited resources, Raymond often relied on his gut instincts in determining whether to acquire a given photograph:

> One of the things that I've always listened to is what I call a buzz in my body. I believe that all things living or non-living have a vibration, and if you take the time to really be with an object or a person, you start to feel that energy and you sense it . . . I've always responded to that when I've acquired a work of art that I didn't necessarily have a lot of background on or know what it was. But it spoke to me and said, "I'm something of significance, and it would be in your best interest to live with me." I would purchase it, if I could, and it always, knock on wood, turned out to be a very good decision.

As a result of Raymond's openness, his holdings are notable for their remarkable breadth. Raymond moved easily across political and cultural boundaries, attracted primarily to European photographers working in France, Germany, Belgium, and the Netherlands as well as Russia, England, Mexico, and the United States. He was engaged by such art movements as Dada, surrealism, and Russian Constructivism, and catholic in his taste, he collected not just work created for artistic or experimental reasons but also images commissioned for advertising or news agency purposes or publication in fashion magazines. For Raymond, the binding aesthetic link is that the artist saw "the world in a different way."

fig. 3 [8] **René Magritte,** *Georgette at the Table,* c. 1928–30

After reaching a level of confidence and expertise, Raymond felt free to ignore prevailing art historical opinions in favor of making his own discoveries. Indeed, the process of stumbling upon a little-known photographer, researching his or her career, and then tracking down outstanding available work was immensely satisfying to Raymond, who said of the enterprise, "I can honestly say it is one of my most favorite things in the world to do—looking at images, discovering work and getting to live with it." Raymond's holdings were broadened, enriched, and made more special by his uncanny ability to home in on photographers not at the forefront of photography's lexicon, such as Herman Bekman, Horacio Coppola, Heinz Hajek-Halke, Vassily Komardenkov, Marcel G. Lefrancq, Marcel Mariën, and Édouard Léon Théodore Mesens.

Raymond relied on two primary sources of material by these and other surrealists: art dealers and auction houses. Although casting a wide net, he frequently worked with a group of gallerists who specialized in surrealist and modernist photography and had a gift for consistently assembling great inventory: Adam Boxer, Barry Friedman, Edwynn Houk, and Virginia Zabriskie in Manhattan and David and Marcel Fleiss in Paris. As a means of upgrading his holdings throughout his collecting of photography, Raymond would acquire and sell through dealers or collaborate with them as a partner on the purchase and sale of art.

Simultaneously, Raymond bought at auction through an expanding network that covered the United States, France, Germany, and occasionally Belgium. He found auctions an excellent and efficient method of staying in touch with potential vendors in distant locations, who in turn had the contacts to bring to market rare images by major surrealist photographers, as well as highly desirable ones by lesser known and appreciated practitioners. The arrival of new auction catalogues produced heart-pounding anticipation. Would they offer prints by artists he wanted to add to his growing collection? Since it was difficult to anticipate when or where vintage surrealist material might come on the market, Raymond was guided by his belief that "you must be ready to act and move when the opportunity comes."

A perfect example of serendipity was Raymond's acquisition of thirty-three Dora Maar photographs, the largest representation in private hands of this gifted artist who produced an impressive body of experimental photomontage and collage work and arresting street photography as well as having a successful commercial career. Of the twenty-three images by the artist acquired from Raymond by the CMA, sixteen were bought at auction. Put on the block in Paris in 1998 and 1999 by the Maar estate, this large body of photographs was unknown to most. Indeed, some French dealers questioned Raymond's sanity for spending so much money on the work. His belief in and admiration for the inventiveness and consistency of Maar's oeuvre never wavered. In fact, Raymond considers Maar's *Double Portrait with Hat* (c. 1936–37) (fig. 4 [9]) among the top ten photographs in his collection.[6] Created in the late 1930s while the artist was living with Picasso—her lover and muse—it is indeed a great example of her experimentation with multiple negatives and hand manipulation. The arresting result is a complex, Cubist-like deconstruction of a female portrait, with eyes gazing in separate directions.

After building his collection for more than a decade, Raymond came to think of his relationship to the photographs as that of "a custodian, a guardian." He felt that the pictures didn't belong to him but were "passing through my hands." Around 2006, as he began to think about the ultimate disposition of the collection, Raymond made a final purchase that, for him, rounded

fig. 4 [9] **Dora Maar,** *Double Portrait with Hat,* c. 1936–37

fig. 5 [10] **Man Ray,** *Lee Miller,* 1930

out his holdings. He had long been on the hunt for a photograph of the model and photographer Lee Miller, who was the assistant and muse of major surrealist photographer Man Ray in the late 1920s and early 1930s. His acquisition of Man Ray's *Lee Miller* (1930) (fig. 5 [10]), a visually perplexing yet beautiful portrait of the model, satisfied what Raymond considered "probably my biggest art crush."

Although Raymond had been generous in loaning art to museum exhibitions, his collection was of a size that only a small portion could be displayed at any one time. The responsibility of maintaining such a historically important body of work in the New York apartment to which he had moved in 2000 had begun to weigh heavily on him. Raymond decided that the time had come to find a new caretaker for the collection. He considered selling at auction, but that would have meant that his holdings would be widely dispersed. Preferring to create a legacy, he decided to sell to an art institution to ensure the collection stayed intact and would be publicly accessible and properly maintained. Fortuitously, a friend and neighbor, Charles Isaacs, was a private dealer in fine art photography specializing in nineteenth- and early twentieth-century material. After becoming the agent for the sale of the collection, Isaacs contacted the Cleveland Museum of Art, among other institutions.

The museum was interested in increasing photographic holdings created by European photographers active during the interwar years to better represent this period of exceptional innovation and creativity. The museum's surrealist holdings were nearly nonexistent and entirely lacking images by the iconic Russian artists El Lissitzky and Alexander Rodchenko. In fact, only thirteen of the sixty-eight photographers in Raymond's collection were represented in the museum's collection. Indeed, all the essential ingredients for a well-rounded, comprehensive addition to the museum's collection are present: unusual breadth and diversity of nationality, subject matter, and artistic intent represented through rare images of exceeding quality and preservation.

Raymond underscored the museum's motivation for the acquisition of his collection in reflecting on the reasons why it was sold: "The Cleveland Museum of Art truly understands and appreciates the uniqueness of this collection and the fact that these photographs are artifacts of the twentieth century. By selling this collection—a product of years of study, care, and great affection—to the CMA, I recognize that the works will be well cared for and present a wonderful opportunity for many to see and study at one of the finest institutions in the world."[7]

NOTES

1. All quotes, unless otherwise noted, are taken from recorded phone interviews between David Raymond and the author made on February 19 and 20, 2013.

2. From notes made during a phone interview between David Raymond and the author in early 2008.

3. This picture is one of only two known prints, the other given to the Fogg Museum at Harvard University by the pioneering dealer and collector of surrealism, Julien Levy.

4. Taken from an e-mail from David Raymond to the author on February 20, 2013.

5. Raymond's personal definition of vintage is that the print was produced within ten years of making the negative.

6. By e-mail on January 28, 2012, Raymond responded to the author's request with a list of favorites in the collection. The illustrations in this essay are from that special category.

7. Taken from notes made during a phone conversation in 2007.

IAN WALKER

The Latest Snapshot: Surrealist Photography Seen through the Raymond Collection

In the winter of 2009–10, the Centre Pompidou in Paris mounted the exhibition *La Subversion des images: Surréalisme, Photographie, Film*. With over four hundred images and other artifacts on display, it was certainly the largest showing of surrealist photography yet assembled. The accompanying catalogue contained 480 pages with texts by five authors and weighed more than seven pounds.[1]

La Subversion des images was the culmination of thirty years of research into the relationship between surrealism and photography. To my knowledge, the first exhibition devoted to the subject was staged in Cleveland: *Photographic Surrealism,* curated in 1979 by Nancy Hall-Duncan for the New Gallery of Contemporary Art.[2] The catalogue was comparatively slim and already the selection was a mix of the canonical (Man Ray, Ubac, Brassaï, Bellmer) and the questionable (Deborah Turbeville). From the start, it would prove difficult to distinguish between what was and wasn't "surrealist" in photography. The first French book on the subject followed in 1982; *Les Mystères de la chambre noire* by Edouard Jaguer was a much more ambitious volume, written by a participant in surrealist activity since the 1940s and containing a rich mix of work that came all the way up to 1980.[3]

For differing reasons, neither of these innovative projects received a great deal of notice. But the 1985 exhibition *L'Amour fou: Photography and Surrealism,* curated by Rosalind Krauss and Jane Livingston for the Corcoran Gallery of Art in Washington, DC, was a very different matter. It received widespread attention for a number of reasons. One was its internationalism: as well as Washington, the exhibition was shown at the San Francisco Museum of Modern Art, the Centre Pompidou in Paris, and the Hayward Gallery in London. The catalogue was also a weighty and authoritative volume, published in New York by Abbeville Press.[4]

But the most important element in this fame—notoriety even—was the status of its guest curator Krauss, one of the most combative and challenging art writers of the time. In her key essays in *L'Amour fou,* she set up a polemic that deliberately read the surrealism of the interwar years through the prism of 1980s post-structuralist theory. This led to some stretching of historical accuracy and an emphasis on images that bolstered Krauss's own arguments. Despite the all-encompassing implications of its subtitle, *L'Amour fou* in fact laid a heavy emphasis on surrealist photography that was manipulated, fragmented, or constructed; most of this work was made in the studio and had a claustrophobic air to it. But, in the process, the exhibition misrepresented or simply excluded other, contradictory areas of work—most notably that which reflected the surrealist fascination with the life of the city street.

Nevertheless, the polemical force of *L'Amour fou* was such that for a while it seemed to define the field of surrealist photography. But in the succeeding years, there appeared a series of publications and exhibitions that extended and often challenged the Kraussian hegemony. Books and catalogues published in Austria, the Czech Republic, the United Kingdom, Germany, and the United States have demonstrated just how widespread surrealist photography was and is, and how important it has been both for surrealism and for photography.[5] Few areas of surrealist practice have received so much recent attention, and by now any substantial account

fig. 1 [11] **Dora Maar,** *Fashion Study,* c. 1934

of surrealism would need to include photography alongside painting, sculpture, collage, and film as primary media with which surrealist artists worked.

We might, however, pause to look back and ask how it was that if surrealist photography was such a large and important subject, it had not been identified as such until the end of the 1970s, six decades after the founding of the surrealist movement. If one looks at, say, the massive catalogue for *Dada and Surrealist Art,* the major exhibition curated by William Rubin at the Museum of Modern Art, New York, in 1968, the overwhelming emphasis is on painting and sculpture, with the only photographic examples being Dadaist photomontages, Man Ray's rayographs, and Hans Bellmer's photographs of his doll (probably chosen not because they are remarkable photos but because the doll was a remarkable sculpture).[6]

But if one then jumps forward a decade to the equally large and seminal exhibition *Dada and Surrealism Reviewed,* staged in 1978 at the Hayward Gallery in London, one can see a seismic shift in the understanding of surrealism.[7] The major argument of the exhibition was that surrealism was best understood by examining the magazines that peppered its history. Due importance was given to those journals produced between the 1920s and the 1960s by the founding surrealist group in Paris led by André Breton, but there were also sections that acknowledged the importance of surrealism in Belgium, England, the United States, and Mexico (though Czech surrealism was not properly represented, presumably due to the political conditions of the time). Moreover, another section was centered on *Documents,* edited by Georges Bataille in 1929–30 in explicit opposition to the Bretonian version of surrealism. All this gave a much richer understanding of both the possibilities and the contradictions of surrealism. And, of course, when one looks closely at the range of images in all those surrealist journals, one realizes that many of them were photographs and, moreover, that the contributions made by Man Ray to *La Révolution surréaliste,* Jacques-André Boiffard to *Documents,* or Brassaï to *Minotaure* were absolutely central to the identity of each of those magazines.

What one was seeing in the shift between *Dada and Surrealist Art* in 1968 and *Dada and Surrealism Reviewed* in 1978 can also be put in broader terms: it was the shift from modernism to postmodernism. The more complex and indeed contradictory view of surrealism fitted with a more complex and contradictory view of art then emerging. In 1986 Dawn Ades, who had been the major author of the catalogue for *Dada and Surrealism Reviewed,* wrote, "It could be suggested . . . that it was precisely [s]urrealism's efficacity to have maintained a series of contradictions *without* resolution. But this is uncomfortable for a discipline [art history] which tends to work towards a unified view of individuals and movements, and to bestow value on them according to the measure of their unity."[8] But art history was also changing, and it was this very lack of unity in surrealism that was now compelling. As Simon Baker put it in 2007, surrealism "was not curated or assembled by a single author. It resulted from the gradual agglomeration of the diverging, often conflicting interests of individuals working both for and against the surrealist movement."[9]

It is not only surrealism that defies a closed and unified definition; so does photography. This was probably one of the reasons why the medium was not fully accepted into the canon of modernism and why it also came to be of great interest to artists, theorists, historians, and curators at the same time that surrealism did in the late 1970s. Later on in the same volume in which Ades remarked on the contradictions of surrealism, the photographic historian Ian Jeffrey ironically commented, "A 'history of photography' verges on the unimaginable. Such a history, if meant to be comprehensive, would be bewilderingly tangential and discontinuous. . . . Photography never lent itself readily to progressive narrative, to totalizing history, or to any sort of Great Unfolding, and in the general histories is always forced into shape, arbitrarily connected."[10] Thus it is that in studying surrealist photography, one must look at wildly different sorts of objects—great individual images by "master photographers" like Man Ray and Brassaï, certainly, but also the vestiges of popular culture: postcards, snapshots, and photo-booth pictures. Some pictures will stand on their own, but the surreality of others can only be understood by examining their context: the images they are placed next to, the text that accompanies them, or the publication in which they are sited.

These arguments are now three decades old, and we have come to accept and indeed celebrate fragmentation, lack of unification, and the permeable borders between media. In this context, *La Subversion des images* may have seemed like a definitive summing up of the field of surrealist photography, but in fact (and I'm sure the organizers were quite aware of this) no such finality is possible. Even in such a massive collection, there were still things missing. The latest work in the show dated from around the Second World War, but one couldn't, for example, understand the achievement of Czech surrealist photography without discussing the postwar work of Emila Medková and Vilém Reichmann.[11] And even within the exhibition's chosen time frame, there were geographical omissions: next to nothing from the United States, for example (one David Hare but no images by Frederick Sommer or Clarence John Laughlin).

What this account demonstrates above all is just how complex and entangled the relationship between surrealism and photography was and continues to be. In delving into it, one must take a dual approach. On the one hand, one needs to be as rigorous as possible in the placement of any particular work. Was it made by a member of a surrealist group? Was it shown in an exhibition organized by the surrealists themselves or reproduced in a book or journal published by them? Such a purely factual set of criteria will of course limit the range of eligible work, but perhaps such strictness is necessary. I recall a visit I made in 1979 to meet one of the surviving founding surrealists, Philippe Soupault, in Paris. What, I asked him, had been the surrealist position on photography? There had not been one, he replied, and, as regards surrealist photography, there was only Man Ray and perhaps, later on, Raoul Ubac, and they were surrealists first and photographers second.

As the field of surrealist photography has developed and spread, as volume after volume, essay after essay, exhibition after exhibition has appeared, with the number of photographs and photographers increasing exponentially, I have remembered that comment and wondered how to respond. One way would be of course to simply say that Soupault was wrong, or, more specifically, limited in his perception. But, as a member of the premier surrealist group in its earliest days, Soupault's view should be taken seriously; there *were* a lot of photographs in *La Révolution surréaliste,* but the fact they weren't necessarily thought about *as* photographs per se is instructive and tells us something about the surrealists' (anti-modernist) disinterest in media specificity. As Soupault might have put it, the magazine's illustrations were surrealist images first and photographs second (or perhaps, when they were photos of paintings or objects, even third).

But in all those books and exhibitions of "surrealist photography" that have appeared over the past decades, a good deal of the work exhibited and discussed was made not by core participants in surrealism but rather by artists and photographers whose relationship with surrealism was more peripheral and tangential. To place their work in relationship to surrealism is to find affinities rather than actual attachment to any particular surrealist group. But, as long as this is fully acknowledged, the claims made for these artists are important, for as one explores the field, one might discover that much of the most interesting work, both for photography and indeed for surrealism, was in fact not necessarily made within surrealism but rather in relationship to it.

So there is still work to do, and each reconfiguration of surrealist photography adds something to our sense of the subject. The Raymond collection is intriguing in this respect since it brings together a range of work that might not in other circumstances sit together. Some of it is well known and some of it previously unseen; some was made within the context of surrealism, but much of it was made at a distance. Both Man Ray and Ubac have work in the collection, but it sits alongside many other images that one would now want to call "surrealist" and to discuss within the context of surrealist ideas and imagery but whose relationship with surrealism is far from straightforward.

It is, however, difficult to generally describe this web of relationships, as each case is different and there are as many different positionings as there are artists. The best way to engage this issue is perhaps to look at some individual cases, and the Raymond collection offers a wide range of examples. Let us take, to start with, the two photographer-artists who are most heavily represented in the collection: Dora Maar with twenty-three images and Marcel G. Lefrancq with twenty-five. Each had a demonstrable relation with surrealism, but in both cases, it must be qualified in its specifics. Moreover, both Maar and Lefrancq made images that ranged across a wide spectrum of photographic genres, raising the question from another direction of just how we might identify photographic surrealism.

It is of course unjust that Dora Maar is best known as Picasso's mistress and that her most reproduced photographs are the (indeed invaluable) sequence documenting the development of his epic painting *Guernica* in 1937.[12] Perhaps, though, such an attachment to male genius is also still predictable. But before that, in the early and mid-1930s, she had made her own reputation as a photographer of verve and invention. As with many practitioners of the period, her work ranges from the commercially driven and commissioned to the personal, though that distinction may also be blurred. In the Raymond collection, there is one *Fashion Study* (fig. 1 [11]) that is clearly intended for a magazine context, but most of the other images seem to be self-initiated, deriving from either psychological, artistic, or social impulses.

Surrealism was certainly one of the contexts in which Maar operated by the middle of the 1930s—a surrealism that was no longer the preserve of a tightly knit revolutionary group, as it had been in Soupault's time a decade earlier, but more diverse and multifaceted, as its influence had filtered into the wider Parisian culture. Maar had good friends in that surrealist milieu—Jacqueline Lamba (the wife of André Breton), Paul and Nusch Eluard, the photographers Man Ray and Brassaï. She was one of the signatories of the 1935 declaration "When the Surrealists were right," attacking the French Communist Party for its refusal to collaborate with the surrealist group.[13] She exhibited three photographic works in the International Surrealist Exhibition staged in London in June 1936, and her photomontage *29, rue d'Astorg* (the address of her studio) was fifth in a series of surrealist postcards produced by Georges Hugnet in 1937.

A few of Maar's straight photographs evince a committed surrealist sensibility, most notably her well-known *Portrait of Ubu* (a close-up study of what seems to be an armadillo fetus in a glass jar), but it is in her photomontages that this affiliation is clearest. A photographic print of one of the best of these—*Forbidden Games* of 1935—is in the Raymond collection (fig. 2 [12]). The setting is a heavily decorated bourgeois room, but in the foreground, such respectability is undermined as a man in a suit (the father?) bends over and allows a semi-naked woman wearing a pince-nez and a severe expression (the mother or perhaps more likely the governess?) to ride him. From beneath the table, this scene is being observed by a small boy—the

fig. 2 [12] **Dora Maar,** *Forbidden Games*, 1935

son, one presumes, though he seems to have come from an alien reality. And indeed he has, for the Raymond collection also holds a print of the original photograph from which Maar took the boy: a photo looking down onto a group of street urchins playing on the pavement and surrounded by the feet of passersby [67].

This picture comes from a different area of Dora Maar's photography, one that might at first glance seem quite contradictory to her surrealist work. In the early 1930s, she photographed on the streets of her native Paris and, on two trips in 1933–34, Barcelona and London. She often concentrated on the poverty and deprivation she found there, and the Raymond collection holds several images in which she photographed, for example, a beggar woman hunched up on a pavement in Barcelona (fig. 3 [13]) or two men in London who seem to be singing for alms; one has a sign pinned to his jacket saying he is medically unfit for work (fig. 4 [14]).

These pictures hardly seem to be by the same photographer who contrived the elegant *Fashion Study* or the social satire of *Forbidden Games*; rather, they connect with the documentary attention to social reality that had developed during the same period in response to the Depression. But this disjuncture can be read as a quality endemic to photography and, as we will see, particularly to the artistic photography of the 1930s. (Her close friend Brassaï is represented in the Raymond collection not by the surrealist-inflected photographs he published in *Minotaure* but by some of the more documentary images of the Parisian demimonde he was making at the same time.) This diversity also of course says something about Maar's own sensibility, reflecting both her leftist beliefs and her attachment to the poetic and uncanny. Some of the most striking photographs she made on the street are of blind peddlers. One is struck not only by their particular vulnerability in adverse times but by the way these people seem to be staring, not into the unwavering eye of the camera, but up, away into space, somewhere unknowable, beyond ordinary vision.

If Dora Maar's work demonstrates one sort of ambiguous and complex relation with surrealism, that of Marcel G. Lefrancq demonstrates another. He was indeed a full member of a tightly knit surrealist group, but it was not the one based in Paris. Rupture was founded in the small Belgian town of La Louvière in 1934. There was of course already a Belgian surrealist group based in Brussels, with whom Rupture had an uneasy relationship; their own development had been profoundly influenced by the industrial unrest in southern Belgium, which had pushed their politics to the left. Lefrancq was the first visual artist to join the group in 1938; soon after, Rupture disbanded to reform as the Surrealist Group in Hainaut, the new title affirming a commitment to their province. At the end of the war, that group in turn reformed as Haute Nuit and Lefrancq took a leading role in its organization; it was he who wrote to André Breton in 1947 asking for their work to be included in the first postwar surrealist show in Paris, *Exposition internationale du surréalisme*. Breton agreed, but, it seems, due to internal politics, Haute Nuit members were not represented in the final show. When another group, CoBrA, was brought together in 1948 by activists from Copenhagen, Brussels, and Amsterdam, Lefrancq had an abstract photograph entitled *Pastorale* reproduced in the second issue of their journal.[14]

This account can only be a sketch of the bewildering shifts in alliances in European surrealism over the decade from the late 1930s to the late '40s, as surrealist groups and their affiliates formed and reformed across the continent. Lefrancq was connected to all that, yet he remained committed to his hometown of Mons, where, in 1946, he opened a photography shop and studio called La Lanterne Magique. He died in 1974, leaving behind a bewildering range of photographic work.[15] As with Dora Maar, some of this material has little apparent connection with surrealism, but that which does also operates across the wide gamut of surrealist photography.

In fact, to look through the twenty-five photographs by Lefrancq in the Raymond collection—all from a portfolio produced in 1948—is to witness a dazzling array of techniques and strategies. At one end are the straight, documentary photographs—the found images—but those in themselves vary from the ambiguous street scene in *Smoke* (fig. 5 [15]) to the tight close-up on a long-legged insect and its shadow in *The Enemy* (fig. 6 [16]). At the other end of the spectrum would be a number of abstracted, *informel* images in which the technique is hard to determine but which carry suggestive titles like *Scientific Objectivity, Crystallized Landscape,* and *Illustration for* The Adventures of A. G. Pym *by E. A. Poe* (figs. 7 [17], 8 [18], 9 [19]). In between those two extremes of the found and the created are a range of varied images, some of which use photographic techniques like photomontage or double exposure while others use different forms of staging. Perhaps the most memorable of the latter is *Eulogy of Carnage* (fig. 10 [20]), in which the camera looks up at a chair placed in an open natural setting. But the chair has been encircled by barbed wire, to which the clouds floating past offer an ironic counterpoint. It is the only one of Lefrancq's images in this collection that asks to be placed in history, for, created in 1946, the image cannot but allude to the recent war. In fact, many of the images by Lefrancq collected here were made in the postwar period and represent a rich outpouring of creativity, one that moreover was occurring at a point when many commentators had decreed that surrealism was over.

The examples of Dora Maar and Marcel G. Lefrancq are of course quite different, even as they together demonstrate the range of possible strategies open to photographers engaged with surrealism. Maar had a somewhat peripheral relationship with the central surrealist group in Paris while Lefrancq was a central figure in the provincial group in southern Belgium. But the point here is not to create a misleading unity but rather to demonstrate the heterogeneity of what we call surrealist photography. Each example, it seems, would offer a different take on that, and we might turn here from the work of Lefrancq and Maar, amply represented in this collection, to other photographers who are represented by just one or two images.

Take, for instance, the single photograph by Emiel van Moerkerken, a figure scarcely known outside his native Holland but whose early work demonstrates the compelling allure that surrealism could have for a young artist in the 1930s. He had discovered surrealism in 1934 at the age of eighteen and, in the following years, made several visits to Paris, where he met members of the surrealist group and made a number of intriguing documentary photographs. Back in Amsterdam in 1938, he encountered the poet Chris van Geel and, with several other artists and writers, they established a Dutch surrealist group that would continue its activities till the early '50s.

Among their first collaborations were a number of staged scenarios for the camera in which van Geel played the main character and van Moerkerken made the photograph. One of these, published in 1982 by Edouard Jaguer, featured a cage enclosing a doll-like mannequin's head, her face covered with fake spiders.[16] Van Geel was pictured leaning into the cage to kiss her. This was truly a joint work; according to van Moerkerken, "The cage belonged to Chris and the decorated doll's head was mine."[17] The photograph in the Raymond collection was obviously taken at the same session, but its effect is very different. In the first image, the room behind the cage is evenly lit and van Geel is being watched by an anxious, out-of-focus female face; in this picture, the background is completely dark and the foreground dramatically lit. Now van Geel has his gloved hands round the mannequin's neck, his hair is wild under a fedora, and he leers toward the camera like Fredric March playing Mr. Hyde (fig. 11 [21]). The effect is melodramatically parodic, playing off both popular images from horror movies as well as the

fig. 3 [13] **Dora Maar,** *Beggar Woman, Barcelona,* 1933

fig. 4 [14] **Dora Maar,** *Medically Unfit,* 1934

fig. 5 [15] **Marcel G. Lefrancq,** *Smoke,* 1948

fig. 6 [16] **Marcel G. Lefrancq,** *The Enemy,* 1935

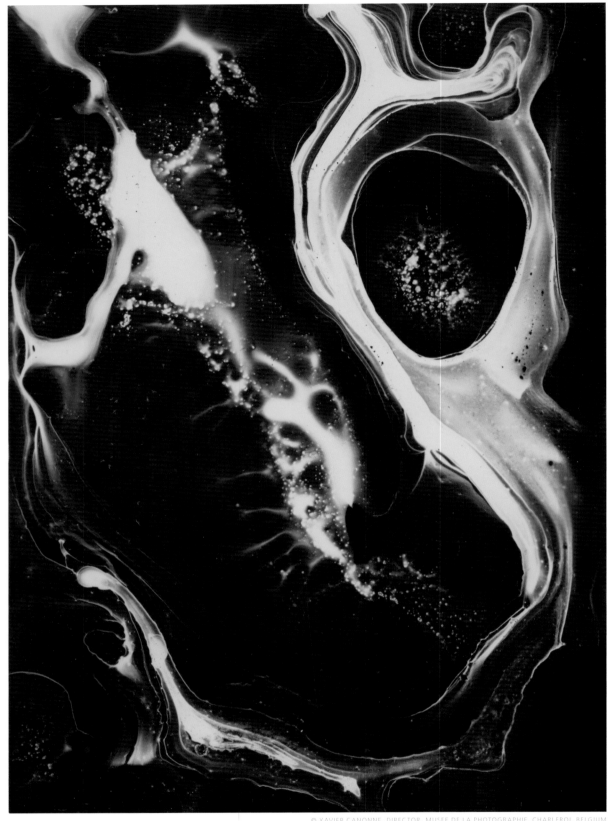

fig. 7 [17] **Marcel G. Lefrancq,** *Scientific Objectivity,* c. 1947

fig. 8 [18] **Marcel G. Lefrancq,** *Crystallized Landscape,* 1948

fig. 9 [19] **Marcel G. Lefrancq,** *Illustration for* The Adventures of A. G. Pym *by E. A. Poe,* 1948

fig. 10 [20] **Marcel G. Lefrancq,** *Eulogy of Carnage,* 1946

Dalían icon of the distressed mannequin in a cage. But it is a celebratory parody, the work of two young artists entranced by surrealism and its possibilities.

The photomontages of Dora Maar, the actions or proto-"happenings" staged by van Geel and van Moerkerken, and the sheer range of imagery produced by Lefrancq can be taken together to represent the diversity of surrealist experimentation with photography. None of these techniques was particularly new, and most had been exploited in the earliest decades of photography. What was new in the interwar years was how all these different ways of working with the medium came together in a rich mix of imagery. Sometimes it might seem like experimentation for its own sake, rather formulaic and repetitive, but in the best examples, it carries a genuine *frisson* that undercuts normality to arrive at something very unexpected. It continues to connect with our enduring fascination with effects that can only be achieved through photography: infinitely subtle and ineffable plays of light, different realities irrevocably soldered together, twists and distortions that yet acknowledge the factuality of the original object.

The manipulated photography of the interwar period represented something of a pan-European language and did not usually carry much national or regional cultural specificity. The other major impulse in surrealist-inspired photography, documentary or street photography, was usually much more particular to the place it was made. Brassaï, for example, was a photographer of Paris; indeed, his friend Henry Miller called him "the eye of Paris," and his photographs have become part of the mythology of the city.[18] Elsewhere, other photographers who felt an affinity for surrealism but, like Brassaï, resisted absorption into the movement likewise took an often askance and poetic view of their own cultures and, in the process, made images that now seem to be iconic representations of that culture.

Two such photographers, otherwise very different, were Bill Brandt in England and Manuel Álvarez Bravo in Mexico. Both are represented in the Raymond collection by a pair of photographs, each of which can be taken to represent a particular aspect of their work. It is perhaps ironic that Bill Brandt should have become the best known English photographer since he was born in Germany and always retained a heavy accent. But after he moved to London in 1933, he identified with English culture as perhaps only an émigré could. His position as an outsider also enabled him to see more clearly the uncanny and eccentric in that culture, and to this he brought his informed understanding of surrealism, gained while working as Man Ray's assistant in Paris in 1930. Yet he maintained his distance from the movement itself, as he developed a distinctive style of his own across a wide range of genres.

The two prints by Brandt in the Raymond collection come from opposite ends of his career and represent the range of his work (though, in fact, neither of them was made in England). The first is one of the earliest images that Brandt kept in his oeuvre: a picture taken on a visit to Barcelona in 1932 of an apparently blind beggar holding out his bowl for alms (fig. 12 [22]). It will of course remind us of Maar's images made in the city two years later, and together, the pictures suggest the sense in which pre–civil war Spain was a sort of "go-to" place for northern photographers looking for an acute sense of impoverishment. However, Brandt's beggar is not kneeling on a city pavement but in a deserted wasteland, which gives the picture an almost biblical quality. Overtly, the picture points toward the path of socially concerned documentary that Brandt would pursue after he settled in Britain the following year. But as with much of his documentary work, there is an unsettling quality to the image, and it might fruitfully be placed next to the documentary film *Land without Bread* that Luis Buñuel made in Spain in 1932, which dwells on a reality so extreme that it edges over into surrealism.

fig. 11 [21] **Emiel van Moerkerken,** *Surrealist Act with Chris van Geel,* 1938

The other photograph by Brandt is one of the few in the Raymond collection made after the Second World War. It dates from 1954, two decades after the Spanish beggar, and is one of a group of images entitled *Perspective of Nudes* in which Brandt photographed fragments of nude female bodies on the beaches of the English Channel;[19] this one, shot in Normandy, shows a giant foot, distorted by the wide-angle, deep-focus camera that Brandt used to make the images (fig. 13 [23]). Again, we might make connections with the "natural" surrealism of other English artists like Paul Nash, Eileen Agar, or Henry Moore, or with the biomorphism of Continental artists such as Arp or Miró, but, as elsewhere in his work, Brandt found his own distinctive way to work with such ideas. The very particular look of these images was in fact mainly due to his large and cumbersome camera—originally designed for the police to take all-inclusive images of crime scenes.

Another artist whose relationship with surrealism is tantalizing yet ultimately detached is the great Mexican photographer Manuel Álvarez Bravo, also represented in the Raymond collection by two images (though they join fifteen other photographs by Álvarez Bravo in the Cleveland Museum of Art's collection that help to amplify this discussion). When André Breton came to Mexico in 1938, he famously declared it "*the* Surrealist country," and back in Paris, he expanded on that perception in his essay "Souvenir du Mexique." He used a selection of photographs by Álvarez Bravo as key evidence: "The ability to reconcile life and death is doubtlessly the principal lure of Mexico. In this regard, it offers an inexhaustible range of sensations, from the mildest to the most insidious. There is nothing like Manuel Álvarez Bravo's photographs to reveal to us its extreme poles."[20]

One of the photographs Breton reproduced was *Ladder of Ladders* (fig. 14 [24]), and he described it thus in his text: "That workshop where they make caskets for children (the infant mortality rate in Mexico is 75%); the relationship between light and shadow, between the stacks of boxes by the ladder and the one by the gate, and the poetically dazzling image created by placing the phonograph horn inside the lower coffin are exceptionally evocative of the emotional atmosphere in which the whole country is steeped."[21] Breton starts here on a strikingly unromantic note, quoting the statistics of infant mortality, and he ends with a "poetically dazzling image," quite able to bring together, as in the picture itself, the apparent contradictory impulses of sociology and poetry. He sees a number of parallel relationships—between light and shadow, the stack of boxes and the one on its own, the coffin and the phonograph horn—which amplify and echo that duality between life and death with which he began.

But Álvarez Bravo had made that photograph seven years earlier in 1931, well before his encounter with surrealism. And he would later always resist a co-option into surrealism, arguing that he was rather documenting the reality of his own culture: "Many times my work, taken as a whole, has been related to surrealism. I believe that this is an equivocation. I believe that when a person is attentive to reality he finds all that is fantastic. People don't realize the fantasy that life itself contains. . . . When people look for it, they find a contact with that enormous surprise: reality."[22] The other photograph by Álvarez Bravo in the Raymond collection might exemplify that encounter. *The Balloon Seller* dates from much later, 1947, and is not a well-known image like *Ladder of Ladders*; it does not seem to appear in any of the major anthologies of Álvarez Bravo's work. It also looks much simpler: a record of a man on a Mexican street holding a bunch of balloons (fig. 15 [25]). Yet the way that the balloons occupy the center of the image, their vaguely biomorphic forms exploding outward and pushing the man himself to one side, makes one look again and find in this everyday encounter something strange and disorienting.

fig. 12 [22] **Bill Brandt,** *Barcelona,* 1932

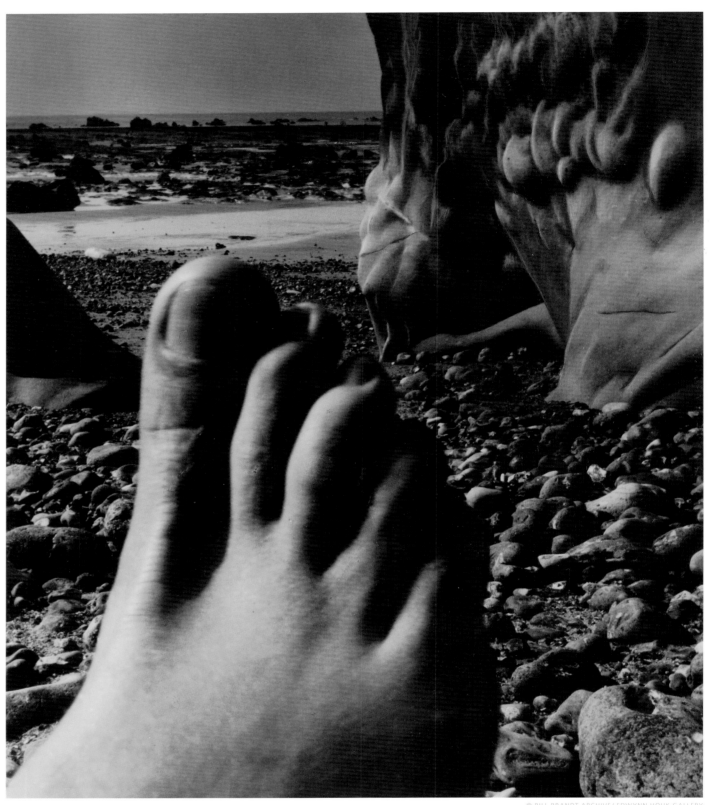

fig. 13 [23] **Bill Brandt,** *Nude, Vasterival, Normandy,* 1954

fig. 14 [24] **Manuel Álvarez Bravo,** *Ladder of Ladders,* 1931

fig. 16 [26] **Eli Lotar,** *The Day After,* 1929

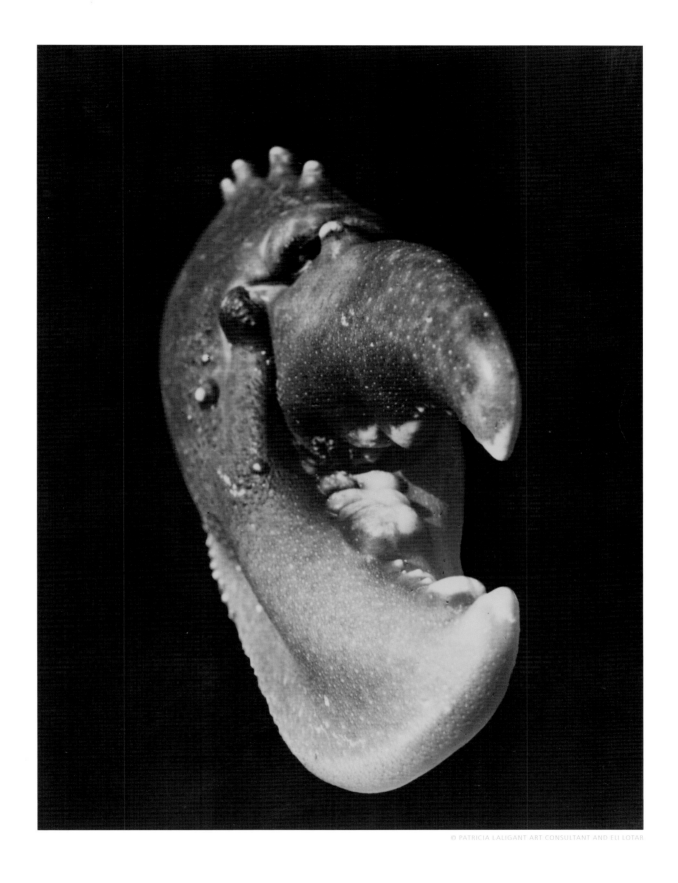

fig. 17 [27] **Jean Painlevé with Eli Lotar,** *Lobster Claw,* c. 1929

images like *The Day After* and the lobster claw. One can see a connection of course across these different pictures—a very conscious use of the photographic strategies of cropping and extreme point of view to construct the image—but the results are radically diverse and seem to sit in different places in the photographic landscape of the time.

Looking back, there are a number of different tendencies discernible in European photography during the interwar years. Pictorialism, the dominant trend in the art photography of previous decades, was still influential but often attacked for its soft-focus impressionism. In quite a different vein, there was photo-reportage, made with increasingly small cameras and published in the new illustrated magazines that were appearing first in Germany and then across Europe; the very terms "documentary" and "*documentaire*" had been coined in the late 1920s and by the '30s were commonplace. The two other forms of photographic practice—surrealism on the one hand and New Objectivity on the other—had their centers of gravity in France and Germany, respectively, and seem quite opposed in their fundamental values, both to each other and to Pictorialism and photojournalism.

Yet in practice, as we see with Dora Maar, individual photographers would wander across the apparent boundaries between these different types of work. If we were to look more widely—at the work of Brassaï, André Kertész, or Bill Brandt, for example—we would find a range of approaches to a range of subject matter. In a similar way, photographers who might appear on the periphery of a history of surrealist photography in Paris—figures like Roger Parry, Maurice Tabard, or Erwin Blumenfeld—also worked across genres and styles in ways that can be quite bewildering. Partly this was for financial imperatives since the only way to make a photographic career was by taking on a variety of projects and placing one's work where one could. But it was also because the very medium itself was in an inchoate state; nobody was quite sure what it could do, and a bubbling state of enquiry and invention was dominant.

So even those photographers most associated with New Vision photography could also produce surrealist-flavored work. Germaine Krull is represented in the Raymond collection not by one of her trademark images of dynamic industrial structures but by an arrangement of a woman's hands below the shadows of two nooses thrown up on a screen as well as a nude. Even artists working in Germany and committed to the New Vision in photography could produce images that emphasized strangeness and the uncanny. Examples in this collection might include Moholy-Nagy's heavily sarcastic collage *Mother Europe Cares for Her Colonies* (1925), Heinz Hajek-Halke's double-exposure *The Princess in the Backyard* (c. 1930), or Franz Roh's use of a negative image in *Woman with a Comb* (c. 1930).

Roh had also been the author of one of the key publications of the new German photography: *Foto-auge* (*Photo-eye*), published in 1929 to accompany the major exhibition *Film und Foto* in Stuttgart.[27] The first image in the book, leading this anthology of the latest New Vision photography of the period, was a photograph of a corset shop made by the Parisian photographer Eugène Atget before his death two years earlier. Thus, this photograph and Atget's work more generally was claimed for the New Objectivity. Yet this same picture had, in 1926, been reproduced in *La Révolution surréaliste* in a section entitled *Rêves* (*Dreams*). Even a single photograph could carry different meanings, depending on the context in which it was viewed.

The photograph by Atget in the Raymond collection is different yet again. It is a study of a large plant, a mullein, in bloom, made much earlier in 1897–99 (fig. 18 [28]). If this reminds us of anything, it is the intense scrutiny that the German Karl Blossfeldt was giving to his plant samples in photographs made during the same years but not published until 1928, when the

fig. 18 [28] **Eugène Atget,** *Mullein in Bloom,* c. 1897–99

images also became icons of New Objectivity.[28] Yet even Blossfeldt's images could cross over into a surrealist discourse, when Georges Bataille used them in *Documents* as illustrations for his essay on "The Language of Flowers."[29] In Atget's photo of the mullein, the sheet hung up behind it was of course used to provide a plain background when the image was cropped; the resulting photograph would have looked very much like one of Blossfeldt's studies. But, looking now at this print made from the full negative, we see a different and more ambiguous picture. As Maria Morris Hambourg remarked of a similar image of an artichoke plant posed against a sheet, "[t]he device produced . . . a better artichoke, but it made for odd pictures."[30] We look past the plant at the ad hoc and provisional presence of the white cloth in this rocky environment (rather like the *terrain vague* surrounding Brandt's Spanish beggar), a juxtaposition that gives this image an unexpected and unintended edge of surreality.

We could go on, subjecting each of the 178 photographs in the Raymond collection to the same scrutiny, and in the end, we would have 178 different and sometimes competing versions of this account of the hybridity of interwar photography. Our overall understanding of that history would grow ever more complex with each photograph. The photographs collected here suggest a range of connections and disconnections but not a further resolution. Loose ends are perpetually left dangling, the disregarded becomes the rather interesting, images made for one reason connect with others made for quite a different purpose.

This complexity is of course partly to do with the nature of a collection put together by one individual in response to his own taste; in that, it will differ from a more institutional collection that is, in theory at least, intended to be more objective and measured. But I think the hybrid and unsettled nature of this collection is also an effect of surrealism—how exactly can we define it and why does it continue to fascinate in ways that other modernist movements do not? It is also more specifically an effect of the uncertain status of photography within surrealism, within the avant-garde, and within the wider culture of the interwar period. And it's also to do with photography more broadly, which is almost impossible, it seems, to define, to categorize, and to control, always offering us tantalizing fragments from the dual realities—internal and external—that André Breton insisted must come together to constitute surreality.

The title of this essay incorporates a phrase from the recent translation by J. A. Underwood of Walter Benjamin's 1929 essay "Surrealismus: Die letze Momentaufnahme der europäischen Intelligentz" as "Surrealism: The Latest Snapshot of the European Intelligentsia" in Walter Benjamin, *One-Way Street and Other Writings* (London and New York: Penguin, 2009), 143–60. This supplements the previous translation by Edmund Jepcott, "Surrealism: The Last Snapshot of the European Intelligentsia" in Benjamin, *One-Way Street* (London: New Left Books, 1979), 225–39.

1. Quentin Bajac, Clément Chéroux, Guillaume Le Gall, Phillippe-Alain Michaud, and Michel Poivert, *La Subversion des images: Surréalisme, Photographie, Film* (Paris: Centre Pompidou, 2009).

2. Nancy Hall-Duncan, *Photographic Surrealism* (Cleveland: New Gallery of Contemporary Art, 1979).

3. Edouard Jaguer, *Les Mystères de la chambre noire* (Paris: Flammarion, 1982).

4. Rosalind Krauss and Jane Livingston, *L'Amour fou: Photography and Surrealism* (Washington, DC: Corcoran Gallery / New York: Abbeville Press, 1985). The catalogue also contains an important essay by Dawn Ades, "Photography and the Surrealist Text," 153–87.

5. Monika Faber, *Das Innere der Sicht* (Vienna: Osterreichisches Fotoarchiv im Museum moderner Kunst, 1989); Petr Král, *Fotografie v surrealismu* (Prague: Torst, 1994); Ian Walker, *City Gorged with Dreams: Surrealism and Documentary Photography in Interwar Paris* (Manchester: Manchester University Press, 2002); David Bate, *Photography and Surrealism: Sexuality, Colonialism and Social Dissent* (London: I. B. Tauris, 2004); Uwe M. Schneede, ed., *Begierde im Blick: Surrealistiche Photographie* (Hamburg: Kunsthalle / Ostfildern: Hatje Cantz, 2005); Therese Lichtenstein, *Twilight Visions: Surrealism and Paris* (Berkeley: University of California Press / Nashville: Frist Center for the Visual Arts, 2009).

6. William S. Rubin, *Dada and Surrealist Art* (New York: Abrams, 1968).

7. Dawn Ades, ed., *Dada and Surrealism Reviewed* (London: Arts Council of Great Britain, 1978).

8. Dawn Ades, "Reviewing Art History," in A. L. Rees and Frances Borzello, eds., *The New Art History* (London: Camden Press, 1986), 18.

9. Simon Baker, *Surrealism, History and Revolution* (Bern: Peter Lang, 2007), 22.

10. Ian Jeffrey, "Photography, History and Writing," in Rees and Borzello, eds., *The New Art History,* 98.

11. On the complex history of Czech surrealist photography, see Krzysztof Fijalkowski, Michael Richardson, and Ian Walker, *Surrealism and Photography in Czechoslovakia: On the Needles of Days* (Farnham and Burlington, VT: Ashgate, 2013).

12. See Mary Ann Caws, *Dora Maar: With and Without Picasso* (London: Thames and Hudson, 2000).

13. The text is translated in Krzysztof Fijalkowski and Michael Richardson, eds., *Surrealism Against the Current: Tracts and Declarations* (London: Pluto, 2001), 106–11.

14. For more detail on the history of Belgian surrealism, see Xavier Canonne, *Surrealism in Belgium 1924–2000* (Brussels: Mercatorfonds, 2007) and Patricia Allmer and Hilde van Gelder, eds., *Collective Inventions: Surrealism in Belgium* (Leuven: Leuven University Press, 2007).

15. See the web site run by Marcel G. Lefrancq's son Michel: www.lefrancq.be.

16. Jaguer, *Les Mystères,* 115.

17. Emiel van Moerkerken, *Foto's* (Amsterdam: De Bezige Bij, 1989), 170.

18. Henry Miller, *Max and the White Phagocytes* (Paris: Obelisk Press, 1938), 240–52.

19. Bill Brandt, *Perspective of Nudes* (London: The Bodley Head, 1961).

20. André Breton, "Souvenir du Mexique," in *Minotaure* 12–13 (1939): 32; Breton, "Memory of Mexico" in *Free Rein,* trans. Michel Parmentier (Lincoln: University of Nebraska Press), 24–25.

21. Breton, "Souvenir du Mexique," 32–35; "Memory of Mexico," 25.

22. Statement by Manuel Álvarez Bravo in Jain Kelly, ed., *Nude Theory* (New York: Lustrum Press, 1979), 9–10.

23. Lotar's photographs accompanied a dictionary entry by Bataille: "Abattoir," in *Documents* 6 (November 1929): 328–30.

24. For these images, see Annick Lionel-Marie, *Eli Lotar* (Paris: Musée national d'art moderne, 1993).

25. See Andy Masaki Bellows and Marina McDougall, *Science is Fiction: The Films of Jean Painlevé* (Cambridge, MA: MIT Press, 2000), 114.

26. See Kim Sichel, *Germaine Krull: Photographer of Modernity* (Cambridge, MA: MIT Press, 1999).

27. Franz Roh, *Photo-eye* (Stuttgart: Akademischer Verlag, 1929; reprinted in fascimile, New York: Arno Press, 1973).

28. Karl Blossfeldt, *Urformen der Kunst* (Berlin: Verlag Ernst Wasmuth, 1928).

29. Georges Bataille, "Le Langage des fleurs," *Documents* 3 (June 1929): 160–68; translated as "The Language of Flowers" in Allan Stoekel, ed., *Visions of Excess: Selected Writings 1927–1939* (Manchester: Manchester University Press, 1985), 10–14.

30. John Szarkowski and Maria Morris Hambourg, *The Work of Atget: Old France* (New York: Museum of Modern Art, 1981), 164.

fig. 1 [29] **Franz Roh,** *Nude in Light,* 1925

In discussing the Raymond collection, photomontage includes photographs made from more than one negative, producing effects of simultaneity and the conflation of several moments; much as in Cubist painting or in film, different viewpoints can be overlapped and presented seamlessly in a single image. By 1920 artists in Dada centers across Europe were experimenting with photomontage, understood then as an additive technique combining found photographic images with typographic elements. While this sort of photo collage work is fractured and full of jump cuts, the composite image favors effects of the film montage—smooth and seamless, without evidence of manipulation on the surface. First developed in the late 1920s and coming to full bloom around 1930, this second wave of photomontage took place in the darkroom and demanded skills honed in the service of consumer advertising. What began with the Dadaists and Russian Constructivists as a revolutionary call to arms became an effective tool of persuasion that quickly dominated high-end magazines in Europe and the United States. Among the surrealists, these techniques were adopted to convey interior states of mind and alternative, idealized realities with convincing renditions of objects shot in the studio. The virtue of these techniques—indeed, of photography itself—was debated throughout the international photography community around 1930.

A variety of photographic techniques contribute to the effect of photomontage, including double exposure, sandwiched negatives, and the addition of handpainting on the negative. In the Raymond collection, the earliest example is *Nude in Light* by Franz Roh (1925) (fig. 1 [29]), an art historian and contemporary art critic who championed the New Vision.[1] Roh's 1929 book *Photo-eye (Foto-auge),* designed with Jan Tschichold and based on the groundbreaking *Film und Foto* exhibition of 1929, was influential in establishing photography as a modernist tool. In seventy-six single-page images, Roh included photographs by well-known artists as well as anonymous police blotter crime scenes,

corporate advertising images, and film montages. In his accompanying essay, photomontage is cited as an exemplary vehicle for expressing the modernity of contemporary life.

Roh's photography consisted of personal photographs that he transformed into layered, multivalent images in ways that reveal his curiosity about the medium's properties and psychological capabilities. Overlapping nudes with quiet street scenes in a negative sandwich technique, Roh combined a long sequence of poses into one visual moment. His use of the Leica and 35 mm film increased his ability to sequence and conflate images. In some instances, he spliced together negatives outside of the camera, as in an image illustrated in *Photo-eye* that includes a negative image from the Raymond collection [125].

Anton Stankowski's *Photo Eye* photomontage (fig. 2 [30]), also produced in Germany, was a product of his influential study with graphic designer Max Burchartz in Essen in 1927–28.[2] This, like all the work of the later 1920s, exhibits a montage aesthetic produced in camera while also drawing on multiple techniques of darkroom manipulation. In this case, Stankowski transformed his mentor's most well-known image, *Lotte (Eye)*[3] (fig. 3), into a conflation of near and far, inner and exterior realities. The miniature portrait is Burchartz, seen gazing up at Lotte looming over him. Laid over her face is Burchartz's hairline, lifted from another Stankowski portrait of Burchartz behind the camera. The final result is a puzzling interpretation of an otherwise highly controlled New Vision portrait.

Heinz Hajek-Halke's experiments with photogram and photomontage techniques were admired and well known throughout Germany and Europe by 1930 when he made *The Princess in the Backyard* (fig. 4 [31]). Expressing the layering of time as a cinematic effect in his negative sandwich image, Hajek-Halke allowed the full view of the female portrait to be superimposed over the urban courtyard. His composite imagery was

fig. 3. *Lotte (Eye),* c. 1928. Max Burchartz (German, 1887–1961). Gelatin silver print; 32.5 x 44.2 cm. Von der Heydt-Museum Wuppertal Inv. F0321. © 2013 Artists Rights Society (ARS), New York / VG Bild-Kunst, Bonn

popular with both art magazine publishers and advertisers. He began using montage techniques in 1925; his "combi photographs" appeared in *Das Deutsche Lichtbild* magazine as early as 1928, and he published many books and articles on photographic technique, including *Light Graphic (Licht Graphik)* in 1964.

François Kollar's 1930 *Wood-Milne* (fig. 5 [32]) montage advertising rubber shoe soles is an early use of photomontage for advertising campaigns.[4] Photography in the service of advertising was well regarded in Paris. The photomontage was created after Kollar had established his own studio in Paris in April 1930. Signed "Kollar" in the negative as well as on the mount, this print may have been made for an early solo exhibition.[5] Kollar assembled a series of masked images that he applied in various combinations in both personal and advertising work throughout the 1930s. Thus, the globe in this image, signifying the international reach of Wood-Milne products, reappears elsewhere.

Maurice Tabard and Roger Parry worked closely together from 1929 to 1932, while Tabard was perfecting a double exposure method he dubbed "simultaneous impressions." An acquaintance of the Paris surrealists, Tabard extended his technical prowess to explore the dream states of surrealist painting and film. Exhibited in the *Film und Foto* exhibition, *Dancer Georges Pomiès* (1929) (fig. 6 [33]) is one of a series he made of the popular modern dancer at the Salle Pleyel, Paris.[6] Using multiple negatives and expressive shadows, Tabard captured the elastic expressiveness of Pomiès, who often performed alone on stage to avant-garde music.

Roger Parry's *Double Exposure, Woman on Bed* (1933) (fig. 7 [34]) best exemplifies what modernist photography gained from contemporary cinema: the shared

interest in expressing the passage of time, private emotional states, and conflicting public narratives that were central themes of the surrealists. In the early 1930s, both film and still photography relied on the same 35 mm film stock, thus presenting enormous opportunity for darkroom experimentation favored by Man Ray and others. Commissioned as the set photographer on Jean Vigo's film *L'Atalante* (released in 1934), Parry printed two shots from different moments of the film in this image, giving form to the heroine's sexual longing for her missing husband through the superimposed memory of their shared adventure earlier in the film. This conflation is Parry's alone and does not appear in the film. He relied on the favored surrealist dream state to establish a visual round robin in this image: the protagonist, featured upside down, stares up at the photographer (and viewer) while a smaller version of her gazes at her recumbent self. Thus, we are all implicated in imagining the sensual daytime dalliance in this image.

NOTES

1. In 1925 Roh penned his best-known essay, "Nach Expressionimus," in which he coined the term *magical realism* for the highly defined German painting style. With Jan Tschichold, he organized the 1929 *Photo-eye (Foto-auge)* book based on the *Film und Foto* exhibition in Stuttgart in 1929. Roh published essays on Aenne Bierman and Lázsló Moholy-Nagy. Correspondence with Raoul Hausmann at the Getty Research Institute as early as 1921 suggests Roh was involved with photographic theory by this early date.

2. An image that Stankowski considered one of his most important, it was reprinted at different times: once in 1927, in a late edition in the 1980s, and during his time in Stuttgart, 1938–40, when the Raymond collection print was made.

3. *Lotte (Eye)* was included in both the *Film und Foto* exhibition and the *Photo-eye (Foto-auge)* publication that emerged from the show. It also appeared in Arts et Métiers Graphiques annual *Photographie* 16, no. 31 (March 1930), edited by photographer Emmanuel Sougez, also represented in the Raymond collection.

4. Wood-Milne, a British company, had a robust advertising campaign in billboard posters as well as illustrated magazines. Kollar published his campaign in *L'Illustration.*

5. The print also carries the stamp of the following studio, where he moved in 1934. Kollar's work was singled out in the European photography survey *Das Lichtbild* in Munich. He also showed at the Galerie de la Pléaide, Paris, in 1934. For the rise of advertising photography studios in Paris, see François Denoyelle, "La Lumière de Paris-Les usages de la photographie 1919–1939," in *Collection Champs Visuels* (Paris: Éditions L'Harmattan, 1997), 2:149–226.

6. A variant of this image was reproduced in the *Photographie* annual of 1930, no. 125. The complete series of portraits by Tabard and Parry were included in Pomiès's memoir: *Danser c'est vivre. Georges Pomiès, témoignages et documents* (Paris: Éditions Pierre Tisné, 1939). Parry befriended Pomiès during his student years. See also Inka Graeve, "Internationale Ausstellung des Deutschen Werkbunds Film und Foto," in *Stationen der Moderne,* exh. cat. (Berlin: Berlinische Galerie, 1989), 269.

fig. 2 [30] **Anton Stankowski,** *Photo Eye,* 1927

© MICHAEL RLETZ

fig. 4 [31] **Heinz Hajek-Halke,** *The Princess in the Backyard,* c. 1930

fig. 5 [32] **François Kollar,** *Wood-Milne,* 1930

WOOD-MILNE

KOLLAR

© MAURICE TABARD

fig. 6 [33] **Maurice Tabard,** *Dancer Georges Pomiès,* 1929

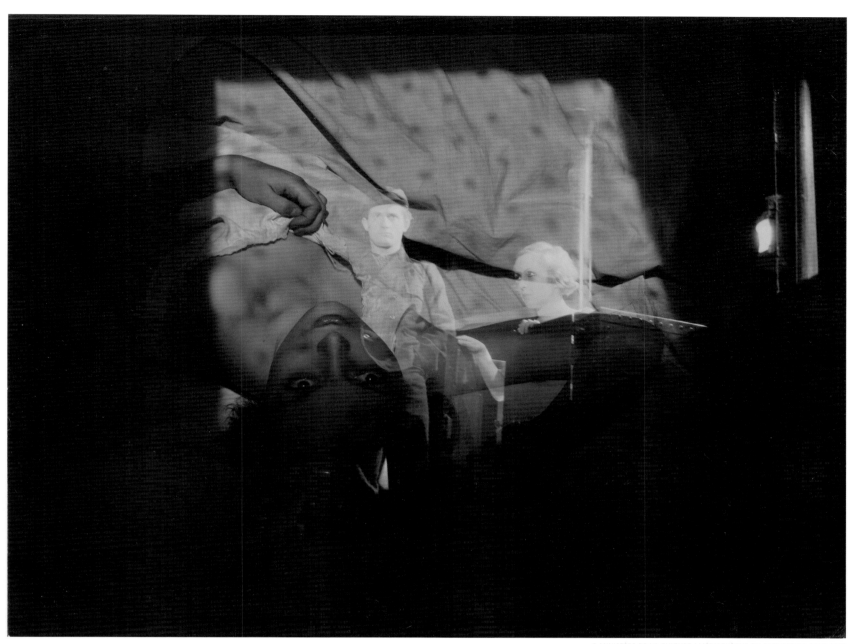

fig. 7 [34] **Roger Parry,** *Double Exposure, Woman on Bed,* 1933

[35] **Ernst Schieron,** *Montage,* 1930s

[36] **John Gutmann,** *That Inward Eye,* 1949

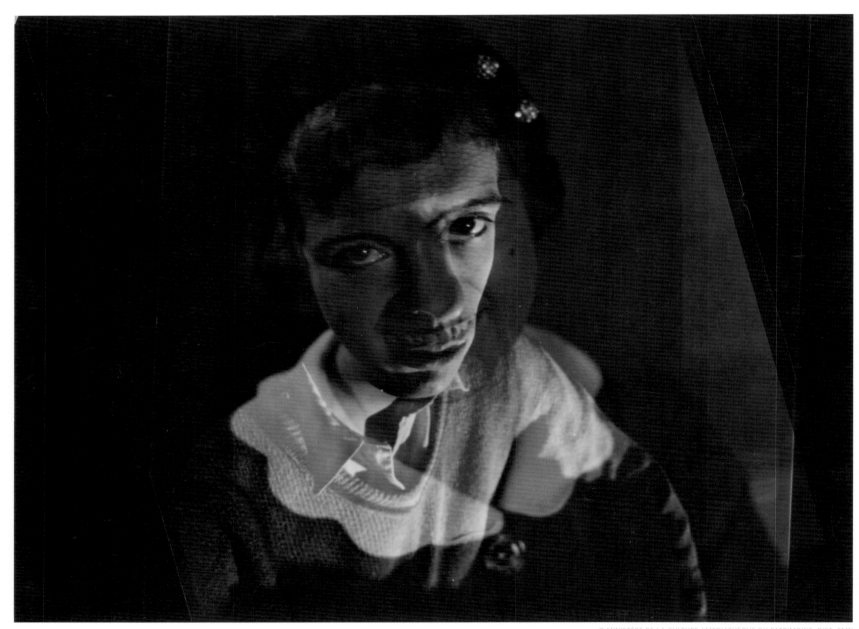

[37] **Roger Parry,** *Double Exposure, Robert Couturier,* 1931

[38] **Thurman Rotan,** *New York Montage,* 1928

LISA KURZNER **PHOTO COLLAGE**

Following World War I and into the 1920s, the Dada movement gained momentum in European capitals: Berlin, Moscow, and Paris. Founded in Zurich in 1916, Dadaism rejected conventional, premeditated notions of aesthetics in visual, literary, and performing arts and prompted a strong visual voice through its followers' inventive use of photographic imagery via collage. By grafting images from popular sources onto photographs, artists offered surprising, often shocking juxtapositions, creating many more interpretations than could the original images. At the center of the Berlin group was John Heartfield, working with his brother Wieland Herzfelde, and George Grosz. Best known for collaged images conceived as newspaper covers for the *AIZ* (*Arbeiter-Illustrierte-Zeitung*) magazine, Heartfield adapted the moniker *monteur* to support the practice of cutting and pasting photographic imagery, much like an engineer would assemble machines from various industrial parts. Interestingly, the photo collage technique initially telegraphed leftist concerns of classless society and social change, but it eventually aligned with the mercantile interest of the consumer advertising community that blossomed in Europe by 1930.[1]

The Raymond collection includes photo collages spanning several countries and purposes by key artists of the genre. Erwin Blumenfeld, an early advocate of the Dada photo collage, often collaborated with his childhood friend Paul Citroen. Indeed, Citroen credited Blumenfeld with inspiring his popular *Metropolis* collage (1923) (fig. 1). George Grosz and John Heartfield shared Blumenfeld's passion for American sports and popular culture, all celebrated in the Weimar-era illustrated press. *Boxers over New York* (fig. 2 [39]) is one of several Blumenfeld collages on boxing, a popular sport in the 1920s.[2] Blumenfeld took images of Jack Johnson fighting Jim Jeffries in 1910 for the world heavyweight championship and glued them to an aerial photograph of Manhattan, probably taken from the zeppelin's 1924 transatlantic flight from Germany.[3] Conscious of Europe's mounting anti-Semitism, Blumenfeld focused

on racial injustice and the marginalized classes in his photographic work of the 1920s. In *Boxers,* all the photographic prints date from about 1910 to the mid-1920s; similar stock images of these celebrities exist in the Berlin-based Ullstein picture agency archives.[4] As in his other early montage works, Blumenfeld fixed cut-out images atop a complete photograph rather than a background assembled from many sources. The collage is signed in block letters directly on the image: "BLOOMFIELD," an Americanized pseudonym, interlocked with "DADA HOLLAND," clearly placing this work within the international Dada movement.[5] Though steeped in the activities of his Berlin Dada associates, by 1923 Blumenfeld had moved to Zandvoort, where he made collages perhaps as an outlet to combat the docile society there. This particular collage was most likely made in this context, years after he left the volatile milieu of Weimar Berlin.

fig. 1. *Metropolis,* 1923. Paul Citroen (Dutch, 1896–1983). Collage; 76.1 x 58.4 cm. Collection Leiden University Library, Special Collections. © 2013 Artists Rights Society (ARS), New York / Pictoright Amsterdam

72

fig. 2 [39] **Erwin Blumenfeld,** *Boxers over New York,* early 1920s

László Moholy-Nagy's *Mother Europe Cares for Her Colonies* (fig. 3 [40]), alternately entitled *Birthmark Salome (Muttermal Salome),* was made in 1925 at the Bauhaus. It was exhibited in his first retrospective exhibition in 1935 in Brno and reproduced in the May 1936 issue of *telehor,* which was dedicated to his work and writings by the architect František Kalivóda.[6] That print remained in Brno in the collection of architect Otto Eisler and eventually found its way into the Raymond collection.[7] In Moholy-Nagy's seminal 1925 book *Painting Photography Film,* he first defined his practice of photo collage—*fotoplastik*—as a more advanced form of Dada's cut-and-paste activity, one only fully realized in the reproduction of an original collage.[8] Fotoplastik, translated roughly as "photo-sculpture," consists of mounted, applied, and retouched elements of different photographs, says Moholy-Nagy, "assembled on one plane . . . making for easier intelligibility, even revelation of an otherwise hidden meaning."[9] The compressed interpenetration of activity in the layered photo collage aptly captured for Moholy-Nagy the fragmentation of the modern urban environment. Here, the fotoplastik is a photograph of a collage of reassembled newspaper images. An African mother with a distressed child is named *Mother Europe,* suggesting the artist's attention to ethnography, a new field of cultural study dovetailing with criticism of European colonialism.

In post-revolutionary Russia, graphic arts and montage were components of the workshops of VKhUTEMAS (state artistic and technical workshops), where Vassily Komardenkov was active in theater and set design in the early 1920s. In his study for a film poster (fig. 4 [41]), photomechanical images and type lyrically interact on a large sheet of drawing paper. This fanciful image belongs to the Dada spirit more than to the political *faktura* of the early Russian Constructivists and indicates a date in the mid-1920s.

In Barcelona, Pere Català i Pic applied montage theory to business and political revolution, creating deft photo collage advertisements for corporate clients while also providing graphics and broadsides to the Catalan government. *Advertising Montage* (fig. 5 [42]), an amalgamation of several of his original photo collage advertisements, illustrated an article on psychology's effect on changing public opinion in 1933.[10] Like his Russian counterparts, Pic applied the sleight-of-hand techniques to both shock and persuade his audience.[11]

Horacio Coppola, who studied photography at the Bauhaus, found a restrained, formalist solution to the political commentary collage in *Royal Wedding* (fig. 6 [43]). Assembled by arranging newspaper text and photomechanical imagery into a three-dimensional composition, the collage conflates the image of a royal wedding with London stock exchange tables.

As supported by the surrealists and their wider circle, collage allowed the maker to splinter meaning with the intention of circumventing received ideas in favor of a more private, nuanced significance.

NOTES

1. For montage as an allegory of disruption and illustration of Apollonian and Dionysian duality see Hanne Bergius, "'Dada Triumphs!' Dada Berlin, 1917–1923, Artistry of Polarities," in *Crisis and the Arts: The History of Dada* (New York: G. K. Hall, 1996), and Brigid Doherty, "'See: "We Are All Neurasthenics"!' or, the Trauma of Dada Montage," *Critical Inquiry* 24, no. 1 (Autumn 1997): 82–132.

2. Helen Adkins, *Erwin Blumenfeld: I was nothing but a Berliner, Dada Montages 1916–1933* (Ostfildern: Hatje Cantz, 2008), 123, 126, pl. M88.

3. On German adulation of American skyscraper culture, see Beeke Sell Tower, *Envisioning America: Prints, Drawings, and Photographs by George Grosz and his Contemporaries, 1915–1933* (Cambridge, MA: Busch-Reisinger Museum, Harvard University, 1990).

4. Ullstein Bild archive, image by Philipp Kestner 00046524, 1920 at www.Ullsteinbild.de.

5. Adkins, *Erwin Blumenfeld,* 98–106, especially 61 and note 20 on the format and dating of Blumenfeld's Dada signatures.

6. Lloyd C. Engelbrecht, *Moholy-Nagy: Mentor to Modernism,* 2 vols. (Cincinnati: Flying Trapeze Press, 2009), 355, for the 1935 exhibition checklist from František Kalivóda, ed., *Výstava László Moholy-Nagy katalog* (Brno: Dům umění města, 1965). Fotoplastik discussed on pp. 313–14. The image has been reproduced with both titles: in the 1935 show as *Muttermal (fotoplastik)* and in the 1936 article as *Mutter Europa.*

7. The fotoplastik works begun in 1924 draw as much from the Berlin Dada group as from the Constructivist circles. *Muttermal* can be compared to other works in the J. Paul Getty Museum's collection, in which Molohy-Nagy produced an unaltered photograph of a photo collage assembled from photographic reproductions obtained from various sources.

8. Irene-Charlotte Lusk, *Montagen ins Blaue: Laszlo Moholy-Nagy, Fotomontagen und -collagen 1922–1943* (Giessen: Anabas, 1980), 84–85, and Julie Saul, *Moholy-Nagy Fotoplastiks: The Bauhaus Years* (New York: Arts Press, 1983), no. 48. The original collage of newspaper photomechanical reproductions glued to cardboard is in the Bauhaus-Archiv Berlin (inv. nr. 773), signed in pencil by the artist and inscribed *Muttermal (Salome).*

9. Moholy-Nagy, "Fotografie ist Lichtgestaltung," *Bauhaus* 1 (Dessau: Bauhaus, 1928) as reproduced in Krisztina Passuth, *Moholy-Nagy* (New York: Thames and Hudson, 1985), 303–4.

10. Fritz Giese, *Psicotecnia,* trans. Miguel Gonzáles (Barcelona: Editorial Labor, 1933), 11.

11. Jordana Mendelsohn, "Desire at the Kiosk: Publicity and Barcelona in the 1930s," *Catalan Review* 18, nos. 1–2 (2004): 191–207.

fig. 3 [40] **László Moholy-Nagy,** *Mother Europe Cares for Her Colonies,* 1925

© ROSER CAMBRAY

fig. 5 [42] **Pere Català i Pic,** *Advertising Montage,* c. 1932

fig. 4 [41] **Vassily Komardenkov,** *Film Design,* mid-1920s

fig. 6 [43] **Horacio Coppola,** *Royal Wedding,* 1934

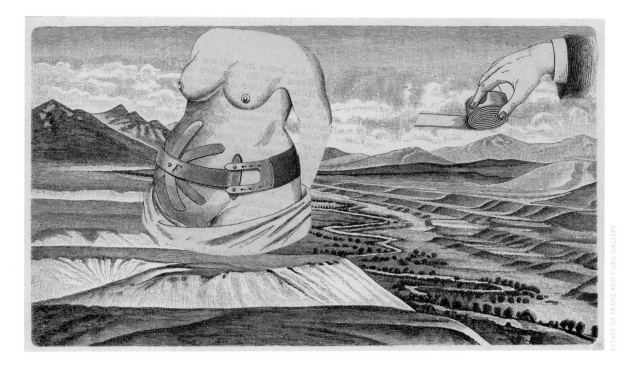

[45] **Franz Roh,** *Fitness Training in the Colonies,* 1930s

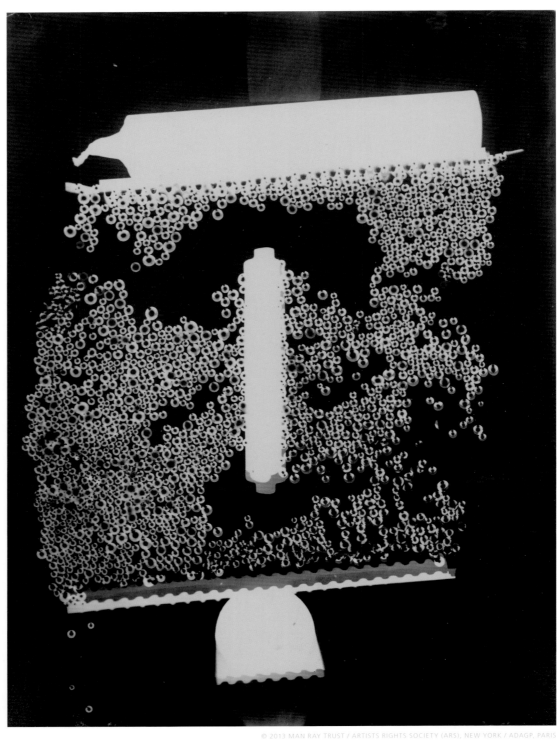

fig. 1 [46] **Man Ray,** *Untitled (Rayograph),* 1926–28

After 1918, when European social and cultural structures were nearly destroyed by World War I, the avant-garde sought innovative visual forms to express a new age and political order. The camera-less technique of the photogram, a common tool for early photographers, was adopted by experimental artists in several European arenas. Its popularity was encouraged by new photographic papers in the marketplace, as well as by the ease in creating without a darkroom or studio. By moving the camera away from the eye and body, the photogram allowed artists to reorder their world in radical ways. Artists could harness reality while circumventing the hierarchal one-point perspective created by the camera lens. The direct contact between the object and the printing surface in this unique form of photographic printmaking appealed to artists who sought the purest expression of material unmediated by emotion or human psychology.

The photogram output of the interwar period, 1918 to 1940, reflects Dada, surrealist, and Russian Constructivist movements, all represented in the Raymond collection. The French circle was dominated by Man Ray, who, after 1922, was well known for his rayographs. His inventive output, early exhibitions, and publications ensured his influence throughout the decade and beyond. *Untitled (Rayograph)* (1926–28) (fig. 1 [46]) capitalizes on the photogram's ability to explore positive and negative space and take translucency itself as a subject. The glass plate in this piece probably holds the glass beads that appear in other compositions of 1926–28 and in the 1923 short film *Le Retour à la Raison.* Also recognizable is a household candle, shown in high relief, and an industrial light tube, making this a composition about light sources—or photography itself.

E. L. T. Mesens, the Belgian artist and surrealist point man in Brussels, was captivated by Man Ray's first photographs in Paris. They engaged in a close correspondence, and Mesens began making camera-less photographs in 1926. His untitled photogram (c. 1926) (fig. 2 [47]) made on printing out paper (or daylight paper) is one of a very small number of photographic prints he produced before turning exclusively to collage in the 1930s. Like Man Ray in his early rayographs, Mesens selected recognizable objects to place across the paper: a drinking glass and a razor blade, part of a grooming ritual he treated reverently.[1] This early work exemplifies Mesens's childlike fascination with the medium, witnessed by the repeated appearance of the blade in varying degrees of resolution.

The 1928 *Film Negative* (fig. 3 [48]) by Emmanuel Sougez takes as its subject a strip of flexible 35 mm film, a product recently brought to the market for the cinema and photography industries. This print was made from a photogram negative that reverses the shade values, rendering the paper white and the strip of film dark. The delicate range of precisely controlled shadows suggests a watercolor effect and remains in keeping with Sougez's focus on pristine negatives and printing. Sougez was a skilled picture editor and promoter of the New Vision aesthetic in French photography, which consisted of highly precise execution in both the studio and darkroom as well as luxurious printing, seen in the photographically illustrated magazines of the 1930s.

By the mid-1920s, Russian Constructivist principles were evident in experimental photography in Russia and Germany. El Lissitzky and Oskar Nerlinger were then exploring the formal and political potential of the photogram to express the essentials of weight, depth, and form in abstract photographic imagery. Nerlinger's *Arrival at Sea* (c. 1928) (fig. 4 [49]) belongs to a series of photogram sketches for a children's fairy tale film that was never produced. Using a simplistic, mechanical vocabulary to underscore the worker's inextricable links to twentieth-century industrial society, Nerlinger created shadowy, geometric forms with cutout layers of tissue paper. He believed these photograms produced a specific magical effect best suited to fantastic subject matter.

Lissitzky's *Mannequin* (c. 1928) [52] similarly represents mankind, specifically the photographer who overcomes the limitations of materiality through the photographic practice. A variant of this image, of a mannequin looking at a photo through a magnifying lens (fig. 5), illustrated a 1929 polemic on "photographic writing (*fotopis*)," in which Lissitzky extolled the virtues of photography, that is, the expression of form through light. He defined form through what is absent: "[W]ithout a camera, we use the conscious organization of the light sources . . . to [construct] shadows which would render the object most characteristically."[2] By a process of reprinting positive and negative images, Lissitzky created form and depth in his silhouettes. In attempting to define the essential properties of photography in terms of the medium alone, he revived a Constructivist aesthetic at a time when content-driven, propaganda images were the norm in the Soviet Union. The artist included a positive variant of this photogram in an oversized print in his installation of the Russian section of the 1929 *Film und Foto* exhibition in Stuttgart.

At the same period in America, however, the photogram retained its telegraphic nature as sleight of hand used for advertising. Edward Quigley's *Photogram (Number 9)* (fig. 6 [50]) (1931) brings the typographic experimentation of Constructivism into bold form, conflating the overhead flatness of the paper into a legible and pleasing pattern. Joseph Breitenbach's *Fireworks* (1949) (fig. 7 [51]) reprises the method used during the photographer's teaching stint for a class on photograms at the Cooper Union school. In selecting the velvety rich Imperato paper to expose a dandelion stem, the photographer invites the viewer to imagine the light-drawn silhouette as a burst of sparks in the night sky.

NOTES

1. George Melly, *Don't Tell Sybil: An Intimate Memoir of E. L. T. Mesens* (London: Heinemann, 1997), 137–38.

2. El Lissitzky, "Photography (*fotopis*)," in Sophie Lissitzky-Küppers, *El Lissitzky: Life, Letters, Texts* (London: Thames and Hudson, 1968), 70.

fig 5. *Untitled (Mannequin)*, c. 1928. El Lissitzky (Russian, 1890–1941). Photogram; gelatin silver print, 29 x 21.4 cm. Russian State Archive for Literature and Art, Moscow. © 2013 Artists Rights Society (ARS), New York

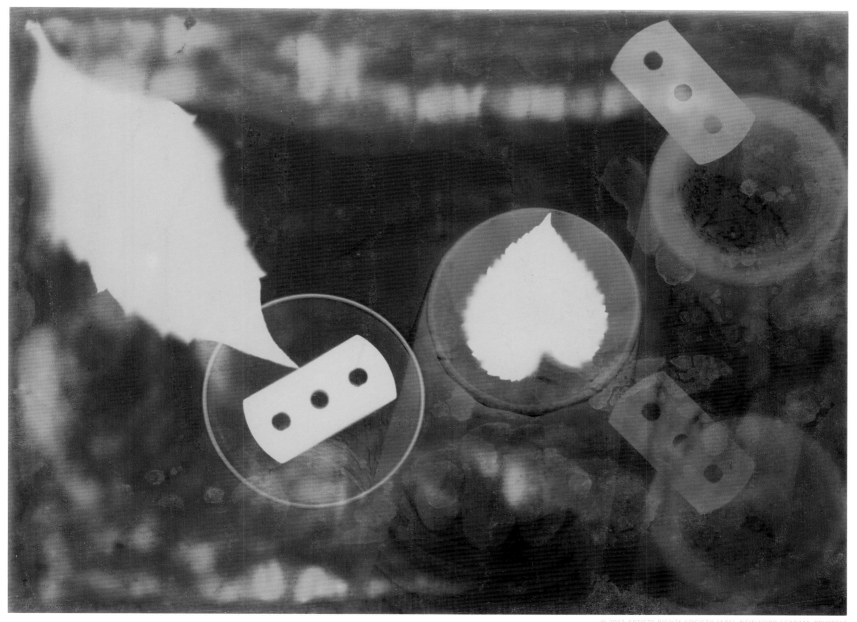

fig. 2 [47] **E. L. T. Mesens,** *Untitled,* c. 1926

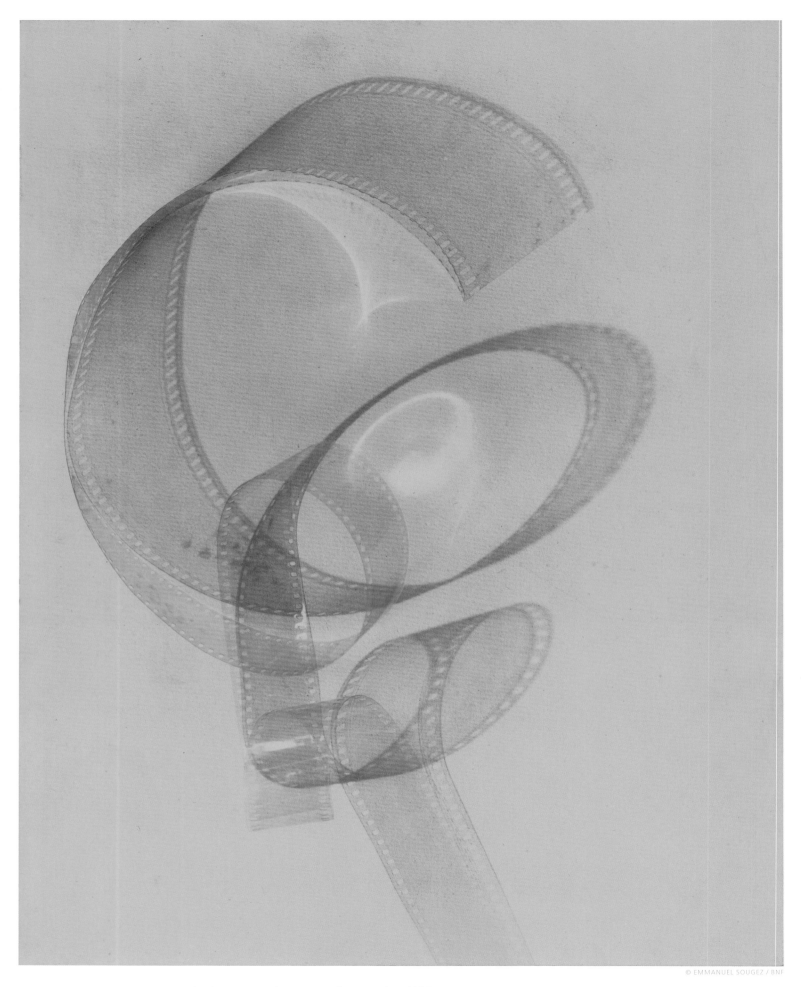

fig. 3 [48] **Emmanuel Sougez,** *Film Negative,* 1928

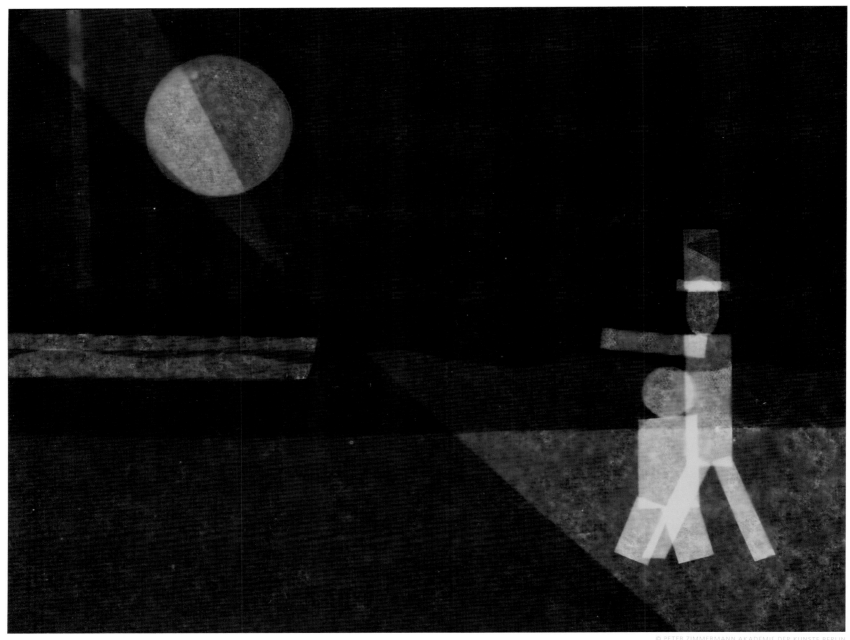

fig. 4 [49] **Oskar Nerlinger,** *Arrival at Sea,* c. 1928

fig. 6 [50] **Edward Quigley,** *Photogram (Number 9),* 1931

fig. 7 [51] **Josef Breitenbach,** *Fireworks,* 1949

The surrealists were fascinated by the culture of the mannequin and doll in theater, literature, and commercial production. As described and depicted in literature and visual work of the 1920s, the doll, in all its imagery, was potent subject matter.[1] Industrial and consumer culture led to increased presence of the doll as shop displays in wax, wire, or porcelain. With their lifelike resemblance, these figurines used to sell fine clothes and luxury items were photographed as early as 1900 by Eugène Atget and were well known to the avant-garde by 1930, if not earlier.[2] But the mannequin was not just an empty shell. The artists also ruminated on and gave power to the supposed, possible interior life of the mannequin. In a 1934 issue of the surrealist journal *Minotaure*, novelist René Crevel closed an essay on the interior life of a female mannequin posed on a Paris sidewalk, writing "[t]he grand mannequin . . . her antennae, her dreams will lead her to the secret of mankind."

The doll's lifelike qualities belie her inanimate form—something Sigmund Freud described in the 1919 essay "The Uncanny," in which the doll is a symbol of death and Eros, an example of "doubling" and of being both alive and static. The photographed doll highlights the parallel relationship of life and death naturally ingrained in photography—the camera freezing a moment that was once alive but now is not. It captures the duality of reality and fiction in its very nature.

Several dolls appear in the Raymond collection that date from the late 1920s and 1930s. From the jointed, wooden architect's model used by El Lissitzky in his *Mannequin* photogram (c. 1928) (fig. 1 [52]) to the mannequins dressed and photographed by artists in the 1938 surrealist exhibition in Paris, the collection reflects how this subject fascinated the avant-garde. Whether faceless and anonymous or a celebrity likeness, handcrafted or extruded from a mold, the doll was a lightning rod for exploring the newest ideas of mass psychology, unconscious desire, and political commentary.

fig. 1 [52] **El Lissitzky,** *Mannequin,* c. 1928

The Doll (1934) (fig. 2 [1]) by Hans Bellmer evokes the private, obsessive aspect of surrealist fascination with the doll. Made of papier-mâché over wire armature by the artist in Berlin, the life-size doll was photographed in a variety of lurid poses in a series intended to protest the idealized Aryan culture of the Nazi regime in Germany.[3] When published by André Breton in *Minotaure,*[4] Bellmer's doll photographs resonated deeply with the Parisian surrealists, who remarked on their psycho-sexual power. This first series of doll images, published as a volume in 1936 in Paris,[5] emphasizes the dissection of separate parts. Yet, this doll image, with the uncanny glance and tilt of the head over the shoulder, displays a shocking sense of vivid humanity that transcends the brutal aspect of its creation.

Herbert List, another German on the surrealist periphery, photographed dolls, mannequins, and tailors' dummies in both the studio and outdoors. Initially attracted by the otherworldliness of Giorgio de Chirico's *pintura metafisica* paintings as well as Man Ray's photography, he mined the double-edged, animate/inanimate qualities of mimetic human likeness in his work.[6] His photographs of classical statuary and commercial display dolls telegraph physical and psychological attributes through select posing and certain photographic angles. *Sant Angelo, Ischia* (fig. 3 [53]), a close-up of a doll resting in the sun on the island of Ischia, Greece, is one of a series List made around 1937. He deepened his surrealist exploration of the theme in studies of the wax figures of famous personalities at the Praüschers Panoptikum, an installation established in 1871 in Vienna. List planned a photographic essay on the wax figures, but it was never published.[7]

Herbert Matter's *Shirley Doll* (fig. 4 [54]) was made on assignment for *Fortune* magazine soon after the artist's arrival in New York in 1936.[8] The accomplished graphic designer immediately began a successful career in editorial photography. His contact prints from the assignment contain both assembly-line shots of mass production as well as other more chaotic images of half-dressed dolls crowded into boxes. This image of dressed dolls missing their hair and tumbling across a bed seems to be taken in a studio, judging by the setting, the strong shadows (from the photographer's lamp?), and a pile of photographic prints arranged in the upper-right corner.

Wols began his artistic career as a photographer before developing the body of painting and graphics of *art informel,* a form of gestural but delicate abstraction, from the 1950s onward. He was in Paris twice, first in 1932–33 and then in 1937–39, when *Antique Seller, Paris* (fig. 5 [55]) was probably made.[9] During his first period in Paris, Wols was attracted by the empty expanses of the city's outskirts and made several photographs of the flea markets located along Paris's periphery.

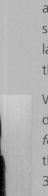

fig. 2 [1] **Hans Bellmer,** *The Doll,* 1934
© 2013 Artists Rights Society (ARS), New York / ADAGP, Paris

The second period marked his great success as a photographer, when he was awarded a lucrative commission as official photographer of the Pavilion of Elegance at the International Exposition in 1937. He made thousands of pictures of fashion mannequins, from straight narratives to disturbing nighttime images that were more fragmented in nature. Wols transposed that experience to the street in *Antique Seller,*[10] the commensurate found surrealist picture. It depicts a faceless soldier mannequin standing guard over the old dame seated outside her shop, a shadowed doorway almost filling the frame. Most noticeable is the elongated shadow of the figure, signaling its double life.

The 1938 *International Surrealist Exhibition* at the Galerie des Beaux-Arts Paris[11] marked the culmination of surrealism as a participatory experience in which the artists acknowledged the movement's adaptation into mainstream culture. Several artists were invited to dress fashion mannequins installed in the exhibition's Street of Mannequins in the exhibition. Raoul Ubac and Gaston Paris were among the photographers who recorded the sensational sculptures created for the show (figs. 6 [56], 7 [57]). While Ubac was well ensconced in the Paris surrealist circle at this time, Paris was a photojournalist working on stories for *VU* and other magazines. His spread on the exhibition appeared in *Marianne,* including the work in the Raymond collection. Both photographers captured the mannequins made by Salvador Dalí and André Masson, respectively, with the electric fervor of the exhibition itself.

Indeed, the photograph—reflective and transparent, a way into an altered world—goes hand in hand with how the doll was treated in this intellectual environment.

NOTES

1. From André Breton's novel *Nadja* (1928) to the mechanized robots and automatons of Dada works and Russian Constructivist theater, the mechanized body prevailed. See Hal Foster, "Exquisite Corpses," in *Compulsive Beauty* (London and Cambridge, MA: MIT Press, 1993), 125–56, and Rosalind Krauss, "Corpus Delecti," in *L'Amour fou, Photography and Surrealism* (New York: Abbeville Press, 1985), 56–112.

2. Atget's photographs were published in 1930. An excellent source for the topic of the doll in twentieth-century art and photography is Pia Müller-Tamm and Katharina Sykora, eds., *Puppen, Körper, Automaten: Phantasmen der Moderne,* exh. cat. (Düsseldorf: Oktagon/ Kunstsammlung Nordrhein-Westfalen, 1999).

3. Bellmer's dolls are the subject of numerous studies. For this interpretation, see Therese Lichtenstein, *Behind Closed Doors: The Art of Hans Bellmer* (Berkeley: University of California Press; New York: International Center for Photography, 2001). Also, Sue Taylor, "Hans Bellmer in the Art Institute of Chicago: The Wandering Libido and the Hysterical Body," *Art Institute of Chicago Museum Studies* 22, no. 2 (1996): 150–65, 197–99.

4. Hans Bellmer, "Poupée: Varations sur le montage d'une mineure articulée," *Minotaure* 6 (Winter 1934–35): 30–31.

5. Hans Bellmer, *La Poupée* (Paris: Editions G. L. M., 1936). Translated from German by Robert Valençay. Bellmer published a second series of photographs of a second doll, *Les Jeux de la Poupée.*

6. Esther Ruelfs, "Mannequin oder Model?," in Müller-Tamm and Sykora, *Puppen,* 336–63, summarizes this tension in the categories of figurines populating early twentieth-century urban culture.

7. Günter Metken, *Herbert List Photographs 1930–1970* (New York: Rizzoli, 1981). Thanks to Peer-Olaf Richter of the Herbert List estate for discussing the theme of the doll in List's work.

8. The final article, "Dolls—Made in America," *Fortune* 14, no. 6 (December 1936): 103, did not publish this image. Many thanks to Dr. Ellen Landau for furnishing the spread and copies of Matter's contact sheets that are part of the artist's archive of his American work at Stanford University.

9. This image is not dated by the scholars of Wols's photographs, Laszlo Glozer and Christine Mehring, nor is it contained in any of the published negative file documents preserved by his widow Gréty. Edouard Jaguer dates it as circa 1937 in *Les Mystères de la Chambre Noire, le surréalisme et la photographie* (Paris: Flammarion, 1982), 107; however, Glozer notes the artist's visual familiarity with Paris in *Wols Photographe,* exh. cat. (Paris: Centre Georges Pompidou, Musée national d'art moderne, 1980), 58.

10. This print carries a stamp from the artist's rue du Varenne studio, where he lived in 1937.

11. The latest work on the exhibition is by Annabelle Görgen, *Exposition Internationale du Surréalisme Paris 1938* (Munich: Schreiber, 2003). See also Lewis Kachur, *Displaying the Marvelous: Marcel Duchamp, Salvador Dali, and Surrealist Exhibition Installation* (Cambridge, MA: MIT Press, 2001), and Uwe M. Schneede, *Die Kunst des Surrealismus Malerie, Skulptur, Dictung, Fotografie, Film* (Munich: Verlag C. H. Beck, 2006), 202–14.

fig. 3 [53] **Herbert List,** *Sant Angelo, Ischia,* 1937

fig. 4 [54] **Herbert Matter,** *Shirley Doll,* 1936

fig. 5 [55] **Wols,** *Antique Seller, Paris,* c. 1937

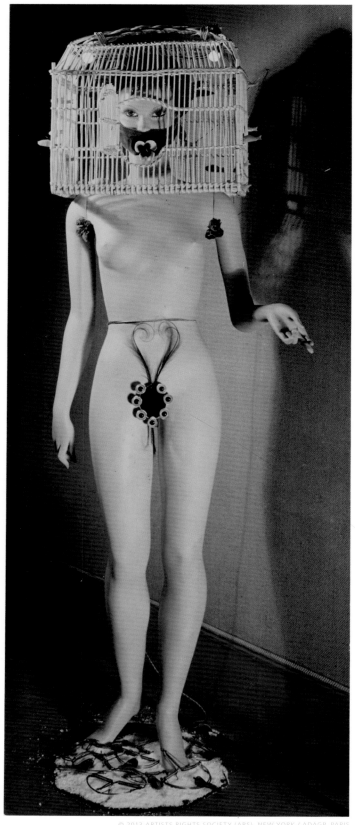

fig. 6 [56] **Raoul Ubac,** *Mannequin (André Masson),* 1938

fig. 7 [57] **Gaston Paris,** *Mannequin (Dali),* 1938

[58] **Roger Parry,** *Carousel Horse,* 1929

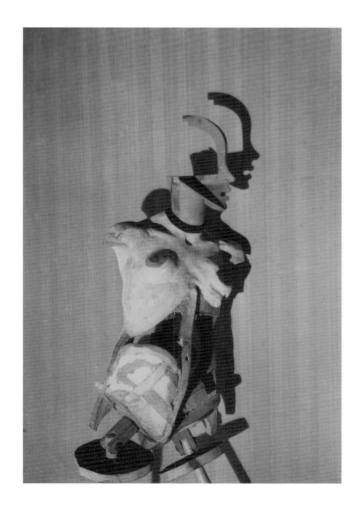

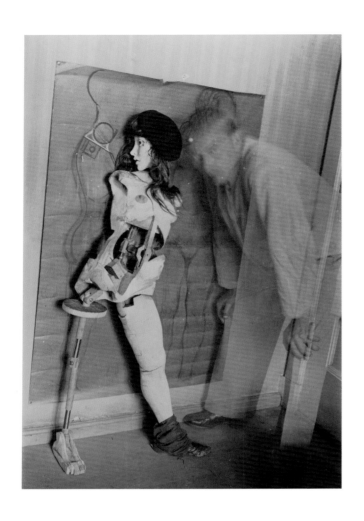

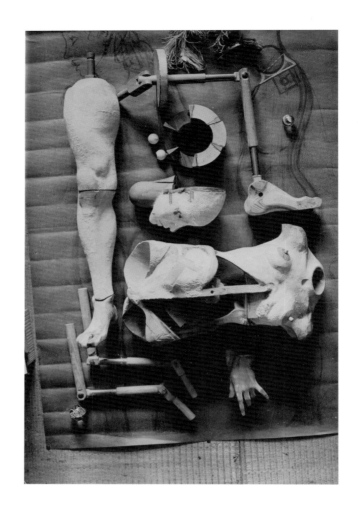

fig. 2 [60] **Dora Maar,** *Street Orchestra, Blind Musicians,* 1934

Dora Maar is the most represented artist in the Raymond collection, with twenty-three works. The arc of her photographic career closely followed the blossoming of the 1930s photography scene in Paris. She published street photography, fashion, advertising, and fine art works in a range of journals including Arts et Métiers Graphique's *Photographie* annual, *Cahiers d'Art, L'Illustration, Votre Beauté,* and many others.[1] Well financed by her parents and groomed by fashionable studio photographers including Man Ray, she found considerable success with her studio partner Pierre Kéfer from 1931 to 1934 and beyond.[2]

Though varied, the Maar photographs in the collection represent a unique viewpoint that is neither documentary nor designed as magazine entertainment. These are private pictures, redolent of the chance encounter defined by Breton's surrealist circles, but without de facto allegiance to political or psychological theories.

Maar's photographic skills included fine prints that would have guaranteed her place in the commercial arena, but she diverted herself from Paris society in pursuit of a different visual language. Her most active period as an independent photographer was 1933–39. In 1933 she traveled to Barcelona and Tossa del Mar, prompted by an assignment for *Beaux-Arts* magazine, photographing many of the same sites as Man Ray, who was also there that summer. This trip and a subsequent one to London in 1934 produced some of her strongest work to date.[3] Back in Paris, Maar exhibited prints from her travels—odd, mysterious images that encouraged new views of her familiar home city.[4] Her street subjects focused on the disenfranchised, with a strong interest in the blind.[5] Among those are *Beggar Woman, Barcelona* (fig. 1 [13]), *Street Orchestra, Blind Musicians* (fig. 2 [60]), *Blind Street Peddler, Barcelona* (fig. 3 [61]), and even *Couple Kissing* (fig. 4 [62]), all of which depict the blind fully exposed in the most public arena.[6]

Another group shows plant images made inside botanical gardens, including the Victorian greenhouses at Kew

fig. 8 [12] **Dora Maar,** *Forbidden Games,* 1935. © 2014 Artists Rights Society (ARS), New York / ADAGP, Paris

in South London (figs. 5–7 [63, 64, 65]). The plants were photographed from below, seen against the glasshouse ceilings, as if Maar were oppressed by the dominating greenery.

In her early Paris years, Maar was an ardent leftist. She met Georges Bataille at gatherings of the Masses[7] and conducted an affair with him that exposed her to the philosopher-critic's exploration of pornography and social taboos in modern society.[8] His interest in sexual activity as a means of transcending the rational sets the tone for Maar's high surrealist works, including the 1935 photo collage *Forbidden Games* (fig. 8 [12]). In this work Maar reconfigured a stuffy fin de siècle salon as the site of illicit sexual activity in which the protagonists (a bustier-clad woman and a stand-in for Sigmund Freud) are spied on by a young Barcelona street urchin, a figure cut from a different Maar photograph [67].[9]

By the mid-1930s, Maar drew upon her extensive negative archive to create montage images in which documentation gives way to the interior reality of

fig. 1 [13] **Dora Maar,** *Beggar Woman, Barcelona,* 1933. © 2013 Artists Rights Society (ARS), New York / ADAGP, Paris

fig. 9 *Negative,* c. 1936. Dora Maar (French, 1907–1997). Negative film; 6 x 9 cm. Musee National d'Art Moderne, Centre Georges Pompidou, Paris, AM 2004-163 (349N). © CNAC/MNAM/Dist. RMN-Grand Palais/Art Resource, NY. © 2013 Artists Rights Society (ARS), New York / ADAGP, Paris

Maar reworked a negative—originally made for a commercial assignment—for personal, expressive ends to create a series of works including the museum's *Double Portrait with Hat.*

[9] Dora Maar, *Double Portrait with Hat,* c. 1936–37. © 2013 Artists Rights Society (ARS), New York / ADAGP, Paris

surrealism. Her high surrealist work benefited from relationships with Paul Eluard, Georges Hugnet, and Yves Tanguy as well as Pablo Picasso, who was her lover from 1936 to 1939. Like many photographers, Maar did not distinguish between her commercial and personal work; aspects of both mix liberally in the finished montages.[10] Such a blend resulted in one of the most powerful and original works in the collection, *Double Portrait with Hat,* c. 1936–37 (fig. 9). By cutting, painting, and rephotographing a negative of a model from a fashion shoot, Maar dismantled the fashion idyll, transforming it into an incisive reflection on the state of the independent female artist and creating a kind of surrealistic self-portrait.

NOTES

1. See Christian Bouqueret, *Les Années folles aux années noirs: la nouvelle vision photographique en France 1920–1940* (Paris: Marval, 1997), 155–64.

2. Victoria Combalía organized the only museum exhibition of Maar's photography during her lifetime. Her research, along with that of Mary Daniel Hobson, forms the basis of this essay.

3. Victoria Combalía, *Dora Maar: más allá de Picasso* (Barcelona: Circe, 2013), 10–12.

4. Her June 1934 exhibition at the Galerie de Beaune was reviewed by Paul Gilson in *L'Intransigeant.* Several images from the Raymond collection are described therein, including *Gypsy Palmist* [70]. I thank Victoria Combalía for pointing out this review.

5. See Mary Daniel Hobson, "Blind Insight: Three Routes to the Unconscious in the Photographs of Dora Maar" (master's thesis, University of New Mexico, 1996), for an informed analysis of this theme in Maar's photography.

6. Sight and blindness appear throughout surrealist imagery and literature.

7. The Masses was a left-wing political action group composed of writers and artists, many linked loosely to the surrealists. For their relationship, see Victoria Combalía, "Dora Maar, Georges Bataille et Tossa de Mar," *Art Press* 260 (September 2000): 52–56.

8. Bataille founded the journal *Documents* in 1930 as an alternative to Breton's surrealist journals. He commissioned many photographs now associated with surrealism, including work by Jean Boiffard and Eli Lotar. See Dawn Ades and Simon Baker, eds., *Undercover Surrealism: Georges Bataille and Documents,* exh. cat. (London: Hayward Gallery, 2006).

9. The photograph of street kids was made in Barcelona, the site of scenes in Bataille's erotic novel *Le Bleu de Ciel,* written in 1934 with the protagonist and his lover, Dorothea/Dirty. See Susan Rubin Suleiman, "Bataille in the Street: The Search for Virility in the 1930s," *Critical Inquiry* 21, no. 1 (Autumn 1994): 61–79. Maar's extensive surrealist photo collages may be seen in Combalía's *Dora Maar: Bataille, Picasso et les Surréalistes,* exh. cat. (Marseille: Musées de Marseille, 2002).

10. Combalía discussed this with Maar and refers to the interview in many of her essays. Maar's negative archive at the Centre Pompidou, comprising almost two thousand negatives, contains many examples of copy negatives that she used to graft figures from one negative onto a different setting.

fig. 3 [61] **Dora Maar,** *Blind Street Peddler, Barcelona,* 1933

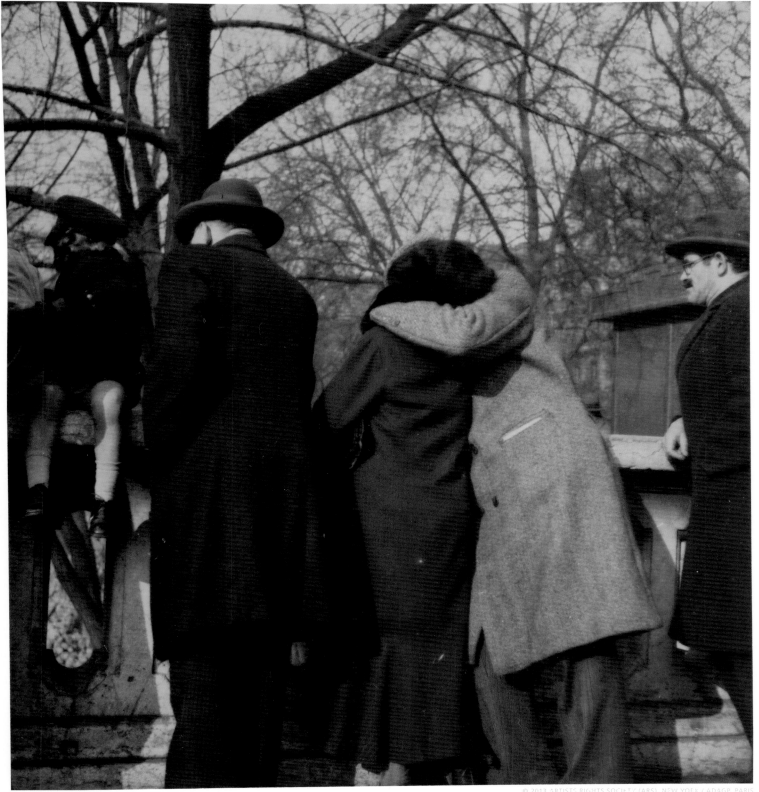

fig. 4 [62] **Dora Maar,** *Couple Kissing,* 1931–36

fig. 5 [63] **Dora Maar,** *Plants in Covent Garden,* 1934

fig. 6 [64] **Dora Maar,** *Plant and Window Study,* 1934

fig. 7 [65] **Dora Maar,** *Stairwell and Plants in Kew Gardens,* 1934

[66] **Dora Maar,** *Headstand, Barcelona,* 1933

[67] **Dora Maar,** *Children Playing,* 1933

[68] **Dora Maar,** *Horse and Carriage,* 1931–36

[69] **Dora Maar,** *Carousel at Night,* 1931–36

[70] **Dora Maar,** *Gypsy Palmist,* 1934

[71] **Dora Maar,** *Repent for the Kingdom of Heaven Is at Hand,* 1934

[72] **Dora Maar,** *Sky Pinwheels and Bottles,* 1931–36

[73] **Dora Maar,** *Trees and Ominous Sky,* 1931–36

[75] **Dora Maar,** *As Seen through the Aquariums on the Quai de la Mégisserie,* 1931–36

[74] **Dora Maar,** *Three Covered Statues,* 1931–36

117

[77] **Dora Maar,** *Crowd in Front of a Car,* 1931–36

[76] **Dora Maar,** *The Grimace,* 1933

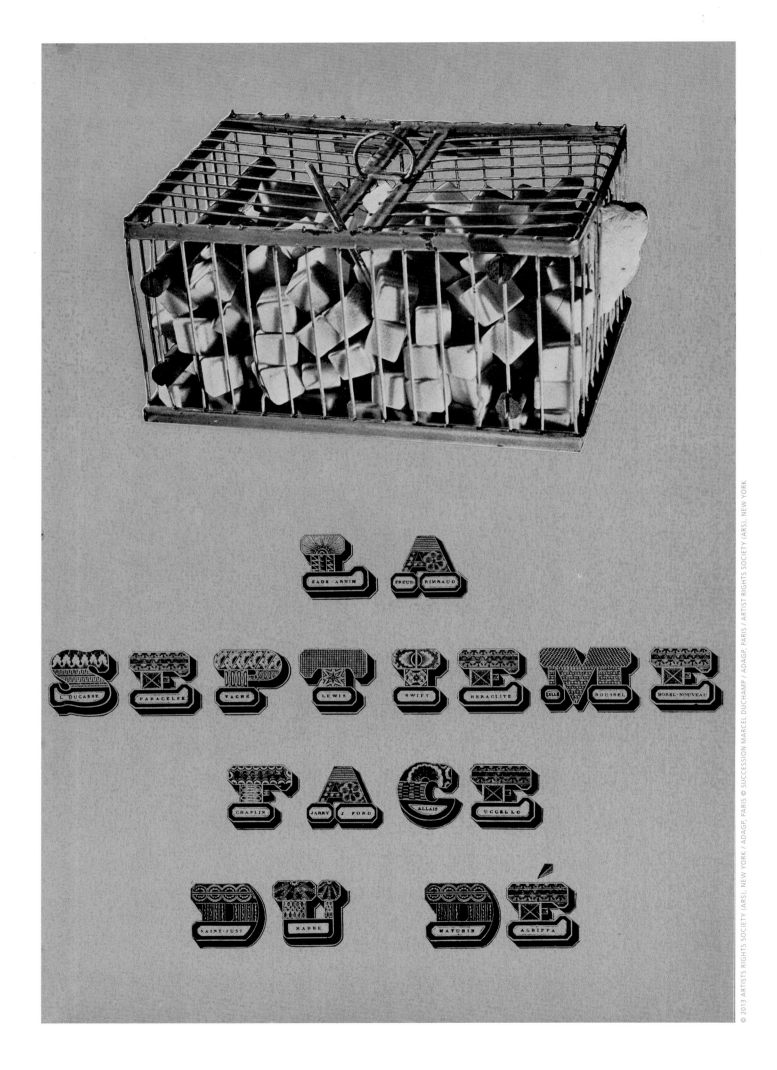

Georges Hugnet plays a significant role in the Raymond collection, one that mirrors his activity as a visual and literary artist, publisher, and beacon of nonconformity in surrealist Paris. First established as a precocious playwright, poet, and translator of Gertrude Stein, Hugnet was soon publishing volumes conceived as surrealist objets d'art, in which layout, illustration, cover, and binding were carefully considered. He collaborated with several Raymond collection artists, including Hans Bellmer and Marcel Duchamp, and interacted with others germane to the collection, including André Breton, Paul Eluard, Dora Maar, Raoul Ubac, and Emiel van Moerkerken. Published in installments in *Cahiers d'Art* in 1932,[1] Hugnet's history of Dada was among the earliest efforts to clarify the complex movement only a decade old at the time. In this series of articles, summarized in Hugnet's contribution to the Museum of Modern Art's 1936 *Fantastic Art, Dada, Surrealism* exhibition, the artist-critic distinguishes Dada as dedicated to disruptive theatrical public gestures and performances compared to the more structured program of surrealism, striving to give form to the idea of chance and dream in the visual and literary arts.[2]

The Raymond collection contains photographic work by Hugnet from four distinct areas: individual photo collages; his book of illustrated poems, *The Seventh Face of the Die: Poems-Decoupages (La Septième face du dé: poèmes-découpages)* in collaboration with Marcel Duchamp; photo collages created for *Eight Days at Trébaumec (Huit Jours á Trébaumec),* a literary send-up of popular tourist guides; and collages made for the *1961* book.[3] The works span Hugnet's collage activity that began in the early 1930s and continued into his final years. His childhood preoccupation with cutting and pasting newspaper images developed into an intuitive form of visual poetry that Hugnet calibrated either to bolster or offset the tone of his written works.

"Collage," in his words, "is a process of creation for the pleasure of the imagination and the one law of *'dépaysement,'*[4] without prejudging the aspect of chance in this process and, finally, to penetrate the domain of the marvelous while redirecting images from their original intention and banal signification."[5]

The appearance of *The Seventh Side of the Die* (fig. 1 [78]) in 1936 coincided with the height of interest in the surrealist object.[6] A surrealist exhibition at the Charles Ratton gallery in Paris that year included seminal works by Alberto Giacometti and Man Ray, as well as several *livres-objets* by Hugnet.[7] His collaborator Marcel Duchamp was then occupied with his *Boîte en Valise,* an editioned collection of miniature reproductions of his own artworks contained in a handcrafted suitcase. Duchamp designed the covers for *The Seventh Side*—photographs of unrolled cigarettes (fig. 2 [80]) replete with cellulose acetate covers—as references to the denuded female form in *The Bride Stripped Bare by Her Bachelors, Even (The Large Glass).*[8] As such, Hugnet's carefully composed layouts of left-hand letterpress text and right-hand collotype collages offer the viewer a surrealist experience channeled through the object. He wanted to amend reality by orchestrating the arrangements of original poems, found language, and image. He applied sophisticated graphic skills to reproduce collages of various media—photographs, wood engravings, and newspaper printed text—with enough detail to satisfy close viewing, but he used printing techniques that suppressed differences to achieve a seamless structure of word and image. Hugnet was creating his own version of Duchamp's assisted ready-made: art full of intention but lacking evidence of the human hand.

Hugnet's photo collages of the 1930s were drawn primarily from reproductions found in a few popular

fig. 1 [78] **Georges Hugnet and Marcel Duchamp,** *The Seventh Face of the Die,* 1936

magazines that enjoyed robust circulation during that decade.[9] A rare example of his use of original photography is *My Wanderings Lead Me* (c. 1936) (fig. 3 [81]), based on a photograph by Jean Moral.[10] This image exemplifies the more pointedly photographic sensibility found in *Eight Days at Trébaumec* (1947), which is markedly different from the all-over nature of the poems-decoupages of the *Seventh Side of the Die*.[11] Another image destined for *Trébaumec, En route, One Visits the Castle* (fig. 4 [82]), entertains the erotic fantasy of finding scantily clothed girls stranded in the setting of an old Breton seaside mansion.

In his individual collages, Hugnet developed the assisted ready-made by cleverly recycling imagery that attracted him. In *Angkor-Thom* (c. 1930) (fig. 5 [83]), Hugnet transformed a gallery announcement into a comment on the chic rage for this type of architecture, which resulted from the 1931 Paris exposition that included a full-scale reconstruction of the temples at Angkor (part of Cambodia, French territory at the time).[12] A gloved hand, lipsticked mouth, and enormous eyes decorate the ink sketch of the ruined temple in a most mocking attitude.

Hugnet's emphasis on text, the book as surrealist object, and his collaboration with Duchamp make his inclusion in the Raymond collection vital to the history of surrealism.

NOTES

1. Georges Hugnet, "L'esprit dada dans la peinture," *Cahiers d'Art* 1, 2, 6–10 (1932); 1–4 (1934); 8–10 (1936).

2. Georges Hugnet and Margaret Scolari, "In the Light of Surrealism" and "Dada and Surrealism: Essays," *The Bulletin of the Museum of Modern Art* 4, no. 2–3 (November–December 1936): 19–32.

3. Sam Stourdzé, "Détournement d'Images," *Georges Hugnet: Collages* (Paris: Editions Léo Scheer, 2003), is seminal to the dating and sources of Hugnet's photo collages.

4. This term, defined in dictionaries as removal from one's ordinary surroundings, was used by André Breton and Louis Aragon in 1930 to describe a state of disorientation, of making the ordinary strange, or making the quotidian unfamiliar.

5. Georges Hugnet, "'Collage' et 'Montage ou photo montage,'" from *Dictionnaire du dadaïsme, 1916–1922* (Paris: J. C. Simoën, 1976), as reprinted in Centre Pompidou, *La Subervsion des Images: Surréalisme Photographie Film* (Paris: Editions du Centre Pompidou, 2009), 431.

6. For an excellent analysis of the work see Robert A. Sobieszak, "Erotic Photomontages: Georges Hugnet's *La Septième face du dé*," *Dada/Surrealism* 9 (1979): 66–82.

7. James Phillips, *Georges Hugnet (1906–1974) le pantalon de la fauvette du Dictionnaire abrégé du Surréalisme: étude et choix de textes* (Paris: Lettres Modernes, 1991), 61–62. The 1936 issue of *Cahiers d'Art*, 11e année, is dedicated to the object and includes examples by Hugnet.

8. Arturo Schwarz, *The Complete Works of Marcel Duchamp* (London: Thames and Hudson, 1997), 2:733–34.

9. Stourdzé, "Détournement d'Images," 167–68, and note 5.

10. Hugnet was at that time close to Jean and Juliette Moral and was romantically involved with Juliette. See ibid., 172, note 13.

11. Stourdzé sorts out the dating of Hugnet's 1930s collages published in 1947.

12. The exhibition comprised sketches of architectural ruins by André Maire, known for his onsite renderings of the Angkor temple complex.

[79] **Georges Hugnet,** *Black Magic,* 1936

aux femmes qui emploient

avec toutes les robes

MAGIE NOIRE

parle, entend
et voit

Mai 1936 GH.

fig. 2 [80] **Marcel Duchamp,** *Cigarette Covers,* 1936

fig. 3 [81] **Georges Hugnet,** *My Wanderings Lead Me,* c. 1936

fig. 4 [82] **Georges Hugnet,** *En Route, One Visits the Castle,* 1934

ANGKOR-THOM. — Baycn.

fig. 5 [83] **Georges Hugnet,** *Angkor-Thom,* c. 1930

[84] **Georges Hugnet,** *Two Women,* 1934

[85] **Georges Hugnet,** *Beach,* c. 1933–36

[86] **Georges Hugnet,** *Bra and Girdle,* 1961

[87] **Georges Hugnet,** *Young Bride,* c. 1933–36

[88] **Georges Hugnet,** *The Architect of the Magus,* 1935

fig. 1 [89] **Marcel Mariën,** *The Spirit of the Staircase,* 1949

BELGIAN AND DUTCH SURREALISM

Established by André Breton in 1920s Paris, surrealism relied on publications, exhibitions, and political actions of artists moving across Europe to disseminate its ideas. Characterized by its detachment from any specific locale (*dépaysement*), surrealism found a welcome reception in Belgium, a new country with three languages and cultural profiles.[1] Embracing its poetic possibilities, Belgian writers, composers, and artists established strong connections to the Paris surrealists, championing their ideas in new journals. Beginning in 1922, the Belgian musician E. L. T. Mesens traveled between Paris and Brussels forging a relationship with René Magritte. The writer Paul Nougé rallied the surrealist cause with his journal *Correspondance* (1924–26), and Mesens followed with his more elaborate *Marie* and *Variétés* journals. Magritte spent three years in Paris (1927–30) before relocating to Brussels, and Nougé, Mesens, and other Belgians contributed to key French publications including *Minotaure, Documents,* and *Bifur,* as well as to surrealist exhibitions in Paris.

Markers for the evolution of the movement include the 1924 and 1929 congresses of surrealists in Paris, Breton's visit to Brussels in the summer of 1925, and Mesens's two photography exhibitions in 1931 and 1932, as well as his important 1934 *Documents* journal out of Brussels. A second thrust of activity emerged around two later shows in Paris: the 1936 surrealist sculpture exhibition at Charles Ratton's gallery, and the 1938 *International Surrealist Exhibition,* which traveled internationally and was shepherded by Georges Hugnet to Amsterdam, complete with an illustrated catalogue containing an essay by Hugnet.[2]

Dutch surrealism thrived first in Utrecht around the art academy and then gained strength as a literary movement in the publication *De Schoene Zakdoek (The Lovely Handkerchief).* The painter Kristians Tonny worked with Hugnet on the 1938 show, but it was Emiel van Moerkerken who spearheaded surrealist photography in Holland.[3] After meeting Man Ray, Salvador

Dalí, and Brassaï in Paris in 1934, he was influenced by automatism and Freudian notions of sexual liberation in his imagery. In 1938, however, Nazi Germany's occupation and annexation of Austria that year dampened further development of surrealism in the Netherlands.

In Belgium the movement branched out beyond the capital and attracted younger artists active during and after World War II. The poet Achille Chavée founded the Rupture group (signifying its break with capitalist society) in La Louvière, a city in the industrial Hainaut region of Wallonia. Linked to the Walloon movement for political independence, Rupture regrouped after the war as Haute Nuit in Mons and exerted influence on a group of avant-garde artists from Copenhagen, Brussels, and Amsterdam (CoBrA) in the 1950s. Contact with Magritte's Brussels group was intermittent, but certainly the spirit of surrealist poetic resistance remained relevant in Belgium through the conceptual work of Marcel Broodthaers.

Marcel Mariën, artist, writer, and creator of *The Spirit of the Staircase* (fig. 1 [89]), defined the peculiarities of Belgian surrealism.[4] He joined Magritte's Brussels circle in 1937, wrote the first biography of the artist in 1943, and in 1968 published Paul Nougé's 1928 photographs and text *La Subversion des images,* now recognized as a seminal surrealist project. Mariën's haunting image of a pair of shoes posed as if ascending a staircase avails itself of photography's unique ability to suggest form and absence at once, and evokes the surrealist waking dream state.[5]

The Belgian surrealists surrounding Magritte lived quietly in the Brussels suburbs, meeting and performing at home rather than in the clubs and cafés favored by the Parisians. As if to illustrate this, the photograph of Magritte's wife, *Georgette at the Table,* revels in domesticity at the breakfast table, though the white canvas, familiar from Magritte's paintings, sets off the young woman from the domestic clutter. In Mons, a medieval Belgian town, Marcel G. Lefrancq founded the Hainaut surrealist group in the 1930s. His *Haunted Eyes* (fig. 2 [90]) belongs to a portfolio of twenty-five images and poems in which scenes of nocturnal Mons merge with abstract images created by photogram and photomontage.[6]

Born in German-occupied Belgium, Raoul Ubac, who lived in Paris, Brussels, and Cologne during the 1930s, excelled in darkroom practices praised by Breton as pure expressions of surrealist form.[7] A literature student and artist, Ubac developed his signature photographic style—dependent on negatives and print manipulation—by the mid-1930s under the influence of Man Ray and painters Yves Tanguy and Salvador Dalí in Paris.[8] Combining his interest in geology with image making, Ubac created photographs of fossilized objects through solarization, superimposition of negatives, and finally, *brûlage,* in which he partially melted his nitrate negatives to convey burning superficial layers—both literal and figurative—in violent images of flayed human forms made in the run-up to the German invasion of Europe. *The Battle of the Penthesilea*[9] (fig. 3 [91]) is one of a series of disfigured humans in a ruined landscape. In another dedication of a similar work, Ubac reiterates his interest in the dissolution of the body.[10]

In Amsterdam around the same time, photographer and filmmaker Emiel van Moerkerken created a potent body of photographic work during a short-lived partnership with sculptor Chris van Geel from 1938 to 1941. *Surrealist Act with Chris van Geel* [21] shows the sculptor wearing a menacing grin and heavy rubber gloves in the process of strangling a doll's neck.[11] The doll, with human hair and elaborate make-up, has spiders painted on her white face, thereby capturing so many of the Freudian themes suggested by Dalí and Hans Bellmer, artists van Moerkerken met in Paris.[12] The performative possibilities of photography were well expressed in this partnership, in which both artists enacted elaborate scenarios.

Belgian and Dutch artists moved surrealism, born in urban, cosmopolitan Paris, further along in its evolution by inventing new techniques and placing it on track to change Western art forever.

NOTES

1. Xavier Canonne, *Surrealism in Belgium, 1924–2000* (Brussels: Mercatorfonds, 2007), 23.

2. Georges Hugnet, *Surréalistische Schilderkunst: inleiding bij de internationale tentoonsteling van het surréalisme gehouden in de Galerie Roubert Keizersgracht 527 te Amsterdam* (Amsterdam: Scheltema & Holkema's Boekandel, 1938). See also, José Vovelle, "Le 'bel été' surréaliste d'Amsterdam 1938: stratégies internationalistes à l'épreuve de la FIARI," *Les Cahiers du Musée nationale d'art moderne* 23 (Spring 1988): 23–74.

3. For the movement see *De automatische verbeelding: Nederlandse surrealisten,* exh. cat. (Amsterdam: Meulenhoff/Landshoff, 1989), and Mattie Boom, "Éxposition du Surréalisme in Amsterdam," *Jong Holland* 4, no. 1 (1988): 5–15.

4. Described as "a linguist and professional in-between figure, a French-speaking artist who grew up in an increasingly Dutch-speaking Antwerp, and a well-read autodidact who preferred to live and work on the margin" in Mieke Bleyen and Hilde van Gelder, "The (De) Construction of National Photography in Minor Photographies: The Case of Marcel Mariën," *History of Photography* 35, no. 2 (May 2011): 117.

5. Mariën made at least three versions of this composition. See Ann Thomas, *Modernist Photographs from the National Gallery of Canada,* exh. cat. (Ottawa: National Gallery of Canada, 2007), cat. no. 120. A variant of Cleveland's print was reproduced in the second issue of Mariën's surrealist periodical *Les Lèvres Nues* 2 (1954): 22.

6. Marcel G. Lefrancq, *Aux Mains de la Lumière Images et Poèmes* (Mons: Éditions de Haute Nuit, 1948).

7. Ubac's place in Belgian surrealism was cemented when he conceived the journal *L'Invention Collective* with Magritte in 1940.

8. The motif of petrification of organic form in Ubac and Tanguy's work is described by Sidra Stich in *Anxious Visions, Surrealist Art* (Berkeley: University Art Museum Berkeley, 1990), 91.

9. Ubac drew the subject of this work from an 1808 play by the German Romantic poet Hermann von Kleist, *Penthesilea* (Queen of the Amazons), which was popular in Germany at that time. Breton describes Brauner's paintings and Ubac's photographs of this series in "Les tendences les plus récentes de la peinture surréaliste," *Minotaure* 12–13 (1939): 16–21.

10. The work, *Untitled (Penthésilée),* 1938, belongs to the collection of the Centre Pompidou, Paris, inv. AM 1988-1726, inscribed: *A Victor Brauner au camarade et á l'ami/pour que la dissolution des corps ne soit pas vaine/Raoul Ubac RU38.*

11. For this relationship and related work, see Hans Renders, *Verijdelde dromen: een surrealistisch avontuur tussen De Stijl en Cobra* (Haarlem: Enschedé, 1989). Also, Bruno van Moerkerken and Minke Vos, *Emiel van Moerkerken* (Zwolle: d'jonge Hond, 2011).

12. The artist commented on this image: "The cage belonged to Chris and the decorated doll's head was mine." With the assistance of Jetty Tielrooy in Emiel van Moerkerken, *E. van Moerkerken Foto's* (Amsterdam: De Bezige Bij, 1989), no. 22.

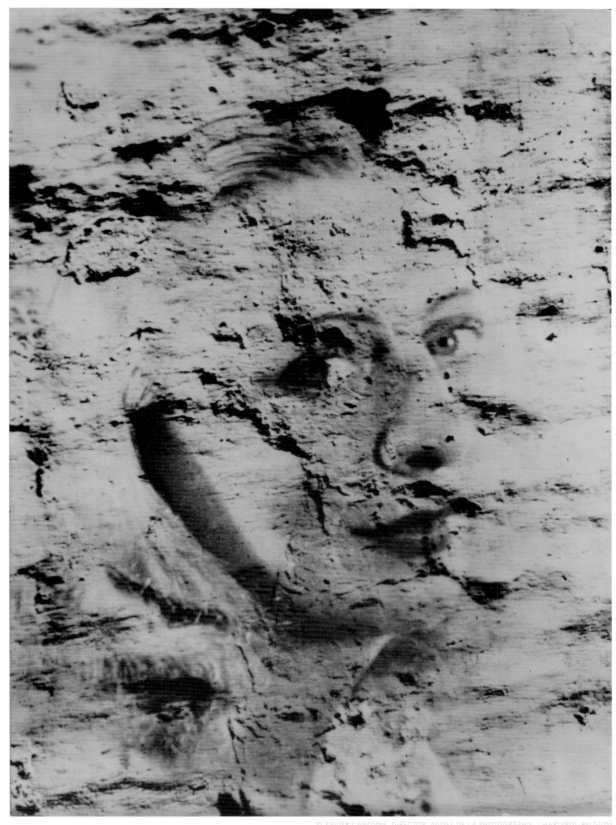

fig. 2 [90] **Marcel G. Lefrancq,** *Haunted Eyes,* 1947

fig. 3 [91] **Raoul Ubac,** *The Battle of the Penthesilea,* 1937

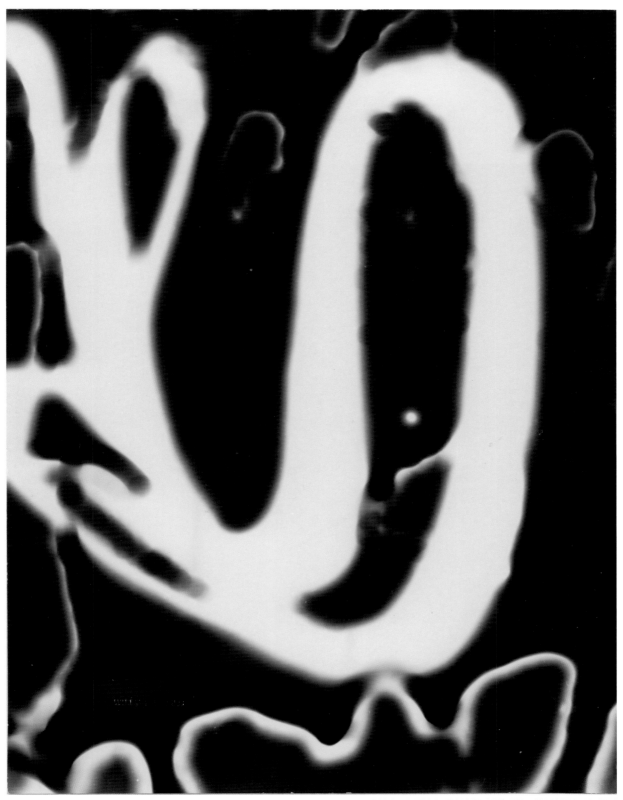

[92] **Willy Kessels,** *Untitled,* 1920s–1930s

[93] **Herman Bekman,** *The Film,* 1930

[94] **Willem van de Poll,** *Paris, Double Exposure of the City of Light,* 1935

[95] **Piet Zwart,** *Typographic Composition,* 1931

[96] **Marcel G. Lefrancq,** *The Melancholy Door,* 1939

[97] **Marcel G. Lefrancq,** *Elected,* 1945

[98] **Marcel G. Lefrancq,** *The Law of Coincidences,* 1938

[99] **Marcel G. Lefrancq,** *Countryside,* 1948

[100] **Marcel G. Lefrancq,** *Heide,* 1942

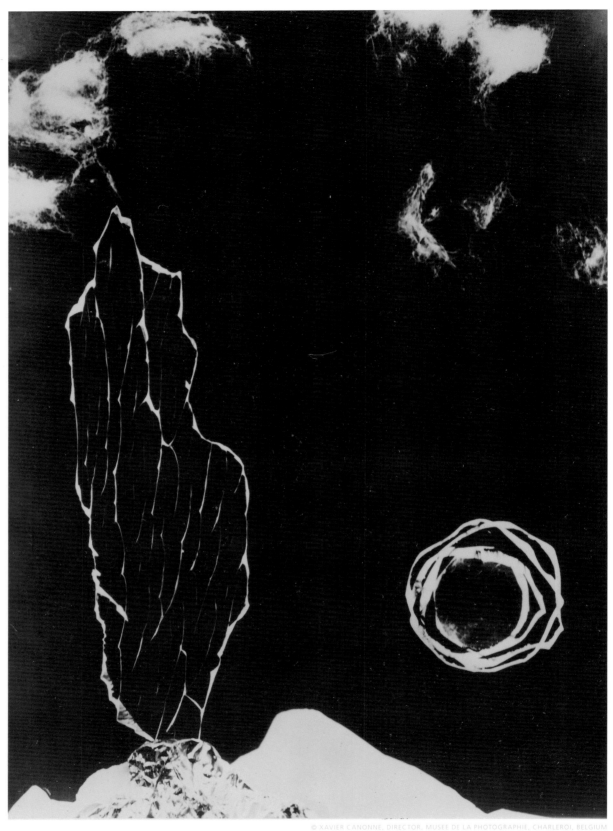

[101] **Marcel G. Lefrancq,** *Photogram,* 1948

[102] **Marcel G. Lefrancq,** *Head of Christ,* 1948

[103] **Marcel G. Lefrancq,** *Hope Is Out the Window,* 1948

[104] **Marcel G. Lefrancq,** *The Song of the Rooftops,* 1948

[105] **Marcel G. Lefrancq,** *Study of Form V,* c. 1942

[106] **Marcel G. Lefrancq,** *Large Nets for Capturing the Wind,* c. 1947

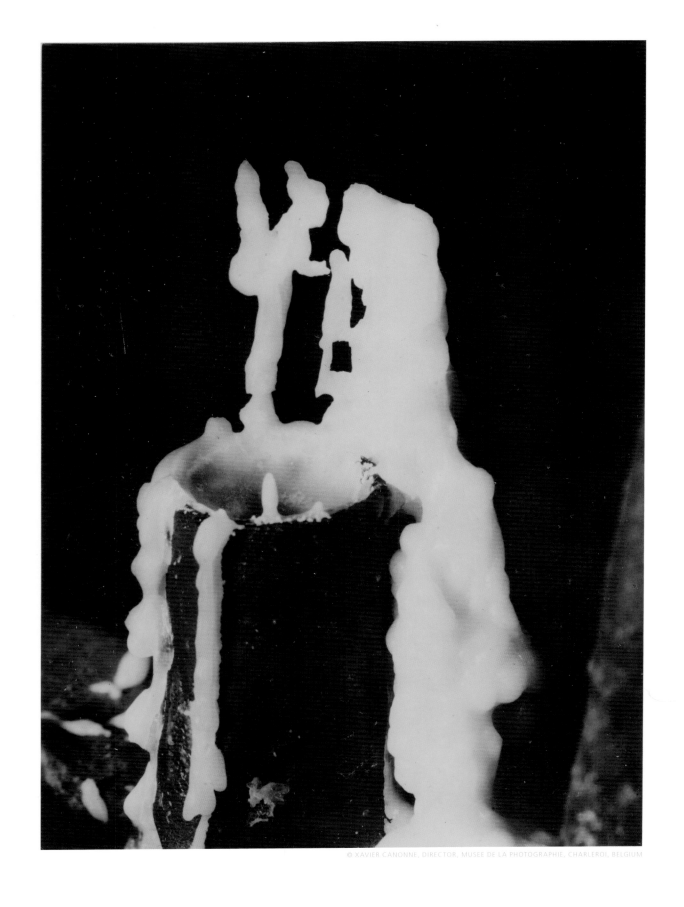

[107] **Marcel G. Lefrancq,** *Statue of Snow,* 1948

[108] **Marcel G. Lefrancq,** *Small Fairy in a Park,* 1948

[109] **Marcel G. Lefrancq,** *In a Far Off Land,* 1948

[110] **Marcel G. Lefrancq,** *Study of Form I,* c. 1942

[111] **Marcel G. Lefrancq,** *Exercise in Purity,* 1948

[112] **Marcel G. Lefrancq,** *Burst of Sunshine,* 1948

[113] **Marcel G. Lefrancq,** *Endless Recurrence,* 1948

[114] **Richard Tepe,** *Eggs of a Stone-curlew or Plover,* 1900s

[115] **Richard Tepe,** *Yellowhammer Nest with Eggs,* 1900s

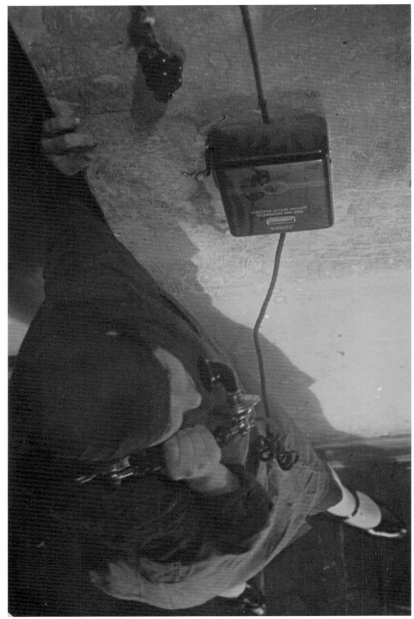

fig. 1 [116] **Alexander Rodchenko,** *At the Telephone,* 1928

Innovative photographic techniques of the interwar period were not limited to complex manipulation or abstracted forms. Indeed, a notable source of radical photographic vision applied Russian Constructivist principles of spatial reorganization to everyday subjects. By the late 1920s and into the 1930s, a formalist aesthetic couched in oblique angles and skewed perspectives dominated photographs that might otherwise be considered documentary—images of street sweepers, architectural subjects, children at play. Radical vision emerged as a dominant trait of interwar photography and remains a visual hallmark of experimentation from that era. Though such formal tropes as the overhead view, the wormhole view, microphotography, and off-center composition existed in varying degrees before the 1920s, they were employed with deliberate fervor by artists who believed photography to be the harbinger of a new technological age.

"We who are accustomed to seeing the usual, the accepted, must reveal the world of sight. We must revolutionize our visual reasoning. Photograph from all viewpoints except 'from the belly button,' until they all become acceptable. And the most interesting viewpoints today are those from above down, and from below up and their diagonals."[1] So wrote Alexander Rodchenko in the August 1928 issue of *Novyi Lef* magazine, the same year he produced *At the Telephone* (fig. 1 [116]), an image taken on commission to report on a newspaper production.[2] The radical foreshortening of the standing figure and the collapsing of space delineated by the telephone cord makes this work a successful blend of aesthetic and political ideals. This mixing of formalism and political content defined Russian Constructivism in ways that filtered only partially to other photographic communities.[3]

In Germany, a similar movement to radicalize photographic vision was also under way in the 1920s, with László Moholy-Nagy's direction of the preliminary course at the Bauhaus serving as ground zero.

Dedicated to the medium's basis in light and chemistry, in 1927 Moholy-Nagy exhorted artists to seek unfamiliar views made by positioning the camera obliquely and experimenting with various lenses in order to subvert the camera's one-point perspective.[4] Erich Consemüller, a Bauhaus student, conformed to the visual language of the grid upheld in Bauhaus design principles in the photograph *Bauhaus Sculptural Study* (c. 1927) (fig. 2 [117]), an example of photography that straddled both the documentary and the artistic.[5] This image includes a wooden sculptural model made by Walter Tralau seen from below with the Dessau Bauhaus glass windows above, a perspective that creates an abstraction of form and space translated through light and shadow.[6]

Photographers throughout Europe quickly adopted the rigorous principles of Germany's New Vision to telegraph commitment to modernity across the commercial spectrum, from fashion and advertising to news essays and applied graphic design.[7] Those trained in Germany, including Ilse Bing and Germaine Krull, found success in their adopted city of Paris, serving the plethora of photographically illustrated magazines. Krull was one of the first photographers hired by Lucien Vogel for *VU* magazine following the publication of her landmark photo book *Métal* (1928), a paean to the steel structure of the Eiffel Tower rendered in contemporary New Vision style. Her *Study of Hands* (1928) (fig. 3 [118]), though possibly commissioned for a story on the market area of Les Halles, describes not the place but the mood, as evoked by oblique shadow play.[8]

Bing was using the new small-format Leica camera for her photo stories, which allowed her greater freedom, the camera nearly part of her body. A hallmark of Bing's outdoor work is a gentle skewing of frontal compositions along strong diagonals, which produce dizzying arrangements of urban vignettes whose actions seem to extend beyond the frame of the image. Her *Paris Fair* (1933) (fig. 4 [119]) presents a dynamic, charming narrative on the popular pastime of the amusement fair, possibly from a commission for *Le Monde Illustré*.[9]

Berenice Abbott, another expatriate in 1920s Paris, learned darkroom techniques from Man Ray while studying ways to reinterpret the modern city, a key lifelong subject. *Hudson River Bridge* (1930) (fig. 5 [120]), an early entry in the large group of architectural New York views, reflects the inspiration of Krull's Eiffel Tower pictures that had been on view in Paris in 1929 before Abbott returned to New York. *Bridge* was one of her earliest assignments upon returning to America.[10] Aiming her camera obliquely under the steel suspension arch, she imbued a solid structure with the momentary fluidity of Bing's couple racing through the air.[11]

Back in Paris, the radical viewpoint flourished in work by successful professional photographers who stepped lightly or not at all in the surrealist milieu. René Zuber's *Grate over Coins* (1932) (fig. 6 [121]) integrates both the overhead and worm's-eye view in a composition of transparent layers. This superb study of pattern, texture, light, and dark probably served as an advertisement. Zuber, a founding member of the Alliance Photo agency in Paris, was one of the French photographers who most successfully assimilated radical visual composition into a style befitting luxury goods.

Brassaï, who published his nighttime photographs of Paris in 1932, also took his camera inside to public events, as witnessed in his *Folies Bergères* (1932) (fig. 7 [122]), which reveals a string of bare-chested women shot in linear formation from above.[12] Already included in Breton's surrealist social circle, he maintained an interest in photographs that documented the life of his adopted city of Paris. He photographed several shows at the Folies from this vertiginous height, often perched backstage at the top of the scenery panels. Giving the viewer the sensation of joining him atop the scene, in this work Brassaï brings the radical view—first used to disguise reality—back to a celebration of the human condition.

NOTES

1. Alexander Rodchenko, "The Paths of Modern Photography," originally published in *Novyi Lef* 9 (1928): 31–39, here cited in translation in Christopher Phillips, *Photography in the Modern Era: European Documents and Critical Writings, 1913–1940* (New York: Metropolitan Museum of Art, 1989), 256–63.

2. On this image and series, see Margarita Tupitsyn, "The Photographer in the Service of the Collective," in *The Soviet Photograph 1924–1937* (New Haven and London: Yale University Press, 1996), 35–63, pl. 34; and Peter Galassi, "Rodchenko and Photography's Revolution," in *Aleksandr Rodchenko,* exh. cat. (New York: Museum of Modern Art, 1998), 100–137, pl. 249.

3. Galassi, *Aleksandr Rodchenko,* summarizes the chronology and historical interpretation of Rodchenko's work within the context of New Vision photography.

4. László Moholy-Nagy, "Unprecedented Photography (*Die beispiellos Fotografie*)," in *Das Deutsche Lichtbild* (Berlin 1927), is reprinted in translation in Christopher Phillips, *Photography in the Modern Era: European Documents and Critical Writings, 1913–1940* (New York: Metropolitan Museum of Art, 1989), 83–85.

5. Leah Dickerman, "Bauhaus Fundaments," in *Bauhaus 1919–1933: Workshops for Modernity,* exh. cat. (New York: Museum of Modern Art, 2009), 14–39.

6. This photograph is erroneously attributed to Tralau in Lutz Schöbe, *Bauhaus Fotografie,* exh. cat. (Firenze: Fratelli Alinari, 2002), no. 54. Roswitha Fricke, *Bauhaus Fotografie* (Düsseldorf: Editions Marzona, 1982), and the English edition, *Bauhaus Photography* (Cambridge, MA and London: MIT Press, 1985), no. 23, publish it as Consemüller's work. Dr. Rolf Sachsse kindly affirmed that Fricke confirmed the attribution with the photographer's widow, Ruth Hollos Consemüller, for her publication.

7. Franz Roh's 1929 introductory essay to the *Photo-eye (Foto-auge)* exhibition in Stuttgart, "Mechanism and Expression: The Essence and Value of Photography," is considered the summary statement for German photography's New Vision movement.

8. This print carries inscriptions and stamps alluding to its commercial purpose. Dr. Robert Knodt of the Germaine Krull Archive, Essen, has proposed the site of the image. Krull made numerous photographs of hands. For an interesting survey of the theme in surrealist photography, see Kirsten H. Powell, "Hands-On Surrealism," *Art History* 20, no. 4 (December 1997): 516–33.

9. Nancy Barrett, *Ilse Bing: Three Decades of Photography* (New Orleans: New Orleans Museum of Art, 1985), 20. Bing moved to Paris in 1930, establishing herself as an independent photojournalist by 1931. The amusement park assignment was important to her career. Krull had done a similar assignment for one of the earliest issues of *VU* (April 4, 1928): 92–93.

10. The image was made for, but did not appear in, E. C. Seibert, "The Design of Masonry Arch Bridges," *Architectural Record* 67, no. 5 (May 1930): 402–10. Peter Barr discusses Abbott's exposure to Krull's modernist photographs in Paris in his doctoral dissertation, "Becoming Documentary: Berenice Abbott's Photographs 1925–1939" (Boston University, 1997), 58, 74.

11. Abbott recalled her experience on this shoot: "I wanted to photograph the George Washington Bridge, which was just going up. I wanted to shoot it from up in the crane. The construction workers put me in the pan and, once I was high in the air they swung the crane back and forth so I couldn't take any pictures. I was *terrified*," as quoted in Melissa A. McEuen, *Seeing America: Women Photographers between the Wars* (Louisville: University of Kentucky Press, 2000), 264.

12. A variant of this image appeared as *The Rainbow* in Brassaï, *Secret Paris of the 30s* (New York: Pantheon Books, 1976), 144.

fig. 2 [117] **Erich Consemüller,** *Bauhaus Sculptural Study,* c. 1927

fig. 3 [118] **Germaine Krull,** *Study of Hands,* 1928

fig. 4 [119] **Ilse Bing,** *Paris Fair,* 1933

fig. 5 [120] **Berenice Abbott,** *Hudson River Bridge,* 1930

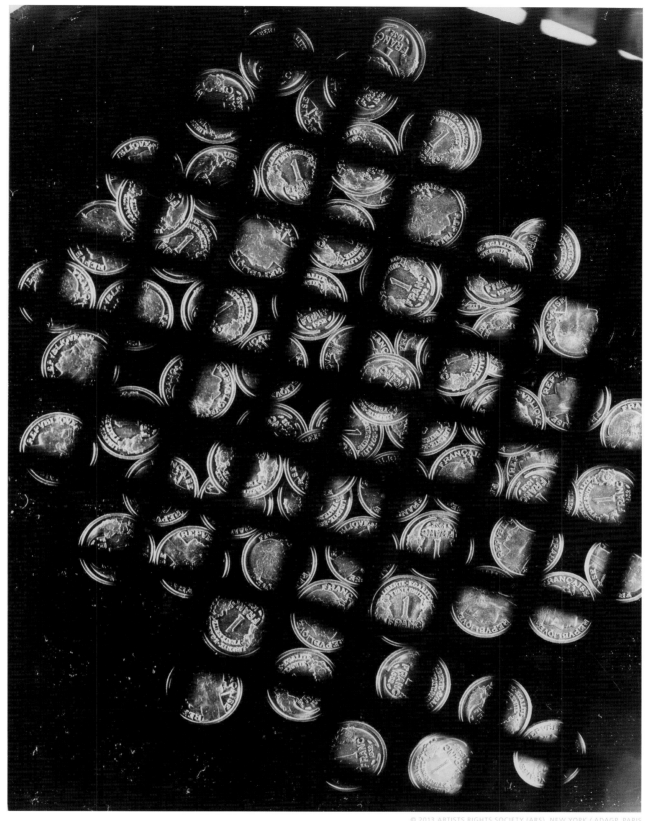

fig. 6 [121] **René Zuber,** *Grate over Coins,* 1932

fig. 7 [122] **Brassaï,** *Folies Bergères,* 1932

[123] **Wols,** *Portrait of a Woman,* 1938

Additional Works

[124] **Werner Rohde,** *Rule Britannia,* 1950s–early 1960s

[125] **Franz Roh,** *Woman with a Comb,* c. 1930

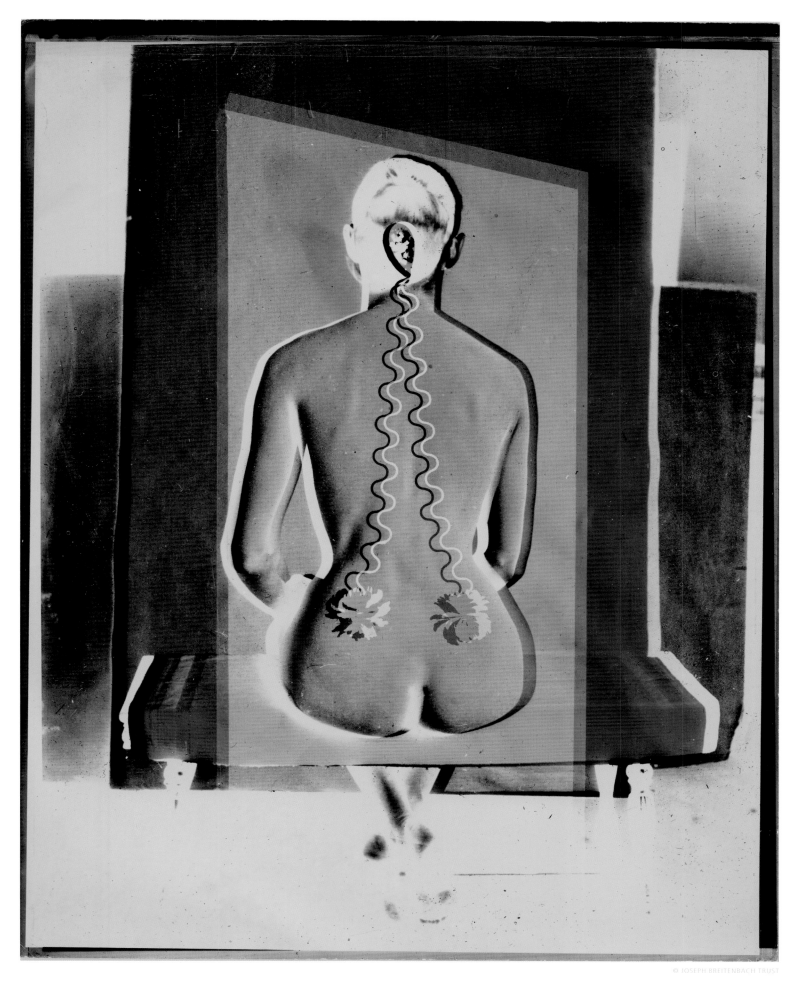

[126] **Josef Breitenbach,** *Electric Back,* 1949

[127] **Alfred Tritschler,** *Wire Strainers,* 1938

[128] **Ilse Bing,** *Paris,* 1933

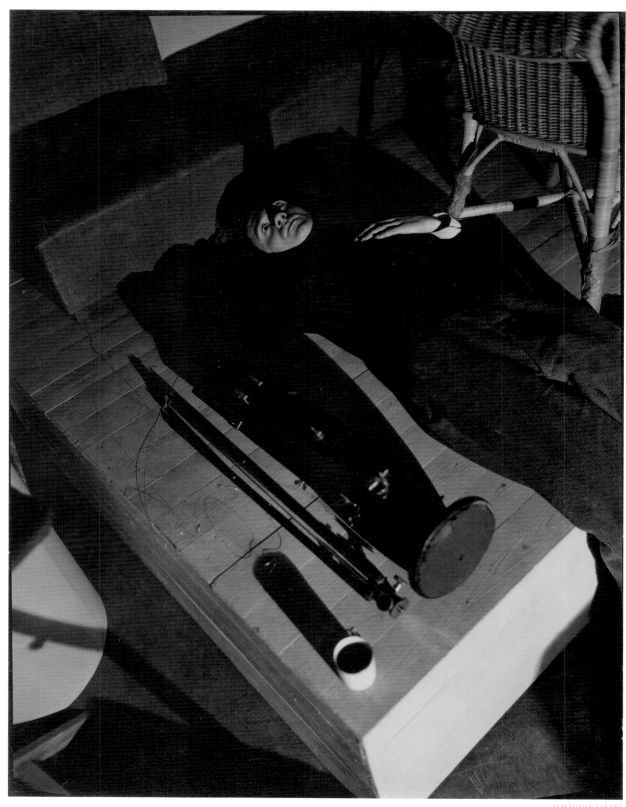

[129] **Maurice Tabard,** *Portrait of Roger Parry,* c. 1930

© ERNST SCHIERON

[130] **Ernst Schieron,** *Vertical: Stuttgart Central Station,* 1929

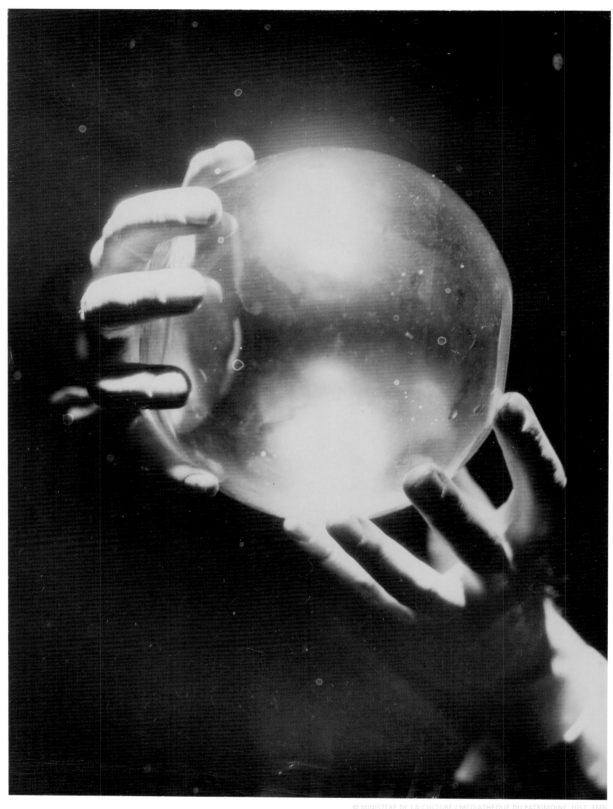

[131] **Roger Parry,** *Hands with Crystal Ball, Variation,* 1930

[132] **Brassaï,** *Two Acrobats, Cirque Médrano in Paris,* 1932–33

[134] **Brassaï,** *Night at Longchamps,* 1937

[136] **Brassaï,** *A Couple at the Ball Quat'z Arts,* 1931

[137] **Brassaï,** *Novice Prostitute, Place d'Italie,* c. 1931

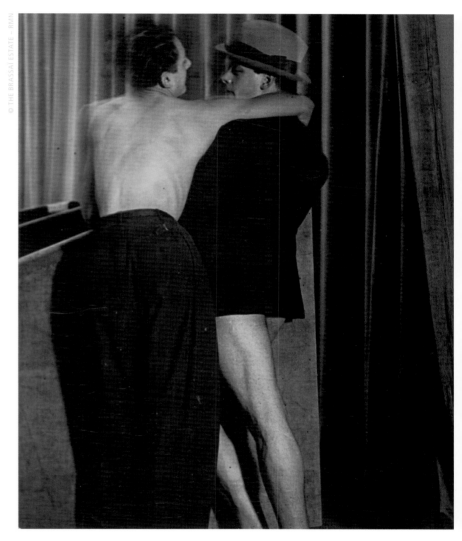

[139] **Brassaï,** *Young Couple Wearing a Two-in-One Suit at the Bal de la Montagne Sainte-Geneviève,* c. 1931

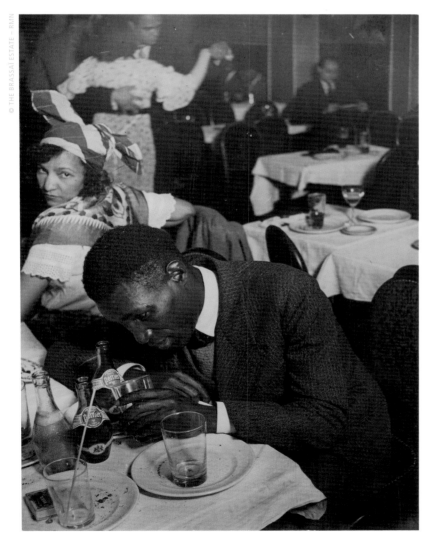

[138] **Brassaï,** *At the White Ball, Montparnasse,* 1932

[140] **Monsieur X,** *Three Graces,* 1925

[141] **Werner Rohde,** *Renate, the Animal Tamer,* 1930

[142] **Gaston Paris,** *Entertainers,* 1930s

[143] **Roger Parry,** *Nude,* 1930

[144] **Louise Dahl-Wolfe,** *Fashion Study,* c. 1930s

[145] **Ernst Schieron,** *In the Mirror,* c. 1930

[146] **Anton Stankowski,** *The Questioner,* 1930

[147] **André Steiner,** *Advertising Image,* 1940s

187

[148] **Jacques-Henri Lartigue,** *In the Studio,* 1931

[149] **Jacques-Henri Lartigue,** *With Lulu in the Bois du Boulogne,* 1931

[150] **Horace Bristol,** *Fortuneteller with Glass,* 1946

[151] **Robert Capa,** *Race Course, Paris,* 1937

[152] **Roger Parry,** *Still Life,* 1930

[154] **Roger Parry,** *Still Life,* 1930

[153] **Roger Parry,** *Dirty Sink,* 1930–31

[155] **Dorothy Norman,** *From 509 Madison Avenue,* 1946

[156] **Ilse Bing,** *Street Cleaners,* 1947

[157] **Berenice Abbott,** *Starrett Lehigh Building,* 1936

[158] **Albert Renger-Patzsch,** *Cactus Leaves (Euphorbia),* 1922–24

[160] **Albert Renger-Patzsch,** *Euphorbia (Codiaeum),* 1922–24

[159] **Albert Renger-Patzsch,** *Annual Blooming of the Cactus Cereus Macrogonus,* 1922–24

[161] **Wols,** *Posts,* 1933

[162] **Théodore Blanc and Antoine Demilly,** *Sign with Hat,* c. 1934

[163] **Ilse Bing,** *Laundry, Frankfurt,* 1929

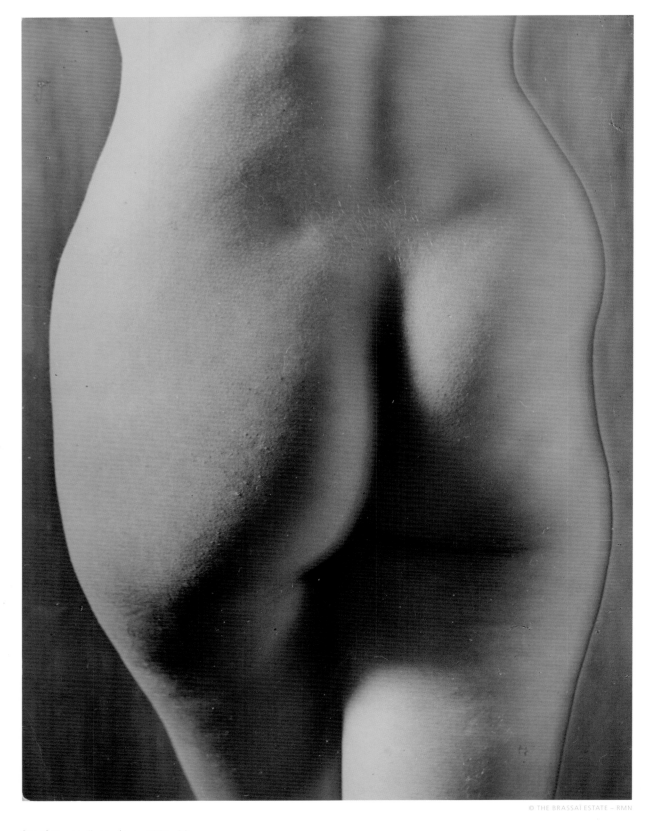

[164] **Brassaï,** *Nude,* c. 1931–33

[165] **Jacques-Henri Lartigue,** *Socoa,* 1931

[166] **Germaine Krull,** *And By Chance,* c. 1930

[167] **Carl Strüwe,** *The Spiral,* 1935

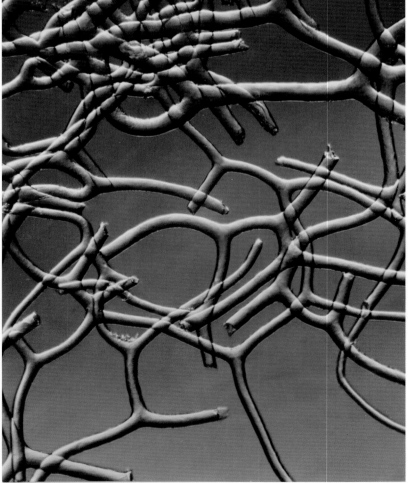

[168] **Carl Strüwe,** *Structure of a Bath Sponge,* 1933

[169] **Carl Strüwe,** *Construction of Chain Algae in Chlorophyll,* 1928

Artist Biographies and Object Entries

Notes: All dimensions are of the image; height precedes width.

All reproductions are of the verso of the print or the cover of the book or portfolio.

Berenice Abbott
American, 1898–1991

A native of Springfield, Ohio, Abbott attended Ohio State University before becoming a journalist in New York in 1918. While there, she met both Marcel Duchamp and Man Ray who later became supporters. In 1921 she moved to Paris to study sculpture, became a studio assistant to Man Ray (1923–25), and in 1926 opened her own portrait studio, photographing artists and intellectuals such as James Joyce. Her portraits were included in prestigious European exhibitions including the Premier Salon Indépendant de la Photographie (Salon de l'Escalier) in Paris (1928) and the 1929 *Film und Foto* show in Stuttgart. Through Man Ray, Abbott met Eugène Atget in 1925. Captivated by his straightforward views of Paris, she became his champion and executor of his estate when he died in 1927. She preserved his glass-plate negatives, brought them to New York in 1929, and actively promoted his work. New York was then undergoing a building renaissance; she used a small, handheld plate camera and a view camera and tripod to capture her city scenes.

Though magazine assignments were plentiful, Abbott focused her work—considered a new form of documentary photography—on the changing shape of the city, both its architectural and social structures. Her intentions dovetailed with new ideas about historical preservation, and Abbott was invited by architectural historian Henry Russell Hitchcock to help organize exhibitions of vernacular architecture. Once the Depression began, Abbott broadened her focus to include those citizens hardest hit in New York and elsewhere in the mid-1930s. She continued making pictures of New York's architecture, both old and new, without financial assistance until she was commissioned by the Federal Art Project to continue this work from 1935 to 1939. Once armed with administrative and technical assistants, Abbott accrued a total of 305 im-

ages in a series titled *Changing New York,* exhibited at the Museum of the City of New York.

In 1935 Abbott moved in with art critic Elizabeth McCausland, who wrote some of the earliest assessments of Abbott's photography of the New York landscape. McCausland also authored the essay for *Changing New York* when the body of work was published as a book in 1939. In later years, Abbott was interested in scientific applications for photography, working at the Massachusetts Institute of Technology. She moved to Maine in the 1960s, where she continued to photograph.

120. *Hudson River Bridge,* spring 1930
Gelatin silver print; 23.7 x 17.3 cm (9³⁄₈ x 6⁷⁄₈ in.).
John L. Severance Fund 2007.20

INSCRIPTIONS
In pencil on verso of print: *Hudson River Bridge* and *Berenice Abbott* [signature]

Black stamp on verso of print: *Courtesy of Julien Levy Gallery*

Purple stamp on verso of print: *Photo/Berenice Abbott/1 W. 67th St. N.Y.C.*

PROVENANCE
The artist, New York; Julien Levy Gallery, New York; Sotheby's, New York, 7 October 1998, no. 87; David Raymond, New York

157. *Starrett Lehigh Building,* July 1936, printed 1950s
Gelatin silver print; 19.8 x 24.5 cm (7⁵⁄₈ x 9⁵⁄₈ in.).
John L. Severance Fund 2007.21

INSCRIPTIONS
Black stamp on verso of print: *Federal Art Project/"Changing New York"/Photographs by Berenice Abbott*

Black stamp with handwriting on verso of print: *Starrett Lehigh Building/601 West 26th Street, Manhattan/July 14, 1936* [illegible markings]

PROVENANCE
Harry Lunn, Washington, DC; Edwynn Houk Gallery, New York; David Raymond, New York

Manuel Álvarez Bravo
Mexican, 1902–2002

Álvarez Bravo studied art at the Academia de San Carlos in Mexico City. A self-taught photographer, his earliest works were Pictorialist-style portraits. During the late 1920s he developed an interest in Mexican literature and indigenous art as well as important relationships with Edward Weston and Tina Modotti that influenced the development of his original modernist style. He assumed Modotti's role as photographer for *Mexican Folkways* magazine in 1930. Befriending Mexican muralist painters, including Diego Rivera, Álvarez Bravo took up revolutionary subject matter but treated it with the abstraction and distance of modernism. At that point he moved away from amateur photographic circles to interact with the international avant-garde artists who visited Mexico in the 1930s. He worked as a cameraman for Sergei Eisenstein in 1930 and met Paul Strand and Henri Cartier-Bresson (1933 and 1934, respectively) in Mexico City.

In 1931 Álvarez Bravo turned to photography full time. A debut solo exhibition at Galeria Posada in 1932 led to an exhibition in Julien Levy's New York gallery alongside work by Walker Evans and Cartier-Bresson. André Breton featured the work in the journal *Minotaure* (1939), thus propelling Álvarez Bravo's photographs into the international surrealist orbit. In Mexico Álvarez Bravo's publication efforts, including articles on Eugène Atget and reprints from

[25]

[28]

[93]

the Parisian journal *Photographie,* encouraged an understanding of the restrained, crystalline style that the photographer admired. Between 1943 and 1959, he worked in the film industry as a photographer and cameraman. He founded El Fondo Editorial de la Plástica Mexicana, a fine art publishing house, directing it from 1959 to 1980.

Álvarez Bravo had a distinguished museum career and was recognized internationally for his contribution to fine art photography. His photographic style was formed by the violence of the Mexican Revolution, his own political engagement, and his appreciation for the radical abstraction of the international avant-garde.

24. *Ladder of Ladders (Escala de Escalas),* 1931
Gelatin silver print; 24.4 x 18.3 cm (9⅝ x 7¼ in.). John L. Severance Fund 2007.142

INSCRIPTIONS
In brown ink on verso of print: *cajas para muertes grandes y chicas* and *MAlvarez Bravo/Mexico*

In pencil on mount: *Manuel Alvarez Bravo*

PROVENANCE
The artist, Mexico City; André Breton, Paris; Private collection, France; David Raymond, New York

BIBLIOGRAPHY
Andre Breton: 42, rue Fontaine, no. 5047. Paris: Calmels Cohen, 2003.

André Breton: La Beauté Convulsive. Exh. cat. Paris: Centre Pompidou, 1991.

Focus on Minotaure: The Animal-Headed Review, no. 5. Exh. cat. Geneva: Musée d'Art et d'Histoire, 1987.

La Revolution Surréaliste. Exh. cat. Paris: Centre Pompidou, 2002.

Surrealismus 1919–1944. Exh. cat. Düsseldorf: Kunstsammlung Nordrhein Westfalen, 2002.

25. *The Balloon Seller,* 1947
Gelatin silver print; 16.3 x 11 cm (6⅜ x 4⅜ in.). John L. Severance Fund 2007.25

INSCRIPTIONS
Signed on verso of print: *M. Alvarez Bravo/Manuel Álvarez/Bravo/ca. 1947* [possible later signature]

PROVENANCE
The artist, Mexico City; Lorenzo Hernandez, CA; David Raymond, New York

Eugène Atget
French, 1857–1927

Atget's long photographic career straddled the nineteenth and twentieth centuries in chronology and outlook. Born near Bordeaux, he studied acting in Paris, but around 1890 he took up photography as a commercial profession, using a box camera with gelatin dry glass-plate negatives to make prints of landscape and architectural details. These he sold to artists, decorators, and craftsmen who then used the images in their own work. By 1898 he was photographing the streets of Paris and arranging his studio output into distinct sets of negatives and paper prints in albums. He referred to these street views and details as *Vieux Paris* (Old Paris), noting the movement to save the old sections of Paris in response to the demolition and modernization of several Right Bank areas in the 1860s. The general nature of Atget's cataloguing work evolved into an exhaustive collection of indoor and outdoor architectural details over a ten-year period. In 1899 he moved to Montparnasse—on the same street Man Ray lived in the 1920s—where Atget remained until his death in 1927. By 1905 Atget had sold six hundred prints of decorative art details to the Musée Carnavalet. Other commissions and sales to public institutions followed.

Before 1900 Atget photographed the gardens and chateaus in the suburbs of Paris, including Versailles and Saint-Cloud. He produced distinctly more lyrical, personal photographs that focused on lighting, atmospheric conditions, and the Cartesian logic of French garden architecture. The cumbersome photographic equipment he used went against popular convenience offered by the handheld cameras in widespread use by the 1880s. Yet the preference was deliberate, offering Atget ample opportunity to capture all aspects of the landscape in great detail. Even as Atget expanded his repertoire to embrace the ragpickers and itinerant travelers beyond the urban borders, his clinical point of view remained steadfast. His métier of straight visual facts jibed with the modernist vision of the New Objectivity/New Vision movement throughout European visual art of the 1920s. He was greatly admired and studied by the

rising avant-garde; eventually, Atget's work achieved recognition as one of the cornerstones of twentieth-century fine art photography.

During the 1920s Atget was befriended by Berenice Abbott, who worked as his studio assistant and became the executor of his estate. Abbott actively promoted Atget's work in her artistic circles in Paris and elsewhere, often asking more for his prints than for her own work. Eventually, Abbott sold most of Atget's studio archive to the Museum of Modern Art.

28. *Mullein in Bloom (Bouillon en fleur),*
c. 1897–99
Albumen print; 21.8 x 17.6 cm (8⅝ x 6⅞ in.). John L. Severance Fund 2007.26

INSCRIPTIONS
In pencil on verso of print: *Bouillon Blanc/En Fleur/133*

Black stamp on verso of print: *E. Atget/Rue Campagne-Première, 17 bis*

PROVENANCE
Millon & Associés, Paris, 16 November 1999, no. 2; David Raymond, New York

Herman Bekman
Dutch or German, 1906–?

Bekman worked as a professional photographer in the Amsterdam area in the 1930s and 1940s. His studio was in Coevorden, an Amsterdam suburb. He participated in the amateur group Union of Netherlandish Photographers and published occasionally in their illustrated journal, the *Nederlandsch Jaarboek voor fotokunst* (1944/46 and 1947).

93. *The Film (Der Film),* 1930
Gelatin silver print; 23.8 x 29.8 cm (9⅜ x 11¾ in.). John L. Severance Fund 2007.29

INSCRIPTIONS
Black stamp on verso of print: *ATELIER BEKMAN/Fotografie–Fotohandel/Heutszingel 19/Coevorden*

In pencil on verso of print: *8 stuk* and *BOVEA*

PROVENANCE
Kunsthaus Lempertz, Cologne, 15 September 2001, no. 35; David Raymond, New York

Hans Bellmer
German, 1902–1975

Born in Kattowitz, Germany (now Katowice, Poland), Bellmer spent much of his childhood in fantasy play with his younger brother Fritz, avoiding his overbearing father who forced him to work in a steel mill and coal mine after high school. In 1922 he exhibited a series of pornographic gouaches, prompting his arrest for "undermining the moral supports of the State." Bellmer's father then enrolled him against his will in the engineering program at the Berlin Technical College in 1923. The disciplined drawing skills he learned there provided a good foundation for his later work as an artist whose focus became the female doll. A drawing class there taught by George Grosz introduced Bellmer to the political artists of the Malik Verlag (Wieland Herzfelde and his brother John Heartfield). During a visit to Paris in 1924–25, Bellmer met the artists associated with the surrealist circle, including René Magritte. Back in Berlin, he opened an advertising and design agency in 1926.

Bellmer's lifelong exploration of the female figure intensified after 1932 when he saw a production of Jacques Offenbach's opera *Tales of Hoffmann* featuring Coppelia, an automated doll. Concurrently, he received a box of his childhood toys, including miscellaneous broken and mismatched doll parts, and met the famed Berlin dollmaker Lotte Pritzel.

By 1933 Bellmer created a life-size doll as a model and published a series of images of it, *Die Puppe*, in 1934. By 1935 he made the first of many trips to Paris for exhibitions and collaborations with surrealist artists and writers. He made a second doll with an articulated ball joint in 1935 and published a second photographic volume, *Les Jeux de la Poupée*.

He moved permanently to Paris in 1938, though he was interned during the war and spent time in Carcassone after 1941. At the war's end, he resumed his illustrations and literary collaborations, working with Georges Bataille and Paul Eluard. Bellmer was very active in the postwar surrealist circles in Paris and was central to the production of a special issue of the periodical *Obliques* (1975) dedicated to his work.

1. *The Doll (La Poupée),* 1934, printed 1936
Gelatin silver print; 11.7 x 7.8 cm (4⁵⁄₈ x 3 in.). John L. Severance Fund 2007.27

PROVENANCE
Paul Hertzmann, San Francisco; David Raymond, New York

BIBLIOGRAPHY
Schaffner, Ingrid, and Colin Westerbeck. *Accommodations of Desire: Surrealist Works on Paper Collected by Julien Levy,* 75. Exh. cat. Pasadena: Curatorial Assistance, 2004.

59. *The Doll (La Poupée),* 1936
Paris: Editions GLM. Translated from German by Robert Valençay. Ten original gelatin silver prints. Book: 16.3 x 12.5 x 1.5 cm (6³⁄₈ x 4⁷⁄₈ x ½ in.); images: 11.7 x 7.8 cm (4⁵⁄₈ x 3 in.). John L. Severance Fund 2007.28.1–10

PROVENANCE
Christie's, New York, 22 April 2003, no. 165; Ubu Gallery, New York; David Raymond, New York

BIBLIOGRAPHY
Lichtenstein, Therese. *Behind Closed Doors: The Art of Hans Bellmer.* Berkeley: University of California Press, 2001.

Ilse Bing
American, born Germany, 1899–1998

Bing was raised in an upper-class family in Frankfurt, where she pursued her doctorate in art history. Her introduction to photography was shooting architectural images with her Voigtländer glass-plate camera for her dissertation. In 1929 Bing purchased a Leica camera that she used exclusively in Europe. That same year she received her first photo essay assignments from *Das Illustrierte Blatt,* a prestigious journal featuring the new photojournalism. An early relationship with artist Ella Bergmann-Michel exposed Bing to the Bauhaus and Russian Constructivist movements, whose formalist rigor matched her own. After seeing an exhibition of modernist photography held in Frankfurt in spring 1930, she moved to Paris.

Lauded for her expertise with the Leica in all kinds of light and atmospheric conditions, Bing found great success in Paris; her reportage work on the Paris

Ballet in 1933 was well known. She received commissions for important journals including *VU* and *Le Monde Illustré* and was also on contract to *Harper's Bazaar* and *Vogue* as well as French publications. Her work was included in several important exhibitions, such as the *International Exhibition of Contemporary Photography* at the Musée des Arts Décoratifs in Paris, *Das Lichtbild* in Essen, *Modern European Photography* at the Julien Levy Gallery, New York, and Beaumont Newhall's groundbreaking survey of the medium, *Photography 1839–1937,* at the Museum of Modern Art.

In 1937 she married pianist and musicologist Konrad Wolff. Two years later they were interned at a camp for enemy aliens in France and in 1941 emigrated to the U.S., settling in New York. Supporting herself with portrait commissions during the war, Bing found a new photographic language in the later 1940s with the Rolleiflex camera. Her style became less fluid and her compositions more abstract, due somewhat, she said, to her new habitat. In the later 1970s, Bing's work was rediscovered by a new generation. She had an active exhibition and museum career, first in the U.S. and then worldwide.

163. *Laundry, Frankfurt,* 1929
Gelatin silver print; 11.5 x 17.4 cm (4⁵⁄₈ x 6⁷⁄₈ in.). John L. Severance Fund 2007.32

INSCRIPTION
In pencil on mount: *IB/FFM/1929*

PROVENANCE
Edwynn Houk Gallery, New York; David Raymond, New York

BIBLIOGRAPHY
Schaffner, Ingrid, and Colin Westerbeck. *Accommodations of Desire: Surrealist Works on Paper Collected by Julien Levy,* 67. Exh. cat. Pasadena: Curatorial Assistance, 2004.

128. *Paris,* 1933
Gelatin silver print; 21.6 x 28.3 cm (8½ x 11⅛ in.). John L. Severance Fund 2007.31

INSCRIPTIONS
In white ink in lower left on recto of print: *Ilse Bing/1933*

Black stamp on recto of mount: *ILSE BING/PARIS/1933*

[156] [162]

Agfa Brovira stamp on verso of print

PROVENANCE
Edwynn Houk Gallery, New York; David Raymond, New York

BIBLIOGRAPHY
Schaffner, Ingrid, and Colin Westerbeck. *Accommodations of Desire: Surrealist Works on Paper Collected by Julien Levy,* 66. Exh. cat. Pasadena: Curatorial Assistance, 2004.

119. *Paris Fair (Paris Foire),* 1933
Gelatin silver print; 28.3 x 22.3 cm (11⅛ x 8¾ in.). John L. Severance Fund 2007.30

INSCRIPTIONS
In white ink on recto of print: *Ilse Bing/1933*

In pencil on mount: *Paris Foire*

Black stamp on recto of mount: *ILSE BING/PARIS*

In red pencil on verso of mount: *Ilse Bing Paris*

PROVENANCE
Edwynn Houk Gallery, New York; David Raymond, New York

BIBLIOGRAPHY
Schaffner, Ingrid, and Colin Westerbeck. *Accommodations of Desire: Surrealist Works on Paper Collected by Julien Levy,* 83. Exh. cat. Pasadena: Curatorial Assistance, 2004.

156. *Street Cleaners,* 1947
Gelatin silver print; 32.5 x 26.8 cm (12¾ x 10½ in.). Gift of David Raymond 2009.477

INSCRIPTIONS
In pencil on verso of print: *Ilse/Bing/1947*

In pencil in top left corner of verso of print: [?]*OB*

In black ink in lower left margin of recto of print: *ILSE BING*

PROVENANCE
Edwynn Houk Gallery, New York; David Raymond, New York

BIBLIOGRAPHY
Schaffner, Ingrid, and Colin Westerbeck. *Accommodations of Desire: Surrealist Works on Paper Collected by Julien Levy,* 69. Exh. cat. Pasadena: Curatorial Assistance, 2004.

Théodore Blanc and Antoine Demilly
French, 1898–1985 and 1892–1964, respectively

Brothers-in-law Blanc and Demilly inherited the photography studio of Édouard Bron in 1924 in Lyon, where Demilly was a studio apprentice and Blanc a local amateur photographer. They enhanced Bron's portrait business studio by adding street and landscape work, often shot with the new Rolleiflex and Leica cameras.

Their work reflected the popular Pictorialist mode as well as more experimental compositions favored by the avant-garde. Their work was included in several illustrated periodicals including *VU* and *L'Amour de l'Art* featuring André Kertész and Germaine Krull among others, and in the 1933 French historical photography survey exhibition at Galerie Braun in Paris. Interspersed with their more conventional work are semi-abstract urban views that reveal a modernist eye and an urge to record social change during the interwar years.

Their best-known work, a collection of twelve portfolios of atmospheric city views published in heliogravure under the title *Les Aspects de Lyon,* appeared in 1933–35. They opened a gallery offering oversized prints for sale. Blanc and Demilly were appreciated for the high quality of their prints as well as their support for local artists. They sold and promoted the new German cameras, published a monthly technical bulletin on photography, and established a yearly award in photography, Le Concours Blanc et Demilly.

162. *Sign with Hat,* c. 1934
Gelatin silver print; 29.7 x 29.6 cm (11¾ x 11⅝ in.). John L. Severance Fund 2007.33

INSCRIPTIONS
In red pencil on recto of print: *Blanc et Demilly*

In red pencil on verso of print: *Le Chapeau* and *30 x 30* and *29 x 29* and writing lower left and lower right [illegible]

PROVENANCE
Étude Tajan, Paris, 18 November 2000, no. 313; David Raymond, New York

Erwin Blumenfeld
American, born Germany, 1897–1969

Blumenfeld took up photography as a teenager in Berlin. Having befriended Dutch artist Paul Citroen during his student years, the pair frequented the Café des Westens, a hub for the radical artists of the German Expressionist group. Among their cohorts were George Grosz and the Wieland brothers of the Malik Verlag, a left-wing publisher supporting the socialist movement in Germany. Blumenfeld became engaged to Lena Citroen, Paul's niece. During World War I he was an ambulance driver (1916–18).

After the war, Blumenfeld moved to Amsterdam, married Lena, established an unsuccessful gallery with Citroen (1919–21), and embarked on a rich period of artistic activity centered on the Dada movement, then blossoming throughout Europe. He established the Hollandse Dadacentrale with Citroen as a means to connect with other Dada centers of activity. He delved into collage work, combining found and original photography with newsprint and other texts, signing these works under the pseudonym Jan Bloomfield, an Americanized version of his name.

In 1932 Blumenfeld exhibited his photography in Amsterdam and published work in several illustrated magazines in France and Germany. Inspired, he moved and set up a studio in Paris in 1936, working on commercial assignments and portrait commissions while pursuing personal work. Through Cecil Beaton he made contact with *Vogue,* publishing there and in *Harper's Bazaar* in 1938–39. As soon as the Second World War began, Blumenfeld was interned in a holding camp but by 1941 was able to move his family to New York. Most of his work during the 1940s and 1950s was with *Vogue,* where his one hundred cover images established his reputation as one of the preeminent fashion photographers of the era. Blumenfeld's technical prowess with color processes and his sophisticated grasp of art history created a rich legacy of imagery.

39. *Boxers over New York,* early 1920s
Gelatin silver print of photomechanical reproductions, collage; 19.4 x 24.4 cm (7⅝ x 9⅝ in.). John L. Severance Fund 2007.34

INSCRIPTION
In black ink on recto of print: *BLOOMFIELD DADA HOLLAND*

[6]　　　　[22]　　　　[23]　　　　[136]

PROVENANCE
Estate of Paul Citroen, Wassenar, Netherlands; Egidio Marzona, Berlin; Hendrik Berinson, Berlin; Ubu Gallery, New York; Barry Friedman Ltd., New York; David Raymond, New York

BIBLIOGRAPHY
Adkins, Helen. *Erwin Blumenfeld. I Was Nothing but a Berliner: Dada Montages 1916–1933,* 216. Ostfildern: Hatje Kantz, 2008.

6. *Profile Study,* c. 1944
Gelatin silver print, ferrotyped; 31.6 x 26.3 cm (12½ x 10⅜ in.). John L. Severance Fund 2007.35

INSCRIPTIONS
In pencil on verso of print: *Hand printed by Erwin Blumenfeld for the Collection of Yorick Blumenfeld*

Blue estate stamp on verso of print: *FROM THE ESTATE OF ERWIN BLUMENFELD*

PROVENANCE
The artist's estate, England; U.S. art market; Sotheby's, New York, 27 April 1989, no. 443; David Raymond, New York

Bill Brandt
English, 1904–1983

Son of a British father of Russian descent and a German mother, Brandt was raised primarily in Germany and experienced the anti-British sentiment of World War I. As a child he spent almost six years in a Swiss sanatorium recovering from tuberculosis, was psychoanalyzed in Vienna, and began to paint and photograph with a Brownie camera. He traveled throughout Europe, spending time in Vienna, Paris, Hungary, and Barcelona between 1927 and 1932, making pictures in the streets, some of which he sold to illustrated magazines in England and France. Brandt was self-trained, apart from a few months spent as an apprentice in Man Ray's Paris studio in 1929 when he absorbed the culture of the surrealist avant-garde. Yet by the early 1930s, his connections with astute artists and editors on both sides of the Channel led to publication of his images in Arts et Metiers Graphique's *Photographie* annual as well as the surrealist journal *Minotaure*. At that point his career as a photojournalist took off.

Back in London in 1931, Brandt began photographing the stratified society of England, publishing *The English at Home* (1936), followed by *A Night in London* (1938). His interest in capturing England's class system extended beyond the city to the working class with trips to the Midlands industrial towns in 1937. During the Blitz in 1940, he photographed London citizens in underground bomb shelters and subway stations. Although Brandt made straight pictures of his surroundings, he did not consider his work documentary and often took liberal license in posing his characters as well as manipulating his prints in the darkroom.

After the war, Brandt focused on nudes shot in interiors and along the beaches of Britain and northern France, as in *Nude, Vasterival, Normandy* (1954). Using a Kodak wide-angle camera, he created the sequence of distorted forms that were published in his hallmark volume *Perspective of Nudes* (1961). These surrealist-tinged images were shown at New York's Museum of Modern Art in 1948 and in a retrospective exhibition in 1969 that traveled to London.

22. *Barcelona,* April 1932
Gelatin silver print; 29.2 x 22 (11⅝ x 8¾ in.). John L. Severance Fund 2007.143

INSCRIPTIONS
Signed in pencil on mount: *Bill Brandt*

In black marker on verso of mount: *Barcelona (April 1932)*

PROVENANCE
The artist's family, England; Edwynn Houk Gallery, New York; David Raymond, New York

23. *Nude, Vasterival, Normandy,* June 1954, printed mid- to late 1950s
Gelatin silver print with hand-applied manipulation; 23 x 19.8 cm (9 x 7⅞ in.). John L. Severance Fund 2007.36

INSCRIPTIONS
Artist's stamp on verso of print: *BILL BRANDT*

In blue ink on verso of print: *June 1954*

PROVENANCE
New York auction market; Ramer collection, San Francisco; Christie's, New York, 8 April 1998, no. 240; David Raymond, New York

Brassaï (Gyula Halász)
French, born Hungary, 1899–1984

The child of a French literature professor in Transylvania, Brassaï studied at the Budapest Fine Arts Academy and moved to Berlin for a year (1921–22) where he studied painting and socialized with Wassily Kandinsky and László Moholy-Nagy. In 1924 Brassaï moved to Paris, supporting himself as a reporter for German and Hungarian newspapers and spending time with the avant-garde artists of Montparnasse. He only began to consider photography after meeting André Kertész, newly arrived in Paris in 1926, who sometimes accompanied Brassaï on journalism assignments as his photographer. After 1929 Brassaï made his own photographs to illustrate his articles.

Brassaï made nocturnal journeys through the rougher neighborhoods of Paris around 1930, often with Kertész or American writer Henry Miller, then living in Paris. Brassaï loved these heady escapades in which he photographed the pimps, prostitutes, and the demimonde, images gathered in his first book, *Nuit de Paris,* published in 1932.

Having changed his name to Brassaï, he met the politically active Prévert brothers as well as André Breton and Pablo Picasso. Brassaï's photographs were often featured in the pages of the surrealist publication *Minotaure* in the mid-1930s, beginning with his graffiti pictures in 1933. Other work in the magazine included a series of nudes and images of his so-called Involuntary Sculptures, created with Salvador Dalí—photographs of quotidian objects considered from a surrealist viewpoint. Throughout 1933 and 1934, Brassaï actively continued his personal street photography and worked on assignment in Paris for the popular *Détective* magazine, among others. His work was shown at Julien Levy Gallery in New York in 1932, and his first solo exhibition was at the Batsford Gallery, London, in 1933. By 1935 Brassaï began reporting for the Rapho picture agency, using the Rolleiflex for the first time. His series on Henri Matisse appeared in the first edition of *Verve* magazine (December 1937). A selection of photographs illustrated Breton's novel *L'Amour fou* in 1938, which cemented Brassaï's reputation as a surrealist, though he never held any allegiance to the group beyond a shared poetic vision.

In the later 1930s, Brassaï found commercial success with *Harper's Bazaar* and other illustrated magazines in England and the U.S. During the German occupa-

tion of Paris, he concentrated on personal work and photographed Picasso's sculpture. After the war, he published several books of photographs including *Conversations with Picasso* (1960). Brassaï's work received recognition in American museums beginning in 1951 with *Five French Photographers* at the Museum of Modern Art.

136. A Couple at the Ball Quat'z Arts (Un couple le Bal des Quat'z Arts), 1931, printed 1950s
Gelatin silver print, ferrotyped; 28.5 x 20.9 cm (11¼ x 8¼ in.). John L. Severance Fund 2007.144

INSCRIPTION
In black ink on verso of print: *Un couple/Le bal des Quat'z arts, vers 1931/Brassaï* [signed]/*Pl. 746*

Black stamp on verso of print: *BRASSAÏ/81, rue de St. Jacques/PARIS-XIV-PORt-Royal 23-41*

Purple stamp on verso of print: *© COPYRIGHT by BRASSAÏ/81, Faubourg St. Jacques/PARIS 14ème Tél. 707.23.41*

PROVENANCE
Mme Brassaï, Paris; Edwynn Houk Gallery, New York; David Raymond, New York

BIBLIOGRAPHY
Schneede, Uwe M., and Hamburger Kunsthalle. *Begierde im Blick: Surrealistiche Photographie,* no. 58. Exh. cat. Ostfildern: Hatje Cantz, 2005.

137. Novice Prostitute, Place d'Italie (Novice Prostituée, Place d'Italie), c. 1931, printed 1950s
Gelatin silver print, ferrotyped; 23.5 x 17.5 cm (9¼ x 6⅞ in.). Gift of David Raymond 2007.282

INSCRIPTIONS
In pencil on verso of print: *Brassaï* [signed]/*Fille en robe printanière* [illegible] *Italie vers 1931; No. 16* [circled]; *41* [circled]; *11/15 Pl. 327*

Stamps on verso of print: *BRASSAÏ/81, rue de Faub.-St. Jacques/PARIS XIV-PORt-Royal 23-41; © COPYRIGHT by BRASSAÏ/81, Faubourg St. Jacques/ PARIS 14ème Tel. 707.23.41*

PROVENANCE
Mme Brassaï, Paris; Edwynn Houk Gallery, New York; David Raymond, New York

BIBLIOGRAPHY
Schneede, Uwe M., and Hamburger Kunsthalle. *Begierde im Blick: Surrealistiche Photographie,* no. 57. Exh. cat. Ostfildern: Hatje Cantz.

139. Young Couple Wearing a Two-in-One Suit at the Bal de la Montagne Sainte-Geneviève, c. 1931, printed mid-1950s
Gelatin silver print, ferrotyped; 29.8 x 22 cm (11¾ x 6¾ in.). John L. Severance Fund 2007.40

INSCRIPTIONS
In blue ink on verso of print: *Pl. 444*

Purple stamp on verso of print: *BRASSAÏ/81, rue de Faub.-St. Jacques/PARIS-XIV-PORt-Royal 23-41*

PROVENANCE
Mme Brassaï, Paris; Edwynn Houk Gallery, New York; David Raymond, New York

BIBLIOGRAPHY
Combalía Dexeus, Victoria. *Paris y los surrealistas,* 230. Exh. cat. Bilbao: Museum de Bellas Artes de Bilbao, 2005.

164. Nude, c. 1931–33
Gelatin silver print, solarized; 23.3 x 17.6 cm (9⅛ x 6⅞ in.). Gift of David Raymond 2008.174

PROVENANCE
Private collection, Paris; Jane Corkin Gallery, Toronto; Phillips, New York, 24–25 April 2003, no. 99A; David Raymond, New York

BIBLIOGRAPHY
Schneede, Uwe M., and Hamburger Kunsthalle. *Begierde im Blick: Surrealistiche Photographie,* no. 59. Exh. cat. Ostfildern: Hatje Cantz.

138. At the White Ball, Montparnasse (A la Boule Blanche, Montparnasse), 1932
Gelatin silver print, ferrotyped; 24 x 18 cm (9½ x 7⅛ in.). John L. Severance Fund 2007.39

INSCRIPTION
On verso of print: *A la Boule blanche/Montparnasse/ vers 1932/Brassaï* [signed]

PROVENANCE
Mme Brassaï, Paris; Edwynn Houk Gallery, New York; David Raymond, New York

BIBLIOGRAPHY
Combalía Dexeus, Victoria. *Paris y los surrealistas,* 224. Exh. cat. Bilbao: Museum de Bellas Artes de Bilbao.

122. Folies Bergères, 1932
Gelatin silver print, ferrotyped; 22.3 x 15 cm (8¾ x 5⅞ in.). Gift of David Raymond 2007.281

PROVENANCE
Mme Brassaï, Paris; Edwynn Houk Gallery, New York; David Raymond, New York

BIBLIOGRAPHY
Schaffner, Ingrid, and Colin Westerbeck. *Accommodations of Desire: Surrealist Works on Paper Collected by Julien Levy,* 62. Exh. cat. Pasadena: Curatorial Assistance, 2004.

132. Two Acrobats, Cirque Médrano in Paris (2 Equilibristes Cirque Médrano à Paris), 1932–33
Gelatin silver print, ferrotyped; 27.7 x 23.4 cm (10⅞ x 9¼ in.). John L. Severance Fund 2007.38

INSCRIPTIONS
In pencil on verso of print: *2 equilibristes Cirque Médrano à Paris/Bd. Rochechouart vers 1932–1933/ 7/30; Pl. 1155 circus; No. 25* [circled]

In pencil on verso of print: *Lilliput dec 1948/"Conversation avec Picasso" pp. 30–31 Gallimard/pp. 20–22 Doubleday NY*

Purple copyright stamp on verso of print: *© COPYRIGHT by BRASSAÏ/81, Faubourg St.-Jacques/PARIS XIV/Tel. 707.23.41*

Black stamp on verso of print: *BRASSAÏ/81, RUE DU St. JACQUES/PARIS-XIV/TÉLÉPH.: PORT-ROYAL 23-41*

Black agency stamp on verso of print: *RAPHO GUILLUMETTE PICTURES . . . New York* [crossed out]

PROVENANCE
Mme Brassaï, Paris; Edwynn Houk Gallery, New York; David Raymond, New York

BIBLIOGRAPHY
Brassaï and Popper. "Tigers, Tumblers and the Flying Trapeze." *Lilliput* 23, no. 6 (December 1948): 70.

Combalía Dexeus, Victoria. *Paris y los surrealistas,* 230. Exh. cat. Bilbao: Museum de Bellas Artes de Bilbao, 2005.

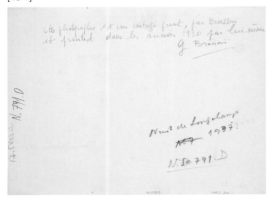

134. *Night at Longchamps (Nuit de Long-champs),* 1937
Gelatin silver print, ferrotyped, montage; 17.6 x 23.2 cm (7 x 9⅛ in.). John L. Severance Fund 2007.37

INSCRIPTION
In pencil on verso of print: *Nuit de Longchamps 1937/Cette photographie est un montage, fait par Brassaï/et printed dans les années 1930 par lui même/G. Brassaï/N.791.D* [negative number]

PROVENANCE
Mme Brassaï, Paris; Edwynn Houk Gallery, New York; Simon Lowinsky; Foster Goldstrom, CA; David Raymond, New York

BIBLIOGRAPHY
Schaffner, Ingrid, and Colin Westerbeck. *Accommodations of Desire: Surrealist Works on Paper Collected by Julien Levy,* 63. Exh. cat. Pasadena: Curatorial Assistance, 2004.

Josef Breitenbach
American, born Germany, 1896–1984

Born into a Jewish family in Munich, Breitenbach studied chemistry, philosophy, and art history at the Ludwig Maximilian University, Munich (1914–17). He worked in several offices and professions, eventually returning to the family wine business in 1919. During business trips abroad, he began photographing landscapes, winning his first medal in a Milan photo competition in 1928. The wine business folded in 1931, and Breitenbach opened a photography studio in Munich, doing portraits and taking advertising assignments. As a member of the Sozialdemokratische Partei Deutschlands (SPD, the main left-wing political party in Weimar Germany), he participated in rallies and avant-garde theater circles in Munich. In 1933, after the Nazis assumed power in Germany, he moved to Paris and was included in André Breton's circle, though he never officially joined the surrealist group. Breitenbach exhibited odd-angled portraits, solarized landscapes, and nudes that increasingly took on modernist qualities. He exhibited alongside avant-garde photographers in Paris and associated with the German exiles there, including Berthold Brecht (1938). In 1939 Breitenbach became the Paris correspondent for the British International News Agency and joined the Association of Foreign Press Photographers, traveling to England and Germany

for assignments before being interned as a foreigner for two months in a camp in central France. In 1941 he left France and eventually landed in New York in 1942, just as the United States joined World War II.

In New York Breitenbach applied his confident surrealist techniques to fashion and portrait work while also gathering experience as a journalistic photographer. He shot stories for *Fortune* and *McCall's,* among others, and established a successful teaching career at Cooper Union and the New School for Social Research. After becoming a naturalized American citizen in 1946, he was hired to cover the Korean War in 1952–53. During the 1960s, Breitenbach traveled extensively in Southeast Asia. At home he pursued studies of plein-air nudes in nudist camps in New Jersey.

Breitenbach's documentary work from the 1950s was included in Edward Steichen's *Family of Man* exhibition at the Museum of Modern Art in 1955.

126. *Electric Back,* 1949
Gelatin silver print, montage; 34.2 x 26.7 cm (13½ x 10½ in.). John L. Severance Fund 2007.145

INSCRIPTIONS
Estate and studio stamps on verso of print: *ESTATE OF JOSEF BREITENBACH/Credit to Joseph Breitenbach, A.R.P.S., 210 Central Park South, New York City, Columbus 5-0468*

PROVENANCE
Private collection, New York; Swann Galleries, New York, 13 December 2005, no. 391; David Raymond, New York

51. *Fireworks,* 1949
Gelatin silver print, photogram; 35.4 x 27.9 cm (14 x 11 in.). John L. Severance Fund 2007.41

INSCRIPTIONS
Estate stamp on verso of print: *ESTATE OF JOSEF BREITENBACH*

In pencil on verso of print: *150 Fire Works/FEUER-WERK P 18/Imperato*

PROVENANCE
Sothebys.com, c. 2001; David Raymond, New York

BIBLIOGRAPHY
Die Sammlung Josef Breitenbach zur Geschichte der Photographie, no. 150. Exh. cat. Munich: Fotomuseum im Münchner Stadtmuseum, 1979.

Holborn, Mark. *Josef Breitenbach, Photographer,* 23. New York: Temple Rock Company, 1986.

Horace Bristol
American, 1908–1997

Bristol was born and raised in California where he briefly attended the University of Southern California and Stanford. Married in 1929, he and his wife traveled to Germany where he studied architecture and photography using both a Rolleiflex and the new Leica. By 1930 the couple was back in San Francisco where Bristol attended photography classes at the Art Center in Los Angeles. He befriended Ansel Adams and others in meetings of Group *f*/64, though he preferred the documentary ethos of Dorothea Lange's work to Group *f*/64's strictly formalist rigor. He joined Lange and Paul Taylor on photography trips to migrant worker camps in California's central valley, initiating Bristol's career as a photojournalist. In 1935 he joined the Western Photographic Group and by 1937 was under contract to *Life* magazine.

Inspired by Margaret Bourke-White, Bristol wanted to study the western movement of farmers from the Dust Bowl and joined John Steinbeck on several trips to document the plight of workers facing harsh conditions. For *Life* magazine he traveled to Indonesia to explore that culture and territory for American audiences in 1939. After Pearl Harbor he was recruited by Edward Steichen to join the Naval Aviation Photographic Unit and followed General Patton's flotilla to North Africa, to the Aleutian Islands in 1945, and to Tokyo in 1946. He remained in Japan, hosting foreign correspondents and selling pictures through his East West Photo Agency. Bristol explored human interest stories in and around Tokyo, shooting geisha culture and *yakuza,* the Japanese organized crime network. His numerous picture books on Asian communities were popular with the GI population. Bristol returned to California in the late 1960s.

150. *Fortuneteller with Glass,* 1946
Gelatin silver print; 5.6 x 5.6 cm (2¼ x 2¼ in.). John L. Severance Fund 2007.42

INSCRIPTIONS
Signed in black pen on mount: *Horace Bristol*

Chop mark in red ink on recto of mount

PROVENANCE
Butterfields, San Francisco, 14 December 1995, no. 1680; David Raymond, New York

Robert Capa
Hungarian, 1913–1954

Born André Friedmann in Hungary to Jewish tailors, Capa was a politically savvy teenager forced to leave Hungary for his alleged support of the Communist Party in 1931. He pursued political studies in Berlin but adopted photography as a trade when the family experienced a reversal of fortune. Capa successfully shot events for the German illustrated press, most often for the Ullstein family of magazines, beginning with a 1932 photograph of Leon Trotsky speaking in Copenhagen. Capa also printed for the Dephot agency in Berlin. In 1933 he left Berlin for Vienna and then for Paris, where he remained between location shoots until 1939. There he blossomed amid the Hungarian and other immigrant artist populations. He met photographers David Chim and Gerda Taro, who became his lover and agent. Conscious of rising anti-Semitism, Taro gave him the name Robert Capa in 1935 in order to attract higher prices for his freelance photographs. In short order he was affiliated with the French photo agencies Hug Block, Agence Centrale, and finally Alliance Photo founded by Maria Eisner. He worked often for Lucien Vogel, publisher of *VU* in the 1930s. Ernest Mayer, one of three founders of the Black Star photo agency, brought Capa's work to New York just after *Life* magazine was founded in 1936. In 1939 the photographer immigrated to the United States.

Best known as a war photographer starting with his pictures of the Spanish Civil War (1936), Capa photographed conflicts and newsworthy political events everywhere; his work redefined the standard for immediacy in news photography. In China in 1938 he followed Chiang Kai-shek and the rise of Mao's Communist Party. He was a correspondent for *Life* magazine during the war, and in Paris in 1947, along with Chim, Henri Cartier-Bresson, George Rodger, and Bill Vandivert, he founded Magnum, the cooperative picture agency run by its member photographers. In the post-World War II era, Magnum was the gold standard for independent photojournalists worldwide, insisting that copyright rest with the photographers rather than the publisher.

Capa died on the battlefield in Indochina in spring 1954 after the fall of Dien Bien Phu. His brother Cornell Capa established the International Center for Photography in New York, which houses his archive. Most recently the discovery of a suitcase full of Capa's negatives (the "Mexican Suitcase") has brought this great career into the limelight once again.

151. *Race Course, Paris (Concours Hippique, Paris),* 1937
Gelatin silver print; 24 x 17 cm (9½ x 6¾ in.). John L. Severance Fund 2007.43

INSCRIPTIONS
In pencil on verso of print: *G./French Group/Concours Hyppique in Paris/France, 1937*

Signed in marker on verso of print: *Robert Capa*

Stamps on verso of print: *Photo Robert Capa* and *Black Star/Graybar Building, New York*

In pencil on verso of print: *Seeds 100*

PROVENANCE
Private collection, New York; Swann Galleries, New York, 13 December 2005, no. 391; David Raymond, New York

Pere Català i Pic
Spanish, 1899–1971

Català i Pic was born in Valls, Tarragona, Spain, where he studied photography with Rafael Arenas (1913–14). In 1915 the young artist established his own photography studio. He is considered to be the first photographic theorist of the modernist period in Spain, bringing theory, psychology, and design to the field of advertising photography. He translated the newest articles and taught the newest techniques developed in Germany and France, and suggested how these were best applied to Spanish subjects.

His commercial work developed in an avant-garde direction through the use of photomontage and superimposition, techniques that appear in his magazine and poster work. Though his activity remained commercial and pedagogical, he admired Man Ray above all other photographic artists. From 1932 to 1935, Català i Pic wrote actively for *Mirador* and traveled widely in Europe. Among his clients were large Spanish companies as well as international brands such as Ford.

During the Spanish Civil War, he directed the Publication Department of Visual Propaganda for Catalonia. At that time, he adopted the signature PIC on all his studio work. Photomontage, his visual trademark, appeared in his work throughout the war years and beyond.

42. *Advertising Montage,* c. 1932
Gelatin silver print; 13 x 9.3 cm (5 x 3⅝ in.). John L. Severance Fund 2007.109

INSCRIPTION
Blue stamp on verso of print: *Fotos PIC Barcelona* [address illegible]

PROVENANCE
Pere Català i Roca, son of the artist, Barcelona; Gallery Kowasa, Barcelona; David Raymond, New York

Erich Consemüller
German, 1902–1957

Born in Bielefeld, Consemüller apprenticed with a local carpenter (1920–22) and studied at the local institute for arts and crafts. He spent 1922–27 at the Bauhaus in Weimar, first as a student in Johannes Itten's foundation course (the *Vorkurs*) and then in the furniture workshops. He toured Iceland in 1924 and returned to the Bauhaus, this time as an architecture student under Adolf Meyer. From 1925 to 1927, responsible for the interior design and furniture, Consemüller worked on the architectural planning of the new Bauhaus complex in Dessau. In 1927 he was commissioned to prepare photographic documentation of the Bauhaus including interiors, theater, and *Vorkurs* work. He used both a Leica as well as a plate camera. While his images of Oscar Schlemmer's *Triadic Ballet* are perhaps his best known, many of his photographs were published as documents of Bauhaus culture and products in various magazines and brochures.

"Royal Wedding" London 1934. Horacio Coppola Esq.

Consemüller's photographic work fits clearly within the New Objectivity movement, and its visual austerity shows the influence of László Moholy-Nagy. His architectural work for Marcel Breuer and Hans Wittwer at the Bauhaus continued once he left the school at the end of 1929. Consemüller taught in Halle and supervised building projects in the region until he was dismissed from his post in 1933, when he found work as an architectural draftsman in offices in Halle, Erfurt, and Leipzig. After the war, he became the town planner for Halle.

117. *Bauhaus Sculptural Study,* c. 1927
Gelatin silver print; 10.6 x 7.6 cm (4⅛ x 3 in.). John L. Severance Fund 2007.44

INSCRIPTION
Typed label on verso of mount: *(24) # 12/1. mounted on black paper/2. Erich Consemüller/3. Sculptural study shot from below with Bauhaus building visible through design forming a complex abstraction./4. BF* [Bauhaus Fotografie], *p. 26, study c. 1927–Consemüller/5. Bauhaus student, self taught in photography/produced fine/work, especially abstraction*

PROVENANCE
Egidio Marzona, Berlin; Barry Friedman Ltd., New York; David Raymond, New York

BIBLIOGRAPHY
Bauhaus Photography, no. 23. Cambridge, MA: MIT Press, 1985.

Frick, Roswitha. *Bauhaus Fotografie,* no. 54. Düsseldorf: Edition Marzona, 1982.

Horacio Coppola
Argentina, 1906–2012

Born in Argentina of Italian parents, Coppola studied art and philosophy in Buenos Aires where he promoted early cinema and contributed photographs to publications by Jorge Luis Borges. He attended Le Corbusier's 1929 series of lectures and traveled to Europe to study modernist photography in Berlin at the Dessau Bauhaus in the photography department established by Walter Peterhans. There he met Grete Stern and Ellen Auerbach, of the ringl & pit studio, and collaborated on commercial projects as well as an experimental film titled *Dream* in 1933. He and Stern fled to London and married shortly thereafter.

They shared interests in surrealism and psychoanalysis, making experimental films and photo collage work together and shooting commercial assignments for Christian Zervos's *Cahiers d'Art* and the British Museum, among other clients. Coppola bought a Leica camera in 1936 and moved permanently back to Buenos Aires.

Photographically, Coppola worked in two styles: the street work influenced by New Vision and the additive studio work that he learned from Peterhans at the Bauhaus. He used both a 35 mm and a large-format camera throughout his career. Upon returning to Argentina, he published *Buenos Aires (vision fotográfica);* exhibited work under the auspices of *Sur,* the leading avant-garde literary journal; and opened a commercial studio in which he continued to photograph sculptural collections for museums. He also published work by other photographers. After the war he returned to Europe with his second wife, Raquel Palomeque, to photograph cultural sites and museums. He continued to produce and write about film as well as photography and architecture. Several exhibitions of his photographic work took place in Argentina in his later years. Though recognition of his work lapsed during the 1970s, interest in his career has recently revived.

43. *Royal Wedding,* 1934
Gelatin silver print; 13.5 x 20.4 cm (5¼ x 8 in.). John L. Severance Fund 2007.45

INSCRIPTION
In pencil by artist on verso of print: *"Royal Wedding" London 1934. Horacio Coppola Esq.*

PROVENANCE
The artist, Buenos Aires; Michael Hoppen Gallery, London; David Raymond, New York

BIBLIOGRAPHY
Horacio Coppola, 19. London: Michael Hoppen Gallery, 2000.

Louise Dahl-Wolfe
American, 1895–1989

Dahl was born in San Francisco into a progressive upper-middle-class family. In 1914 she enrolled at San Francisco Institute of Art where she studied design with Rudolph Schaffer, an early proponent of color theory in applied design in the U.S. She pursued interior design professionally with the San Francisco design firm Armstrong, Carter, and Kenyon. Dahl began to photograph after meeting Anne Brigman in 1921, entering the circle of Edward Weston, Consuelo Kanaga, and the San Francisco Pictorialist group in the early 1920s. Following her mother's death in 1926, she traveled to Europe and North Africa with Kanaga. During this voyage she met her husband, the painter Meyer (Mike) Wolfe.

The couple settled in New York in 1928 but soon moved to Gatlinburg, Tennessee, where Dahl-Wolfe photographed the local people struggling through the Depression. In 1933 they decamped to New York, where Dahl-Wolfe was contracted as a photographer for Saks Fifth Avenue. At this time, her photographs gained notice from the major magazines.

In 1936 she became staff photographer for *Harper's Bazaar,* working with Carmel Snow, fashion editor Diana Vreeland, and Alexey Brodovitch. This team worked together for twenty years, producing groundbreaking fashion spreads on location throughout the world. Dahl-Wolfe used natural lighting extensively on shoots. Her color work of the 1950s in particular represents an apogee for American modernist fashion identity in the postwar environment. She gained tremendous respect from her editors in devising novel locations and narratives for fashion plates. Dahl-Wolfe left *Harper's Bazaar* in 1958 but freelanced for other magazines. Her work first appeared in museum shows in Beaumont Newhall's history of photography show at the Museum of Modern Art in 1937 and has been in numerous museum exhibitions since.

144. *Fashion Study,* c. 1930s
Gelatin silver print; 23.7 x 15.9 cm (9⅜ x 6¼ in.). John L. Severance Fund 2007.46

INSCRIPTION
Signed in black ink on mount: *Louise Dahl-Wolfe*

PROVENANCE
Alice Rohrer, San Francisco; David Howard, San Francisco; David Raymond, New York

Marcel Duchamp
French, 1887–1968

Duchamp was born into a well-off artistic family in a Paris suburb. He attended painting classes at the Académie Julian and remained in Paris until 1912. In 1909 he exhibited paintings in the postimpressionist style at the Salon des Indépendants and Salon d'Automne in Paris. Once he joined his brothers' Puteaux Circle of artists and poets, including Guillaume Apollinaire, Duchamp moved toward a Cubist style in his painting, merging fragmentation of planar surfaces with interest in the time-based photography of Eadweard Muybridge and Étienne-Jules Marey. Once Duchamp's painting *Nude Descending a Staircase, No. 2* was criticized by the jury of the 1912 Salon des Indépendants, he withdrew the work from consideration and reoriented his artistic concerns. He famously stated that he would abandon traditional art materials to focus on conceptual, idea-based art.

The inclusion of *Nude Descending a Staircase, No. 2* in New York's 1913 Armory Show made Duchamp famous. At that show he also premiered his first "ready-made," a mass-produced object displayed in a gallery context.

He came to New York in 1915 for two years and was introduced to collectors Walter and Louise Arensberg and to Man Ray. In the spring of 1920, he and Man Ray worked closely on film, photography, and magazine projects, including the Man Ray photograph of Duchamp dressed as Rrose Sélavy. In 1923 Duchamp returned to France where he remained until the final years of World War II. Having supposedly given up art for the pastime of chess, Duchamp nevertheless supported and collaborated on many projects and exhibitions initiated by the Dada and surrealist artists in Paris, many with photographic components. His collaboration with Georges Hugnet on *The Seventh Face of the Die: Poems-Decoupages (La Septième face du dé: Poèmes-Découpages)* dovetailed with his own 1935 project to create a portable museum of his artistic output, *Boîte en Valise*.

In 1942 Duchamp again returned to New York, working secretly on the *Etant Donnés,* the sculptural installation considered to be his final work of art. His art, writings, and career have had enormous influence on succeeding generations of artists.

80. *Cigarette Covers (Couvertures Cigarette),* 1936
Gelatin silver prints with hand-applied dye; recto: 29.1 x 21.1 cm (11½ x 8¼ in.); verso: 29.3 x 21.4 cm (11½ x 8⅜ in.). Gift of David Raymond 2007.280.a & b

PROVENANCE
Robert Shapazian, Los Angeles; Private collection, Canada; Roth Horowitz, New York; David Raymond, New York

BIBLIOGRAPHY
Krauss, Rosalind, and Jane Livingston. *L'Amour fou: Photography and Surrealism.* Washington, DC: Corcoran Gallery of Art / New York: Abbeville Press, 1985.

78. *The Seventh Face of the Die: Poems-Decoupages (La Septième face du dé: Poèmes-Découpages),* 1936
Paris: Editions Jeanne Bucher. Book of photomechanical offset and rotogravure typography with original gelatin silver prints as back and front covers by Duchamp and original collage by Hugnet, signed by both and numbered 18/20. Overall: 29.3 x 21.4 x 1.5 cm (11½ x 8⅜ x ⅝ in.). Gift of David Raymond 2007.280

John Gutmann
American, born Germany, 1905–1998

Born into a wealthy German Jewish family in Breslau (now Wroclaw, Poland), Gutmann studied with Otto Müller of Die Brücke group of German Expressionists and moved to the urban milieu of Berlin. After traveling through Europe in 1928–29, he returned to Berlin, exhibiting with the Berlin Secession artists and at Fritz Gurlitt's gallery. In 1933 Gutmann purchased a Rolleiflex camera before moving to the United States, where he had contracts with the Pix (New York) agency. He achieved only minor success as a press photographer, his work being too surrealist in tone for the popular picture press. The flattening of space and low viewpoint established by the Rollei camera contributed perhaps to Gutmann's idiosyncratic style. He found steady work teaching at San Francisco State College beginning in 1936. For his commercial photography, Gutmann mined the ebb and flow of

people in that large urban center, from activities at the harbor to striking workers to children playing in the streets. In the 1940s, he met and married artist Gerrie van Pribosic, who belonged to West Coast surrealist circles. She influenced Gutmann's own experimental photographic phase, which included dream-like scenarios and constructed pictures and montages such as *That Inward Eye* (1949).

During World War II, Gutmann was a still- and motion-picture cameraman for the U.S. military in Asia. After the war he returned to teaching in San Francisco and remained active as a photographer until the 1970s. Gutmann exhibited his photography at local institutions such as the de Young Museum, including shows in 1938, 1941, and 1947. In 1976 his work was the subject of a retrospective organized by the San Francisco Museum of Modern Art, and he continued to receive numerous exhibitions from the 1970s onward.

36. *That Inward Eye,* 1949
Gelatin silver print, montage; 22.7 x 17.5 cm (8⅞ x 6⅞ in.). John L. Severance Fund 2007.140

INSCRIPTIONS
In pencil on verso of print: *IN LOVE/1949*

Signed on verso of print: *John Gutmann*

PROVENANCE
The artist's estate, San Francisco; Paul Kopeikin Gallery, Los Angeles; David Raymond, New York

Heinz Hajek-Halke
German, 1898–1983

Hajek-Halke was raised in Buenos Aires but returned to his native Germany in 1910 to study painting. In 1921 he briefly joined the artists' colony at Worpswede. His photographic career began in the early 1920s as a stringer for news photo and advertising agencies. He was completely self-taught but under the tutelage of photographer Willi Ruge learned how to shoot action and sporting scenes.

In complex photomontage works from the mid-1920s onward, Hajek-Halke excelled at employing sandwiched negatives as well as other subtractive

and additive techniques of superimposition in order to alter the straight photograph. By 1927 he had developed this combination technique and was actively publishing work in *Das Deutsche Lichtbild* and other illustrated magazines. By the early 1930s, he had also begun an intensive study of the nude, winning a gold medal in the 1933 Fascist Photography Exhibition in Rome. Due to his great technical skill, he was asked by the Nazi Party to alter the documentation of the Communists. He refused this task, moving in 1936 to Brazil for two years. He returned to Germany in 1938, and during World War II he served as an aerial photographer. Always an intensive naturalist, Hajek-Halke founded a snake farm after the war to collect and sell venom to the pharmaceutical industry.

By 1950 his renewed interest in photographic experimentation led to participation in Otto Steinert's Subjective Photography exhibition and movement, which emphasized the purity of the negative and the gelatin silver print like the Group *f*/64 in America. Hajek-Halke became a leading participant in this and other similar groups in postwar Germany. He became professor at the Academy of Fine Arts in Berlin and published many books, including *Lichtgrafik* and *Experimentelle Fotografie.*

31. *The Princess in the Backyard (Der Prinzessin vom Hinterof),* c. 1930
Gelatin silver print, montage: 23.2 x 17.4 cm (9⅛ x 6⅞ in.). John L. Severance Fund 2007.47

INSCRIPTIONS
Signed in black marker on verso of print: *Heinz Hajek Halke*

Purple stamp on verso of print: *HHH/Inventar/B6612*

PROVENANCE
The artist's estate, Berlin; Priska Pasquer, Cologne; David Raymond, New York

Georges Hugnet
French, 1906–1974

Hugnet spent his early years in Buenos Aires before returning to his native France to study. He excelled at writing and soon befriended the avant-garde poet Max Jacob and the surrealist circle in Paris. Following military service in 1926, he met Virgil Thompson and Gertrude Stein and later translated two Stein novels into French. He published his first book of poems in 1928, and in 1929 he collaborated on the silent film *La Perle,* which premiered to music by Erik Satie, Virgil Thompson, and Duke Ellington. That year he established the first of several publishing operations, Les Editions de la Montagne, which published the French translation of Stein's *The Making of Americans.*

In his writings Hugnet became an important voice for the Dada movement and a link between this circle and the surrealist group after 1930. Having befriended Max Ernst and Tristan Tzara, Hugnet wrote several articles on the history of the Dada movement for *Cahiers d'Art* from 1932 to 1934, bringing the young poet to André Breton's attention. Hugnet soon became the contemporary archivist for the Dada movement, co-producing with Breton the *Petite anthologie poétique du surréalisme* in 1934 and writing the preface for Alfred Barr's *Fantastic Art Dada Surrealism* show at the Museum of Modern Art in 1936. He masterminded the surrealist exhibition at Galerie des Beaux-Arts in 1938 in Paris together with Marcel Duchamp and Paul Eluard, and he re-created this show in Amsterdam later that year with a catalogue translated into Dutch.

Hugnet's artistic contributions to French surrealism revolved around his poetry, his small press publications, and most importantly his photo-collaged novels. In 1935 he opened his bookbinding workshop, Livre-Objet, where he undertook several unique art book projects with bindings incorporating found objects and organic materials. He collaborated on two volumes with Hans Bellmer, including *Oeillades ciselées en branche* (1938). In 1936 Jeanne Bucher published Hugnet's book of poems and photo decoupages, *The Seventh Face of the Die: Poems-Decoupages (La Septième face du dé: Poèmes-Découpages),* made in collaboration with Marcel Duchamp.

Hugnet continued to back the increasingly political nature of the Paris surrealist group under Breton, traveling to Mexico in 1938 during Trotsky's stay there. However, Hugnet broke with Breton over the pronounced militancy of the Stalinist activities in June 1939. Together with Man Ray, Eluard, and others, Hugnet founded another surrealist magazine in 1939, *Plastique,* active until the Germans occupied France. At that time Hugnet turned his publishing skills toward supporting the French Resistance, writing several pamphlets published by the Editions du Minuit in 1943–44. Hugnet continued to publish poetry and plays throughout the 1940s, allied at this time with Pablo Picasso, Eluard, and Dora Maar. In the mid-1940s, he resumed his graphic work and in 1947 published *Huit Jours à Trébaumec,* a short novella illustrated with photomontages, followed in 1948 by the series of collaged postcards *The Love Life of Spumifieres.*

83. *Angkor-Thom,* c. 1930
Photomechanical reproduction, collage; 13 x 10 cm (5⅛ x 4 in.). John L. Severance Fund 2007.54

PROVENANCE
Ferro collection; Florent Jeanniard, Paris; David Raymond, New York

BIBLIOGRAPHY
Stourdzé, Sam. *Georges Hugnet Collages,* no. 145. Exh. cat. Paris: L. Scheer, 2003.

85. *Beach,* c. 1933–36
Photomechanical reproduction on magazine paper, collage; 27 x 17.7 cm (10⅝ x 7 in.). John L. Severance Fund 2007.51

INSCRIPTION
In pencil on verso of mount: *GH43201*

PROVENANCE
Kauffmann family, Los Angeles; Robert Hamburger, New York; David Raymond, New York

BIBLIOGRAPHY
Schaffner, Ingrid, and Colin Westerbeck. *Accommodations of Desire: Surrealist Works on Paper Collected by Julien Levy,* 64. Exh. cat. Pasadena: Curatorial Assistance, 2004.

Stourdzé, Sam. *Georges Hugnet Collages,* no. 70. Exh. cat. Paris: L. Scheer, 2003.

87. Young Bride (Jeune mariée), c. 1933–36
Photomechanical reproduction on magazine paper, collage; 25 x 17.3 cm (9⅞ x 6¾ in.). John L. Severance Fund 2007.52

PROVENANCE
Kauffmann family, Los Angeles; Robert Hamburger, New York; David Raymond, New York

BIBLIOGRAPHY
Stourdzé, Sam. *Georges Hugnet Collages,* no. 71. Exh. cat. Paris: L. Scheer, 2003.

82. En Route, One Visits the Castle (D'Emblée en visite du château), from **Eight Days at Trébaumec,** 1934
Photomechanical reproduction on magazine paper, collage; 21.3 x 14.8 cm (8⅜ x 5⅞ in.). John L. Severance Fund 2007.49

PROVENANCE
The artist's estate, Paris; Zabriskie Gallery, New York; David Raymond, New York

BIBLIOGRAPHY
Stourdzé, Sam. *Georges Hugnet Collages,* no. 79. Exh. cat. Paris: L. Scheer, 2003.

84. Two Women, 1934
Photomechanical reproduction on magazine paper, collage; 16.3 x 12.5 cm (6½ x 4⅞ in.). John L. Severance Fund 2007.48

INSCRIPTIONS
Some inscriptions and markings on verso (recent dealer numbers only)

PROVENANCE
Auction market, Paris; Zabriskie Gallery, New York; David Raymond, New York

88. The Architect of the Magus (L'architecte du Mage), 12 November 1935
Collage; photomechanical reproductions on drawing (graphite, watercolor, black pen, ink); 31.3 x 22.7 cm (12⅜ x 9 in.). John L. Severance Fund 2007.53

INSCRIPTIONS
Signed, titled, and annotated on recto of print: *12 Novembre 1935*

Across the bottom of recto of print: *et Georges Hugnet*

Printed on recto of print: *15 Jun 1876* and *Louis Chassevent*

PROVENANCE
Private collection, Los Angeles; Robert Hamburger, New York; David Raymond, New York

78. The Seventh Face of the Die: Poems-Decoupages (La Septième face du dé: Poèmes-Découpages), 1936
Paris: Editions Jeanne Bucher. Book of photomechanical offset and rotogravure typography with original gelatin silver prints as back and front covers by Duchamp and original collage by Hugnet, signed by both and numbered 18/20. Overall: 29.3 x 21.4 x 1.5 cm (11½ x 8⅜ x ⅝ in.). Gift of David Raymond 2007.280

79. Black Magic (Magie Noire), 1936
Photomechanical reproduction, collage; 29 x 21.1 cm (11⅜ x 8¼ in.). John L. Severance Fund 2007.280.c

INSCRIPTION
In brown ink on recto of print: *Mai 36 GH*

PROVENANCE
Robert Shapazian, Los Angeles; Private collection, Canada; Roth Horowitz, New York; David Raymond, New York

BIBLIOGRAPHY
Krauss, Rosalind, and Jane Livingston. *L'Amour fou: Photography and Surrealism.* Washington, DC: Corcoran Gallery of Art / New York: Abbeville Press, 1985.

81. My Wanderings Lead Me (Mes déambulations m'amènent), from **Eight Days at Trébaumec,** c. 1936
Gelatin silver print, photomechanical reproduction, collage; 20.3 x 19.5 cm (8 x 7⅝ in.). John L. Severance Fund 2007.148

INSCRIPTION
In pencil on verso of print: *6H3712*

PROVENANCE
The artist's estate, Paris; Zabriskie Gallery, New York; Virginia Lust, New York; Adam Boxer, New York; Peter Berg, New York; Ubu Gallery, New York; David Raymond, New York

BIBLIOGRAPHY
Krauss, Rosalind, and Jane Livingston. *L'Amour fou: Photography and Surrealism.* Washington, DC: Corcoran Gallery of Art / New York: Abbeville Press, 1985.

Stourdzé, Sam. *Georges Hugnet Collages,* no. 58. Paris: L. Scheer, 2003.

86. Bra and Girdle, 1961
Photomechanical reproduction on magazine paper, collage; 34.6 x 19.2 cm (13⅝ x 7⅝ in.). John L. Severance Fund 2007.50

PROVENANCE
The artist's estate, Paris; Virginia Lust, New York; Zabriskie Gallery, New York; David Raymond, New York

BIBLIOGRAPHY
Stourdzé, Sam. *Georges Hugnet Collages,* no. 99. Exh. cat. Paris: L. Scheer, 2003.

André Kertész
American, born Hungary, 1894–1985

Born and raised in Budapest, Kertész photographed the rural surroundings of his native city. He rejected a career as a stockbroker and concentrated on photography as a profession. In 1914 he was drafted by the Austro-Hungarian army and photographed action on the front lines using a plate camera. Before the war's end, he had published his first photographs in leading illustrated magazines in Hungary and Germany. In 1925 he moved to Paris to avoid German anti-Semitism. He settled in Montparnasse among the émigré artist community, met Brassaï, and began an active decade of shooting his adopted city on assignment for the illustrated press. He exhibited his photographs in several shows beginning with the 1927 show at Au Sacré du Printemps. In 1928 he purchased a Leica, which gave enormous freedom and flexibility to his Paris wanderings, allowing him to experiment with vertiginous viewpoints, radical foreshortening, and abstract designs of architectural elements.

One of the first photographers for *VU,* Kertész helped define the independent photographic essay. He also published several photographically illustrated books on Paris and other subjects. The pictorialism of his Hungarian years blossomed into a poetic

[7]

[5]

surrealism in Paris. Kertész was championed by the critics and became celebrated for the found still life. In Paris he created his *Distortion* series of nudes. His work evolved into a truncated narrative style, somewhere between abstraction and surrealist magical images of the city. In 1936 Kertész left Paris for New York, where he briefly worked under contract to the Keystone photographic agency. He photographed for the fashion and lifestyle magazines, first with Alexey Brodovitch and then others, through the early 1960s. When he left Condé Nast in 1962, Kertész returned to personal work, photographing downtown New York from his studio windows. He never attained financial stability through his editorial work but continued to show in galleries and museums, including in the Museum of Modern Art's historical survey *Photography 1839–1939*. In 1944 he became a naturalized American citizen.

7. *Clock and Rope,* 1928
Gelatin silver print; 22.5 x 13.4 cm (8⅞ x 5¼ in.). John L. Severance Fund 2007.55

INSCRIPTIONS
In pencil on verso of print: *L'Intransigeant/A Kertész 1928*

Black stamp on verso of print: *PHOTO BY ANDRÉ KERTÉSZ*

PROVENANCE
Sotheby's, New York, 2 October 1996, no. 222; David Raymond, New York

Willy Kessels
Belgian, 1898–1974

Kessels was born in Dendermonde and studied art at the Sint Lucas School and the Royal Academy of Fine Arts in Ghent. He found work with architectural design firms in Brussels, collaborating on furniture and room design and working with leading Belgian modernists including Henry van de Velde. Self-taught in photography, Kessels began photographing new building projects and room interiors and eventually became the leading architectural photographer of the period in Brussels. He shot advertising campaigns and experimented with advanced darkroom techniques such as solarization, photograms, and

photomontage. His photographic work was included in key exhibitions in Brussels organized by E. L. T. Mesens at the Palais des Beaux-Arts in 1932–33.

An important documentary project followed in 1933, when Kessels accompanied leftist filmmakers Joris Ivens and Henri Storck to the Belgian coal country as a still photographer on the set of *Misère au Borinage* (1933). The resulting detailed documentary images were sympathetic to the plight of the mining community. However, they were soon published in the far-right journal *Rex* after Kessels joined the Flemish nationalist movement, the Verdinaso, in the mid-1930s. As a result of his collaborationist wartime activities, Kessels was sentenced to prison in 1947 for four years. During the 1950s, he resumed experimental photographic work in the style of Otto Steinert's Subjective Photography movement. Several exhibitions from the 1990s onward have sought to reexamine his career and contributions to the field.

92. *Untitled,* 1920s–1930s, printed 1960s
Gelatin silver print from a photogram negative; 23.2 x 17.5 cm (9⅛ x 6⅞ in.). John L. Severance Fund 2007.56

INSCRIPTIONS
Blind stamp on recto of print: *Willy Kessels*

Blind stamp on recto of print, in vertical format with horizontal at bottom: *W*KESSELS/BRUX*

PROVENANCE
The artist, Brussels; Barry Friedman Ltd., New York; David Raymond, New York

Edmund Kesting
German, 1892–1970

Born in Dresden, Kesting studied painting at the school of arts and crafts there in 1915, taking a break for military service in World War I. He returned to his art with a strong German Expressionist style influenced by other Dresden artists including Otto Dix and Conrad Felixmüller, both members of the Dresden Secession group. Though he was not politically motivated, Kesting explored the vigorous dynamism of Cubism and expressionism. In 1919 he founded his own art academy, Der Weg, and married one of his students, Gerda Müller, in 1922. Like the Bauhaus, the school merged fine art with dance,

performance, and craft. Through his association with the avant-garde Galerie Arnold in Dresden, Kesting met many influential artists and dealers including Herwarth Walden, founder of *Der Sturm* in Berlin. He exhibited both at Galerie Arnold (1919) and at Galerie Der Sturm (1923), the latter with László Moholy-Nagy, among others.

Kesting only began photographing in the mid-1920s after his formation as an experimental artist, and by 1930 he was exhibiting and publishing his photographic work. He was able to translate his painting style of fragmented planes into seamless photomontages for advertising and portrait studies. In addition to his noteworthy portraiture, Kesting made studies of avant-garde dancers in studios, replete with accentuated shadows and multiple negatives. He was drawn to the Futurist group in Milan and exhibited his photography with his Italian counterparts. He showed throughout Europe in several landmark photography exhibitions, but after his work was labeled "degenerate" by the Nazis in 1937, he returned to industrial photography. After World War II, Kesting continued teaching and working with artists' groups in Berlin and Dresden.

5. *Dancer Dean Goodelle (Tänzer: Dean Goodelle),* 1930
Gelatin silver print, montage; 23.8 x 17.9 cm (9⅜ x 7 in.). John L. Severance Fund 2007.57

INSCRIPTIONS
In pencil on verso of print: *(Edmund Kesting Dresden Allemagne)/Tänzer 1930 Dean Goodelle/Doppelbelichtung*

Purple stamp on verso of print: *kestingfoto*

In pencil on verso of print: *155* [circled] and *Nr. 12*

PROVENANCE
The artist's family, Germany; Kunsthaus Lempertz, Cologne, 5 May 2001, no. 189; David Raymond, New York

BIBLIOGRAPHY
Werner, Klaus. *Edmund Kesting: ein Maler fotografiert,* 94. Leipzig: VEB Fotokinoverlag, 1987.

François Kollar
Slovak, active in France, 1904–1979

Born in a Slovak town that later became part of Hungary, Kollar pursued general and technical studies in Pozsony (modern Bratislava) after the Treaty of Versailles. Photography was a fervent hobby in his youth. From 1920 to 1924, he was employed by the national railway before moving to Paris. He found machine work in Renault's factory outside Paris and gradually sought commissions for commercial photography assignments in the burgeoning advertising sector. In 1927 he began photographing works of art but soon found steady work at the Draeger advertising studio. He left Paris briefly in 1929 to establish a photography studio in Bratislava but returned after a few months. He married Fernande Papillon in 1930 and found work at Studio Chevojon, specializing in industrial commissions, and Lecram Press where his photographer brother-in-law, André Vignon, was the artistic director. By November 1930 Kollar had an independent photography business in Paris, regularly producing advertising campaigns for major enterprises in the city including Alfred Dunhill and Worth perfumes.

Kollar came to advertising work with a strong sense of modernist design expressed in New Vision photography. Embraced by the Hungarian avant-garde in Paris—André Kertész and Robert Capa among them—Kollar was included in many of the exhibitions of radical photography in Paris and Munich (1930) and published in such places as Arts et Metiers Graphique's *Photographie* annual (1930–32). Reviews noted Kollar's mastery of transparency and overlapping images in his complex works, in which several negatives merge together to counteract the static nature of still photography. Kollar was one of the most skilled practitioners of photomontage techniques first employed by the Dadaists in the early 1920s.

Kollar's major commission came in 1931, a four-year project titled *France at Work (La France Travaille),* which grew to more than two thousand images. Covering the most modern aspects of the industrial complex as well as the country life of farms, the first part of the work was exhibited in 1932 in seven portfolios. The second group of eight portfolios appeared in 1934. Kollar's career was very busy throughout the 1930s but tapered off during World War II, when he retired to the country with his family.

32. *Wood-Milne,* 1930
Gelatin silver print, montage; 37.5 x 28.1 cm (14¾ x 11 in.). John L. Severance Fund 2007.58

INSCRIPTIONS
Signed in pencil on mount, below print: *Kollar*

Signed in white ink on recto of print: *KOLLAR*

Copyright stamps on verso of print with two addresses: *Photo par Kollar 17 rue de la Tour, Paris 16 eme* and *Photo par Kollar, 11 bis rue Chardin Paris 16eme*

In blue ink on verso of print: *1930–Pour les Ets Erwin Wasey et Cie. (agence americaine)*

PROVENANCE
The artist's estate, Paris; Zabriskie Gallery, New York; David Raymond, New York

Vassily Komardenkov
Russian, 1897–1973

Komardenkov graduated from the Stroganov Art School in 1919 in Moscow as a design student and made a career in theater and later in film design and production. He participated in the founding of VKhUTEMAS, the Higher State Artistic Technical Workshops, after the revolution as well as the founding of ObMoKhu, Society of Young Artists, in 1919 as part of George Yakulov's theater set and Aristarkh Lentulov's painting workshops. He exhibited in ObMoKhu's exhibitions in 1919 and 1921 and was also included in the *First Russian Show* at the Van Diemen Gallery in 1922 in Berlin and the 1925 Exposition in Paris. He designed posters and agit-prop materials for the new regime including the Special Commission for the Elimination of Illiteracy. Komardenkov's theater career was tied to the avant-garde Meyerhold Theater in Moscow, where he oversaw seventy productions. He was also associated with the Kemerny Theater. After a long career in film during the late 1920s and 1930s, Komardenkov assumed a professorship in painting at the Moscow Industrial Art College (formerly Stroganov Art School) in 1945.

41. *Film Design,* mid-1920s
Photomechanical reproduction, collage; 41.7 x 30.7 cm (16⅜ x 12 in.). John L. Severance Fund 2007.59

INSCRIPTION
In ink on recto of print: *B.K.*

PROVENANCE
Private collection, Vienna; Sotheby's.com (Leon Wilnitsky, Vienna); David Raymond, New York

Germaine Krull
Polish, 1897–1985

Born in Poland into an affluent German family, Krull spent her teenage years in Munich where she studied photography and opened a small photography school. Her passionate leftist politics led to her expulsion from Bavaria in 1920. She traveled to Russia, then to Berlin where she established a photography studio in 1922–25, and finally to Amsterdam with filmmaker Joris Ivens in 1925. A year later she settled in Paris, where she developed an active career and reputation as a leading modernist photographer of the New Photography era. She was included in important European photography shows such as *Film und Foto* (1929) and was featured in articles by leading critics of Paris. Her sound training enabled her to work in a variety of styles and outlets, from early Pictorialist studio nudes to news coverage to the groundbreaking, vertiginous photographs of the Eiffel Tower published in her 1927 volume *Métal.*

Krull trained Eli Lotar during these early Paris years, and they worked together on some of the first photographic stories for Lucien Vogel's influential picture magazine *VU.* Krull was one of the first photographers to shoot and sequence work for illustrated volumes, a form more popular during the 1930s. Though in demand for high-end commercial work, Krull also continued making radical street photographs for the illustrated news magazines throughout Europe, and she regained her interest in political photography shows, contributing to the 1936 AREAR exhibition of photographers against fascism at Galerie de la Pléiade. But her appetite for fighting waned in the later 1930s. She moved her studio to Monte Carlo and then spent most of World War II in French Africa and the Congo. After the war she lived in Asia for many years, settling in Bangkok, until her return to Germany in 1983 shortly before her death.

 [118]

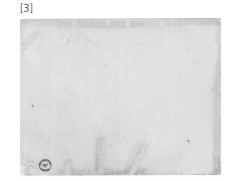 [166]

 [3]

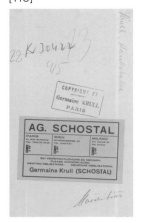 [135]

118. *Study of Hands (Handstudie),* 1928
Gelatin silver print; 22.8 x 13.2 [irregular] cm (9 x 5¼ in.). John L. Severance Fund 2007.61

INSCRIPTIONS
Signed and titled in pencil on verso of print: *Krull Handstudie*

In pencil on verso of print: *Mauritius*

Blue stamp on verso of print: *Copyright by/Germaine KRULL/Paris*

Blue paper photo agency label on verso of print: *AG Schostal*

PROVENANCE
Phillips, New York, 5 October 1999, no. 73; David Raymond, New York

166. *And By Chance (Et du hasard),* c. 1930
Gelatin silver print; 15.2 x 22 cm (6 x 8⅝ in.). John L. Severance Fund 2007.62

INSCRIPTIONS
In pencil on verso of print: *5/Et du Hasard* and *8e paysage* [crossed out]

Blue stamp on verso of print: *Copyright by/Germaine KRULL/Paris*

PROVENANCE
Private collection, Paris; Edwynn Houk Gallery, New York; David Raymond, New York

Nikolai Kubeev
Russian, 1910–1944

Kubeev was born in Pavchino, a village near Moscow. By 1926 he had moved to Moscow and was working as a photographer for TASS, the Soviet news agency. In 1930 he joined the staff of Soyuz Foto (Soviet Photo), first as a researcher and from 1934 to 1941 as a Moscow correspondent, covering state-sponsored parades and events. Photographically his style veered from the Constructivist mode introduced by Alexander Rodchenko in the 1920s to the state-sanctioned Social Realist style prevalent in the 1930s. He exhibited in the 1937 *First All Union Exhibition of Photographic Art*. He was a war correspondent during World War II and died of wounds suffered at the front.

4. *May Day in the Red Capital (Pervoie Maiav Krasnoj Stolitse),* 1932
Gelatin silver print; 15.4 x 22.2 cm (6 x 8¾ in.). John L. Severance Fund 2007.60

INSCRIPTION
Label on verso of print: [in Russian] *Soyuz foto no. 119661/Moscow May 1932/Printed by Kubeev/ 'The First of May in the Red Capital'/Artist made in Sverdlov Square/Maquette of the Shariko–podshibnik manufacture/V.G. 48-0-0/3*

PROVENANCE
The artist, Moscow; Solomon Telingater, Moscow (his archive); Serge Plantureux, Paris; David Raymond, New York

Jacques-Henri Lartigue
French, 1894–1986

Born in Paris, by the 1910s Lartigue was seriously committed to photography, including sports and fashion work in demand by the new illustrated press. His hallmark was stop-action photography, but by 1913 he had expanded his pursuits to film and in 1915 studied painting at the Académie Julian. He photographed both planned and off-the-cuff social interactions in Paris, including the races at Longchamps, the public at leisure in the Bois de Boulogne, and winter sports in the Alps. He sold photographs and some film footage to commercial outlets. Throughout the 1930s and 1940s, Lartigue photographed his personal life and relationships and continued painting. He exhibited paintings at the Salon des Indépendants throughout the 1920s and had solo exhibitions at the Galerie Georges Petit in 1922 and the Galerie Charpentier in 1939.

Only in the 1950s did Lartigue find public interest in his photography. A 1963 exhibition organized by John Szarkowski at New York's Museum of Modern Art—for which Lartigue made new gelatin silver prints of his pre-World War I images—launched his career as a photographic artist. Some of these images were reproduced in *Life* magazine at that time. In 1970 Richard Avedon published *Diary of a Century,* a monograph dedicated to Lartigue. Only in subsequent scholarly writings and exhibitions has the breadth of Lartigue's technical prowess, including his experimental color autochromes, been brought to light. In later years he reconstructed the family

albums of his youth. He donated his entire studio to the French government in 1979.

3. *The Crystal Ball (La Boule de Verre),* 1931
Gelatin silver print, toned; 23.7 x 29.9 cm (9⅜ x 11¾ in.). John L. Severance Fund 2007.149

INSCRIPTION
Black estate stamp on verso of print: *COLL. RENEE PERLE/VENTE/J.H./LARTIGUE*

PROVENANCE
Étude Tajan, Paris, Renée Perle sale, 21 December 2000, no. 69; David Raymond, New York

BIBLIOGRAPHY
Schneede, Uwe M., and Hamburger Kunsthalle. *Begierde im Blick: Surrealistiche Photographie*, no. 103. Exh. cat. Ostfildern: Hatje Cantz, 2005.

148. *In the Studio (Dans L'Atelier),* 1931
Gelatin silver print, toned; 7.7 x 12.9 cm (3 x 5⅛ in.). John L. Severance Fund 2007.64

INSCRIPTION
Black estate stamp on verso of print: *COLL. RENEE PERLE/VENTE/J.H./LARTIGUE*

In pencil on verso of print: *K1*

PROVENANCE
Étude Tajan, Paris, Renée Perle sale, 21 December 2000, no. 14; David Raymond, New York

135. *Painting of a Necklace (Tableau au Collier),* 1931
Gelatin silver print, toned; 13.8 x 7.8 cm (5½ x 3 in.). John L. Severance Fund 2007.65

INSCRIPTIONS
Black estate stamp on verso of print: *COLL. RENEE PERLE/VENTE J.H./LARTIGUE*

In pencil on verso of print: *M3*

PROVENANCE
Étude Tajan, Paris, Renée Perle sale, 4 May 2001, no. 44; David Raymond, New York

165. *Socoa,* 1931
Gelatin silver print, toned; 7.7 x 13.5 cm (3 x 5⅜ in.). John L. Severance Fund 2007.66

[165]

[149]

[133]

At the Hands of Light, cover

INSCRIPTIONS
In pencil on verso of print: *Socoa*

Black estate stamp on verso of print: *COLL. RENEE PERLE/VENTE J.H./LARTIGUE*

PROVENANCE
Étude Tajan, Paris, Renée Perle sale, 4 May 2001, no. 84; David Raymond, New York

149. *With Lulu in the Bois du Boulogne (Bois de Boulogne avec Lulu),* 1931
Gelatin silver print, toned; 15.9 x 24.3 cm (6¼ x 9⅝ in.). John L. Severance Fund 2007.63

INSCRIPTIONS
In pencil on verso of print: *Bois de Boulogne avec Lulu*

In pencil on verso of print: *L30*

Black stamp on verso of print: *COLL. RENEE PERLE/VENTE J.H./LARTIGUE*

PROVENANCE
Étude Tajan, Paris, Renée Perle sale, 21 December 2000, no. 6; David Raymond, New York

Guy Le Boyer
French, 1900s

Active from the 1930s through the post-World War II era, press photographer Le Boyer was an active contributor to *VU* magazine and other French illustrated journals. In the 1930s he received a commission from the association of coal-mining companies to photograph their workers and foundries across France. His collection of negatives and prints, produced through 1951, is now part of the public archive of the National Association of Work in France.

133. *Headlight, Paris,* 1940s
Gelatin silver print; 22.9 x 17 cm (9 x 6¾ in.). John L. Severance Fund 2007.141

INSCRIPTIONS
Signed in pencil on verso of print: *Guy Le Boyer*

Blue stamp on verso of print: *PHOTO/GUY LE BOYER*

PROVENANCE
Paris art market; David Raymond, New York

Marcel G. Lefrancq
Belgian, 1916–1974

A citizen of Mons in the French-speaking region of Belgium, Lefrancq spent his early years in Brussels. He began his photography career as early as 1932 while studying commercial engineering and art. His wide-ranging interests included literature, politics, and archaeology, and he was therefore well suited to the intellectual activity of surrealist circles in the 1930s. After contact with the Rupture group, he established the Hainaut surrealist "Haute Nuit" group in 1939 with Achille Chavée, Armand Simon, and others. These groups all developed in the region around Mons, culturally distinct from Brussels where René Magritte and E. L. T. Mesens forged great connections to Parisian surrealist activities. Many of Lefrancq's activities as a surrealist were devoted to preserving the distinct character of his native region.

Lefrancq photographed his surroundings with an eye for the strange and poetic. To distribute his work, he opened the photographic agency La Lanterne Magique. He contributed to several magazines and journals throughout Belgium and published one photographic volume, *Aux Mains de la Lumière,* in 1948. During World War II he moved to the Dordogne region in France to photograph with an archaeologist and also assist the French Resistance. He was briefly imprisoned for his political activity during the war. He continued his surrealist activities, contributing to CoBrA's journal and also to the American surrealist journal *View,* thereby becoming an important link between pre- and postwar surrealist activities in Belgium.

At the Hands of Light: Images and Poems (Aux Mains de la Lumière: Images et Poèmes), 1948
Mons, Belgium: Editions Haute Nuit; portfolio of printed poems and 25 photographs, 82/100. Overall: 27 x 21.5 x 2.7 cm (10⅝ x 8½ x 1 in.) each, with 25 interleaved gelatin silver prints: 17.6 x 16.4 cm (6⅞ x 6½ in.). John L. Severance Fund 2007.67.1–25

PROVENANCE
The artist's estate, Mons, Belgium; David Raymond, New York

96. *The Melancholy Door (La Porte Triste),* 1939, printed 1948
Gelatin silver print, ferrotyped; 17.6 x 16.4 cm (7 x 6½ in.). John L. Severance Fund 2007.67.1

INSCRIPTION
In pencil on verso of print: *Je certifie que cette photo "la porte triste" de M. G. Lefrancq est réalisé par l'auteur, en 1948/1*

90. *Haunted Eyes,* 1947, printed 1948
Gelatin silver print of a montage, ferrotyped; 22.8 x 16.4 cm (9 x 6½ in.). John L. Severance Fund 2007.67.2

INSCRIPTION
In pencil on verso of print: *Je certifie que cette photo "Haunted Eyes" de M. G. Lefranq est un tirage réalisé par l'auteur en 1948/M. LEFRANCQ 2*

17. *Scientific Objectivity (Objectivité Scientifique),* c. 1947, printed 1948
Gelatin silver print, ferrotyped; 22.8 x 16.3 cm (9 x 6½ in.). John L. Severance Fund 2007.67.3

INSCRIPTION
In pencil on verso of print: *Objectivité scientifique/M LEFRANCQ 3*

15. *Smoke (Fumée),* 1948
Gelatin silver print, ferrotyped; 11 x 16.3 cm (4⅜ x 6½ in.). John L. Severance Fund 2007.67.4

INSCRIPTION
In pencil on verso of print: *Fumée/M LEFRANCQ 4*

97. *Elected (Élue),* 1945, printed 1948
Gelatin silver print, ferrotyped; 22.9 x 15.5 cm (9 x 6 in.). John L. Severance Fund 2007.67.5

INSCRIPTION
In pencil on verso of print: *Elue/M LEFRANCQ 5*

98. *The Law of Coincidences (La Loi des Coincidences),* 1938, printed 1948
Gelatin silver print, ferrotyped; 19.7 x 16.4 cm (7¾ x 6½ in.). John L. Severance Fund 2007.67.6

INSCRIPTION
In pencil on verso of print: *La loi des coincidences/M LEFRANCQ 6*

99. Countryside (Paysage), 1948
Gelatin silver print of a drawing or watercolor, solarized, ferrotyped; 20.5 x 16.4 cm (8 x 6½ in.). John L. Severance Fund 2007.67.7

INSCRIPTION
In pencil on verso of print: *Paysage/M LEFRANCQ 7*

100. Heide, 1942, printed 1948
Gelatin silver print, ferrotyped; 11.9 x 16.4 cm (4⅝ x 6½ in.). John L. Severance Fund 2007.67.8

INSCRIPTION
In pencil on verso of print: *Heide/M LEFRANCQ 8*

101. Photogram (Photogramme), 1948
Gelatin silver print of a photogram, ferrotyped; 22.9 x 16.4 cm (9 x 6½ in.). John L. Severance Fund 2007.67.9

INSCRIPTION
In pencil on verso of print: *Photogramme/ M LEFRANCQ 9*

102. Head of Christ (Tête de Christ), 1948
Gelatin silver print, ferrotyped; 22.7 x 16.1 cm (8⅞ x 6⅜ in.). John L. Severance Fund 2007.67.10

INSCRIPTION
In pencil on verso of print: *Tête de Christ/ M LEFRANCQ 10*

103. Hope Is Out the Window (L'Espoir est Au-delà de la Fenêtre), 1948
Gelatin silver print, ferrotyped; 22.9 x 15.2 cm (9 x 6 in.). John L. Severance Fund 2007.67.11

INSCRIPTION
In pencil on verso of print: *L'espoir est au delà de la fenêtre/M LEFRANCQ 11*

20. Eulogy of Carnage (L'Éloge du Carnage), 20 June 1946, printed 1948
Gelatin silver print, ferrotyped; 10.7 x 16.4 cm (4¼ x 6½ in.). John L. Severance Fund 2007.67.12

INSCRIPTION
In pencil on verso of print: *Eloge du carnage/ M LEFRANCQ 12*

104. The Song of the Rooftops (La Chanson des Toits), 1948
Gelatin silver print, ferrotyped; 22.8 x 15.2 cm (9 x 6 in.). John L. Severance Fund 2007.67.13

INSCRIPTION
In pencil on verso of print: *La chanson des toits/ M LEFRANCQ 13*

18. Crystallized Landscape (Paysage crystallisé), 1948
Gelatin silver print, ferrotyped; 13.9 x 16.4 cm (5½ x 6½ in.). John L. Severance Fund 2007.67.14

INSCRIPTION
In pencil on verso of print: *Paysage cristallisé/ M LEFRANCQ 14*

105. Study of Form V (Étude de Forme V), c. 1942, printed 1948
Gelatin silver print, ferrotyped; 22.7 x 16 cm (9 x 6⅜ in.). John L. Severance Fund 2007.67.15

INSCRIPTION
In pencil on verso of print: *Etude de forme V/ M LEFRANCQ 15*

106. Large Nets for Capturing the Wind (Grands Filets à Capturer le Vent), c. 1947, printed 1948
Gelatin silver print, ferrotyped; 12.2 x 16.4 cm (4¾ x 6½ in.). John L. Severance Fund 2007.67.16

INSCRIPTION
In pencil on verso of print: *Grands filets à capturer le vent/M LEFRANCQ 16*

107. Statue of Snow (Statue de Neige), 1948
Gelatin silver print, ferrotyped; 22.8 x 16.4 cm (9 x 6½ in.). John L. Severance Fund 2007.67.17

INSCRIPTION
In pencil on verso of print: *Statue de neige/ M LEFRANCQ 17*

108. Small Fairy in a Park (Petite Fée dans un Parc), 1948
Gelatin silver print, ferrotyped; 22.7 x 15.5 cm (8⅞ x 6⅛ in.). John L. Severance Fund 2007.67.18

INSCRIPTION
In pencil on verso of print: *Petite fée dans un parc/ M LEFRANCQ 18*

19. Illustration for The Adventures of A. G. Pym by E. A. Poe (Illustration pour Les aventures d'A-G. Pym d'E. A. Poe), 1948
Gelatin silver print, ferrotyped; 11 x 16.4 cm (4⅜ x 6½ in.). John L. Severance Fund 2007.67.19

INSCRIPTION
In pencil on verso of print: *Illustration pour "A. G. Pym"/M LEFRANCQ 19*

109. In a Far Off Land (En Pays Lointain), 1948
Gelatin silver print of a photographically reproduced montage, ferrotyped; 22.8 x 15.3 cm (9 x 6 in.). John L. Severance Fund 2007.67.20

INSCRIPTION
In pencil on verso of print: *En pays lointain/ M LEFRANCQ 20*

110. Study of Form I (Étude de Forme I), c. 1942, printed 1948
Gelatin silver print, ferrotyped; 17.6 x 16.4 cm (7 x 6½ in.). John L. Severance Fund 2007.67.21

INSCRIPTIONS
In pencil on verso of print: *Je certifie que cette photo de Marcel G Lefrancq "Etude de forme I" est un tirage original réalisé par l'auteur en 1948/ M LEFRANCQ*

16. The Enemy (L'Ennemi), 1935, printed 1948
Gelatin silver print, ferrotyped; 11.9 x 16.4 cm (4¾ x 6½ in.). John L. Severance Fund 2007.67.22

INSCRIPTION
In pencil on verso of print: *L'ennemi/M LEFRANCQ 22*

[98] [99] [100] [101] [102]

[103] [20] [104] [18] [105]

[106] [107] [108] [19] [109]

[110] [16] [111] [112] [113]

111. *Exercise in Purity (L'Exercise de la Pureté),*
1948
Gelatin silver print, ferrotyped; 22.1 x 16.1 cm (8¾ x
6⅜ in.). John L. Severance Fund 2007.67.23

INSCRIPTION
In pencil on verso of print: *Exercise de la pureté/
M LEFRANCQ 23*

112. *Burst of Sunshine (Poussière de Soleil),*
1948
Gelatin silver print, ferrotyped; 22.8 x 15.4 cm (9 x 6
in.). John L. Severance Fund 2007.67.24

INSCRIPTION
In pencil on verso of print: *Poussière de soleil/
M LEFRANCQ 24*

113. *Endless Recurrence (Éternel Retour),* 1948
Gelatin silver print, ferrotyped; 22.8 x 15.5 cm (9 x
6⅛ in.). John L. Severance Fund 2007.67.25

INSCRIPTION
In pencil on verso of print: *Éternel retour/
M LEFRANCQ 25*

El Lissitzky
Russian, 1890–1941

Lazar Markovich Lissitzky was born near Smolensk,
studied architectural engineering in Darmstadt,
and traveled throughout Europe before settling in
Moscow in 1916. After the Bolshevik revolution, he
participated in IZO-Narkompros, the artists' association established by the new government. Throughout the war years, though, he dedicated himself to
the blossoming of a Jewish renaissance in the arts,
working as a book illustrator in Moscow and Kiev
and eventually as a professor of graphic arts under
Marc Chagall at the Vitebsk Art Academy. There he
also met Kazimir Malevich and was fervently swayed
by the visual and theoretical rigor of Suprematism,
an abstract art based on the purity of geometrical
forms. Working with Malevich, he helped establish
the UNOVIS group of Suprematist artists.

Lissitzky created work in many media, all dedicated to social change and the utopian values of
the Communist revolution. In 1921 he returned to
Moscow to teach architecture and mural painting

at VKhUTEMAS (Higher State Artistic Technical
Workshops) and thus began a career as a pedagogical leader for the new order. Since he spoke
German, Lissitzky was sent throughout Europe as a
cultural ambassador for the new Soviet government.
In 1921–22 he spent long periods of time in Berlin
where he joined the intellectual circle around Raoul
Hausmann and Hannah Höch and also spent time
with László Moholy-Nagy discussing the principles
of the photogram. In Germany Lissitzky delved more
intensively into book design and publishing, resulting in the creation of the portfolio of the *Prouns*
(architectural painting and graphic compositions)
published by Kestner in Hanover. There he met
Sophie Küppers, his future wife, then working for
the Kestner publishing house. He also collaborated in
Hanover with Kurt Schwitters on his *Merz* publication and exchanged views on extending art into the
environment in Schwitters's *Merzbau.*

Lissitzky contracted tuberculosis in 1923 and spent
1924 in Switzerland where he continued his graphic
projects, including photography and applied design
for advertising clients. Critical writings of this period
include translations of Malevich's texts into German
and preparation of the *Isms of Art* with Jean Arp, a
theoretical text on avant-garde artists and tendencies. Photography and its application in society
dominated his work the rest of the decade, and he
advocated for photography and photomontage in
typographic design.

Lissitzky's interest in photographic imagery and
architectural form was realized in the great exhibition designs he executed for art and trade fairs in
the late 1920s and 1930s. His eventually directed his
typographic talents to government work. In 1928 he
conceived the Russian pavilion at *Pressa,* the exhibition of printing trades in Cologne, including photographs enlarged to mural scale, accompanied by
an accordion book. He also selected and staged the
Russian contribution to the 1929 Stuttgart *Film und
Foto* art exhibition; his photographic self-portrait *The
Constructor* appeared on the cover of the catalogue.
During this final period, Lissitzky's work in utopian
and realized architecture was inextricably linked to
the new Soviet society. After 1932 he was in charge
of design for *USSR in Construction* and continued to
design and write until his death in 1941.

52. *Mannequin,* c. 1928
Gelatin silver print from a photogram negative; 29.4
x 23.5 cm (11⅝ x 9¼ in.). John L. Severance Fund
2007.147

INSCRIPTIONS
Notations on verso of print, initialed by Sophie
Lissitzky-Küppers

In pencil on verso of print: *166* with artist's printing
notes

PROVENANCE
The artist's family, Moscow; Houk Friedman, New
York; Private collection, New York; Bernd Künne, Hanover, Germany; Phillips, New York, 13–14 October
2004, no. 131; David Raymond, New York

BIBLIOGRAPHY
*The Great Utopia: The Russian and Soviet Avant-
Garde, 1915–1932,* no. 472. Exh. cat. New York:
Guggenheim Museum, 1992.

Lissitzky-Küppers, Sophie. *El Lissitzky: Life, Letters,
Texts,* 166. London: Thames and Hudson, 1968.

Tupitsyn, Margarita. *El Lissitsky: Experiments in Photography,* 12–13, pl. 3. New York: Houk Friedman,
1991.

Herbert List
German, 1903–1975

Born in Hamburg, List began photographing during
his travels for the Landfried Coffee enterprise between 1926 and 1928, spending time in South and
Central America and San Francisco. He participated
in the bohemian cultural life of Hamburg, studying
art and literature and meeting writer Stephen Spend-
er there in 1929. Deeply interested in experimental
literature that delved into the unconscious mind,
List began photographing as an exercise in exploring his subconscious. Andreas Feininger gave him
a Rolleiflex camera and rudimentary photography
tutorials, and soon List was making a living with his
photographic work. But in 1936 he was forced to
leave Germany due to his Jewish roots and homo-
sexual lifestyle. He met George Hoyningen-Huene in
London and the two traveled to Greece. Thereafter
List found work with the fashion magazines and
illustrated press. He entered the surrealists' literary
circles as well. During World War II he settled in

Greece but was forced to repatriate to Germany in 1941. After the war, he photographed the ruins of Munich and resumed a commercial photographic career. At the urging of Robert Capa, List joined Magnum in 1951 but was not terribly active in the agency, concentrating instead on his private work: contemplative landscapes with a surrealist bent.

53. *Sant Angelo, Ischia,* 1937
Gelatin silver print; 22.7 x 27.8 cm (8⅞ x 11 in.). John L. Severance Fund 2007.68

INSCRIPTIONS
In black ink on verso of print: *Die beglückende sonne des frühen morgens./San Angelo/Ischia*

Black stamp on verso of print: *Foto Herbert List*

PROVENANCE
The artist's estate, Germany (Max Scheler); Robert Miller Gallery, New York; Jack Banning, Rosa Esman, Adam Boxer, New York; David Raymond, New York

Eli Lotar
French, 1905–1969

Born in Paris to Romanian parents, Lotar studied law in Bucharest but eventually embraced his French nationality and returned to France in 1923. His early art interest was film rather than photography. He spent the years 1924–26 in Nice working as a laborer and extra on film sets before returning to Paris and applying for a position in Germaine Krull's studio. From 1926 to 1928, the two shot many stories together in the streets of Paris. His work was published alongside hers in early issues of *VU* magazine as well as other French illustrated journals, and he exhibited work in important photography shows in Essen and Stuttgart (*Film und Foto*) in 1929. His photographic work varied between found surrealist views of Paris, advertising collage work, and documentary story illustrations.

Lotar's interest in film and radical politics led him to join the surrealist Georges Bataille in his magazine *Documents,* for which Lotar shot his famous *abattoir* (slaughterhouse) photographs in 1930. He also worked closely as cameraman and still photographer with scientific filmmaker Jean Painlevé. From 1931 to 1932, he ran a portrait studio (Studio Unis) with Jacques-André Boiffard but continued film work

with Dutch director Joris Ivens, Krull's husband, in 1932 on *Zuyderzee*. During this time Lotar was active with the political October group in Paris. In 1934 he worked with Luis Buñuel on the social documentary film *Las Hurdes*. By the later 1930s, most of Lotar's photographic and film work was of this type. (See also Jean Painlevé.)

26. *The Day After (Lendemain),* 1929
Gelatin silver print; 15.6 x 22 cm (6⅛ x 8⅝ in.). John L. Severance Fund 2007.69

INSCRIPTIONS
In black ink on verso of print: *Lendemain*

In blue ink on verso of print: *Photo Eli Lotar*

In pencil on verso of print: *Travail* and *No. 1*

PROVENANCE
Sotheby's, London, 10 May 2001, no. 418; David Raymond, New York

BIBLIOGRAPHY
Combalía Dexeus, Victoria. *Paris y los surrealistas,* 228. Exh. cat. Bilbao: Fundacion Museo de Bellas Artes de Bilbao.

Dora Maar
French, 1907–1997

Born Henriette Théodora Markovitch, Maar spent her youth in Argentina where her father was an architect. By 1926 her family returned to Paris. She had both a Rolleiflex and a Leica and began studying art at the Union Centrale des Arts Décoratifs, the École de Photographie, and the Académie Julian, where she studied painting. There she met Henri Cartier-Bresson and Jacqueline Lamba, future wife of André Breton. The art critic Marcel Zahar, editor of *Formes,* hired Maar to photograph statuary at the Musée Guimet and introduced her to Emmanuel Sougez, the influential director of *L'Illustration* magazine. After 1931 Sougez supported Maar through commissions and articles about her work.

Maar was photographing on the streets of Paris while making contacts in the professional photography world. She learned studio practice working for fashion photographer Henry Meerson in 1931 and printing with Brassaï. She established a commercial studio with film set designer Pierre Kéfer in Neuilly;

portrait and fashion contracts soon followed. They worked the streets of Paris together and accrued fashion studio work as well until 1934, when they went their separate ways.

Maar's photography reached its apex in the mid-1930s. She was politically active in left-wing causes in Paris, which propelled her to join the October group of political theater formed by Jacques Prévert. This merged into the activities of the group Contre Attaque, formed in 1935 by Breton and Maar's then-lover Georges Bataille. During trips to Spain in 1933 and London in 1934, Maar photographed the inequalities of working people in urban locales and, upon her return to Paris, also worked for underground pin-up and pornographic magazines. She had a solo exhibition of photographs at the Galerie Van der Berghe in 1934. By 1935 she was well ensconced in the surrealist environment in Paris, reflected in the wealth of her experimental photomontage and collage work that usually repositioned figures from her commercial work into strange environments. Her photography appeared in several surrealist exhibitions and publications, including the international surrealist exhibition in Teneriffe in 1935. Surrealist poet and publishers Paul Eluard and Georges Hugnet were friends and supporters at this time.

Throughout her affair with Pablo Picasso (1936–39), Maar often photographed the artist and his circle, most notably the entire planning and painting of Picasso's *Guernica* mural in the studio. At this time, she experimented more overtly with photographic work that deformed the female body, both in self-portraits and alter-ego images such as *Portrait of Ubu* (1936), a touchstone of surrealist photography in France.

Once Picasso ended the affair, Maar experienced a mental breakdown, institutionalization, and analysis with Jacques Lacan before turning to Catholicism and a pathologically private lifestyle. She did not make photographs after 1940.

[69]   [62]   [77]

75. As Seen through the Aquariums on the Quai de la Mégisserie (A travers les aquariums du quai de la Mégisserie), 1931–36
Gelatin silver print, ferrotyped; 20.2 x 18.3 cm (8 x 7¼ in.). John L. Severance Fund 2007.78

INSCRIPTIONS
Dora Maar estate stamp on verso of print: *DM/1998*

PROVENANCE
The artist's estate, Paris; PIASA, Paris, 20 November 1998, no. 181; David Raymond, New York

69. Carousel at Night, 1931–36
Gelatin silver print, ferrotyped; 25 x 19.8 cm (9⅞ x 7¾ in.). John L. Severance Fund 2007.79

INSCRIPTIONS
Dora Maar estate stamp on verso of print: *DM/1998*

Black stamp on verso of print: *KÉFER–DORA MAAR/ MENTION OBLIGATOIRE* and *45 bis BD. RICHARD–WALLACE/NEUILLY–SUR–SEINE*

PROVENANCE
The artist's estate, Paris; PIASA, Paris, 20 November 1998, no. 180; David Raymond, New York

BIBLIOGRAPHY
Combalía, Victoria. *Dora Maar: Bataille, Picasso et les Surréalistes,* no. 56. Exh. cat. Marseille: Musées de Marseille, 2002.

Combalía, Victoria, and Hubertus Gassner. *Dora Maar,* no. 57. Exh. cat. Munich: Haus der Kunst, 2001.

Johnson, Annabella, and Marcello Marvelli. *Dora Maar: Photographer.* Exh. cat. Long Island City, NY: Dorsky Gallery, 2004.

62. Couple Kissing, 1931–36
Gelatin silver print, ferrotyped; 19 x 17.4 cm (7½ x 6⅞ in.). John L. Severance Fund 2007.80

INSCRIPTIONS
Dora Maar estate stamp on verso of print: *DM/1998*

Black stamp on verso of print: *KÉFER–DORA MAAR/ MENTION OBLIGATOIRE* and *45 bis BD. RICHARD–WALLACE/NEUILLY–SUR–SEINE*

PROVENANCE
The artist's estate, Paris; PIASA, Paris, 20 November 1998, no. 190; David Raymond, New York

BIBLIOGRAPHY
Combalía, Victoria. *Dora Maar: Bataille, Picasso et les Surréalistes,* no. 58. Exh. cat. Marseille: Musées de Marseille, 2002.

Combalía, Victoria, and Hubertus Gassner. *Dora Maar,* no. 59. Exh. cat. Munich: Haus der Kunst, 2001.

Johnson, Annabella, and Marcello Marvelli. *Dora Maar: Photographer.* Exh. cat. Long Island City, NY: Dorsky Gallery, 2004.

77. Crowd in Front of a Car, 1931–36
Gelatin silver print; 18 x 26.6 cm (7⅛ x 10½ in.). John L. Severance Fund 2007.72

INSCRIPTIONS
Dora Maar estate stamp on verso of print: *DM/1999*

Black stamp on verso of print: *KÉFER–DORA MAAR/ MENTION OBLIGATOIRE* and *45 bis BD. RICHARD–WALLACE/NEUILLY–SUR–SEINE*

PROVENANCE
The artist's estate, Paris; PIASA, Paris, 19 November 1999, no. 93; David Raymond, New York

BIBLIOGRAPHY
Combalía, Victoria. *Dora Maar: Bataille, Picasso et les Surréalistes,* no. 63. Exh. cat. Marseille: Musées de Marseille, 2002.

Combalía, Victoria, and Hubertus Gassner. *Dora Maar,* no. 65. Exh. cat. Munich: Haus der Kunst, 2001.

Johnson, Annabella, and Marcello Marvelli. *Dora Maar: Photographer.* Exh. cat. Long Island City, NY: Dorsky Gallery, 2004.

68. Horse and Carriage, 1931–36
Gelatin silver print; 23.5 x 17.6 cm (9¼ x 7 in.). John L. Severance Fund 2007.77

INSCRIPTIONS
Dora Maar estate stamp on verso of mount: *DM/1999*

Purple stamp on mount: *Kefer–Dora Maar*

PROVENANCE
The artist's estate, Paris; PIASA, Paris, 19 November 1999, no. 93; David Raymond, New York

72. Sky Pinwheels and Bottles (Ciel avec moulinets et bouteilles), 1931–36
Gelatin silver print, ferrotyped; 20.5 x 18.3 cm (8⅛ x 7¼ in.). John L. Severance Fund 2007.81

INSCRIPTIONS
Dora Maar estate stamp on verso of print: *CM/1999*

PROVENANCE
The artist's estate, Paris; PIASA, Paris, 19 November 1999, no. 32; Michael Mattis, New York; David Raymond, New York

BIBLIOGRAPHY
Combalía, Victoria. *Dora Maar: Bataille, Picasso et les Surréalistes,* no. 74. Exh. cat. Marseille: Musées de Marseille, 2002.

Combalía, Victoria, and Hubertus Gassner. *Dora Maar,* no. 219. Exh. cat. Munich: Haus der Kunst, 2001.

Johnson, Annabella, and Marcello Marvelli. *Dora Maar: Photographer.* Exh. cat. Long Island City, NY: Dorsky Gallery, 2004.

74. Three Covered Statues (Trois statues revêtues de housses), 1931–36
Gelatin silver print; 39.9 x 29.8 cm (15½ x 11¾ in.). John L. Severance Fund 2007.87

INSCRIPTIONS
Dora Maar estate stamp on verso of print: *DM/1999*

PROVENANCE
The artist's estate, Paris; PIASA, Paris, 19 November 1999, no. 32; Charles Isaacs, New York; Michael Mattis, New York; David Raymond, New York

BIBLIOGRAPHY
Combalía, Victoria. *Dora Maar: Bataille, Picasso et les Surréalistes,* no. 63. Exh. cat. Marseille: Musées de Marseille, 2002.

———. *Dora Maar, fotógrafa,* no. 23. Exh. cat. Valencia: Centro Cultural Bancaixi, 1995.

Combalía, Victoria, and Hubertus Gassner. *Dora Maar,* no. 116. Exh. cat. Munich: Haus der Kunst, 2001.

Johnson, Annabella, and Marcello Marvelli. *Dora Maar: Photographer.* Exh. cat. Long Island City, NY: Dorsky Gallery, 2004.

73. Trees and Ominous Sky (Arbres devant un ciel menaçant), 1931–36
Gelatin silver print, ferrotyped; 28.2 x 24 cm (11 x 9½ in.). John L. Severance Fund 2007.82

INSCRIPTION
Dora Maar estate stamp on verso of print: *DM/1998*

PROVENANCE
The artist's estate, Paris; PIASA, Paris, 19 November 1999, no. 87; David Raymond, New York

BIBLIOGRAPHY
Combalía, Victoria. *Dora Maar: Bataille, Picasso et les Surréalistes,* no. 75. Exh. cat. Marseille: Musées de Marseille, 2002.

Combalía, Victoria, and Hubertus Gassner. *Dora Maar,* no. 77. Exh. cat. Munich: Haus der Kunst, 2001.

Johnson, Annabella, and Marcello Marvelli. *Dora Maar: Photographer.* Exh. cat. Long Island City, NY: Dorsky Gallery, 2004.

13. Beggar Woman, Barcelona (Mendiante, Barcelone), 1933
Gelatin silver print, ferrotyped; 24.2 x 17.9 cm (9½ x 7 in.). John L. Severance Fund 2007.83

INSCRIPTIONS
In black ink on verso of print: *522 DM* and *Mendiante Barcelone* [in same hand]

Black stamp on verso of print: *KÉFER–DORA MAAR/ MENTION OBLIGATOIRE* and *45 bis BD. RICHARD–WALLACE/NEUILLY–SUR–SEINE*

Purple stamp on verso of print: *Edition "Tilleul"/Paris*

In blue pencil on verso of print: [illegible]

PROVENANCE
Étude Tajan, Paris, 18 November 2000, no. 345; David Raymond, New York

61. Blind Street Peddler, Barcelona (Mendiant aveugle, Barcelone), 1933
Gelatin silver print; 39.3 x 29.2 cm (15½ x 11½ in.). Gift of David Raymond 2008.173

INSCRIPTIONS
Signed in pencil on lower right of mount: *Dora Maar*

Dora Maar estate stamp on verso of mount: *DM/1998*

PROVENANCE
The artist's estate, Paris; PIASA, Paris, 20 November 1998, no. 83; Galerie Michèle Chomette, Paris; David Raymond, New York

BIBLIOGRAPHY
Combalía, Victoria. *Dora Maar: Bataille, Picasso et les Surréalistes,* no. 34. Exh. cat. Marseille: Musées de Marseille, 2002.

———. *Dora Maar, fotógrafa,* 72. Exh. cat. Valencia: Centro Cultural Bancaixi, 1995.

Combalía, Victoria, and Hubertus Gassner. *Dora Maar,* no. 35. Exh. cat. Munich: Haus der Kunst, 2001.

Johnson, Annabella, and Marcello Marvelli. *Dora Maar: Photographer,* 2. Exh. cat. Long Island City, NY: Dorsky Gallery, 2004.

Schaffner, Ingrid, and Colin Westerbeck. *Accommodation of Desire: Surrealist Works on Paper Collected by Julien Levy,* no. 95. Exh. cat. Pasadena: Curatorial Assistance, 2004.

67. Children Playing (Enfants Jouant), 1933
Gelatin silver print; 26 x 24.1 cm (10¼ x 9½ in.). John L. Severance Fund 2007.71

INSCRIPTIONS
Dora Maar estate stamp on verso of print: *DM/1998*

PROVENANCE
The artist's estate, Paris; PIASA, Paris, 19 November 1999, no. 88; David Raymond, New York

BIBLIOGRAPHY
Combalia, Victoria. *Dora Maar: Bataille, Picasso et les Surréalistes,* no. 59. Exh. cat. Marseille: Musées de Marseille, 2002.

Combalía, Victoria, and Hubertus Gassner. *Dora Maar,* no. 60. Exh. cat. Munich: Haus der Kunst, 2001.

Johnson, Annabella, and Marcello Marvelli. *Dora Maar: Photographer.* Exh. cat. Long Island City, NY: Dorsky Gallery, 2004.

76. The Grimace (La Grimace), 1933
Gelatin silver print, ferrotyped; 28.2 x 22.9 cm (11⅛ x 9 in.). John L. Severance Fund 2007.88

INSCRIPTIONS
Purple stamp on verso of print: *MENTION OBLIGATOIRE/DORA MAAR*

PROVENANCE
The artist, Paris; Galerie 1900–2000, Paris; David Raymond, New York

BIBLIOGRAPHY
Combalía, Victoria. Dora *Maar: Bataille, Picasso et les Surréalistes,* no. 44. Exh. cat. Marseille: Musées de Marseille, 2002.

———. *Dora Maar, fotógrafa,* no. 23. Exh. cat. Valencia: Centro Cultural Bancaixi, 1995.

Combalía, Victoria, and Hubertus Gassner. *Dora Maar,* no. 49. Exh. cat. Munich: Haus der Kunst, 2001.

Johnson, Annabella, and Marcello Marvelli. *Dora Maar: Photographer.* Exh. cat. Long Island City, NY: Dorsky Gallery, 2004.

66. Headstand, Barcelona, 1933
Gelatin silver print, ferrotyped; 27.3 x 24 cm (10¾ x 9⅜ in.). John L. Severance Fund 2007.86

INSCRIPTION
Dora Maar estate stamp on verso of print: *DM/1998*

PROVENANCE
The artist's estate, Paris; PIASA, Paris, 20 November 1998, no. 88; Sotheby's, New York, 23 April 2003, no. 166; David Raymond, New York

BIBLIOGRAPHY
Johnson, Annabella, and Marcello Marvelli. *Dora Maar: Photographer.* Exh. cat. Long Island City, NY: Dorsky Gallery, 2004.

70. Gypsy Palmist, 1934
Gelatin silver print, ferrotyped; 26.8 x 24 cm (10⅝ x 9½ in.). John L. Severance Fund 2007.150

INSCRIPTION
Dora Maar estate stamp on verso of print: *DM/1999*

PROVENANCE
The artist's estate, Paris; PIASA, Paris, 19 November 1999, no. 33; Michael Mattis, New York; David Raymond, New York

BIBLIOGRAPHY
Johnson, Annabella, and Marcello Marvelli. *Dora Maar: Photographer.* Exh. cat. Long Island City, NY: Dorsky Gallery, 2004.

Schaffner, Ingrid, and Colin Westerbeck. *Accommodation of Desire: Surrealist Works on Paper Collected by Julien Levy.* Exh. cat. Pasadena: Curatorial Assistance, 2004.

14. Medically Unfit, 1934
Gelatin silver print, ferrotyped; 18.2 x 22.7 cm (7⅛ x 8⅞ in.). John L. Severance Fund 2007.75

INSCRIPTIONS
Dora Maar estate stamp on verso of print: *DM/1999*

PROVENANCE
The artist's estate, Paris; PIASA, Paris, 19 November 1999, no. 93; David Raymond, New York

64. Plant and Window Study, 1934
Gelatin silver print, ferrotyped; 22.5 x 26.5 cm (8⅞ x 10⅜ in.). John L. Severance Fund 2007.73

INSCRIPTION
Dora Maar estate stamp on verso of print: *DM/1999*

PROVENANCE
The artist's estate, Paris; PIASA, Paris, 19 November 1999, no. 8; David Raymond, New York

BIBLIOGRAPHY
Combalía, Victoria. *Dora Maar: Bataille, Picasso et les Surréalistes,* no. 77. Exh. cat. Marseille: Musées de Marseille, 2002.

Combalía, Victoria, and Hubertus Gassner. *Dora Maar,* no. 79. Exh. cat. Munich: Haus der Kunst, 2001.

Johnson, Annabella, and Marcello Marvelli. *Dora Maar: Photographer.* Exh. cat. Long Island City, NY: Dorsky Gallery, 2004.

63. Plants in Covent Garden, 1934
Gelatin silver print; 24 x 26.3 cm (9½ x 10⅜ in.). John L. Severance Fund 2007.74

INSCRIPTIONS
Dora Maar estate stamp on verso of print: *DM/1999*

PROVENANCE
The artist's estate, Paris; PIASA, Paris, 19 November 1999, no. 87; David Raymond, New York

BIBLIOGRAPHY
Johnson, Annabella, and Marcello Marvelli. *Dora Maar: Photographer.* Exh. cat. Long Island City, NY: Dorsky Gallery, 2004.

71. Repent for the Kingdom of Heaven Is at Hand, 1934
Gelatin silver print; 28.9 x 23.9 cm (11⅜ x 9⅜ in.). John L. Severance Fund 2007.70

INSCRIPTIONS
Purple stamp on verso of print: *DORA MAAR*

Dora Maar estate stamp on verso of print: *DM/1998*

PROVENANCE
The artist's estate, Paris; PIASA, Paris, 19 November 1999, no. 93; David Raymond, New York

BIBLIOGRAPHY
Combalía, Victoria. *Dora Maar: Bataille, Picasso et les Surréalistes,* no. 38. Exh. cat. Marseille: Musées de Marseille, 2002.

Combalía, Victoria, and Hubertus Gassner. *Dora Maar,* no. 42. Exh. cat. Munich: Haus der Kunst, 2001.

Johnson, Annabella, and Marcello Marvelli. *Dora Maar: Photographer.* Exh. cat. Long Island City, NY: Dorsky Gallery, 2004.

65. Stairwell and Plants in Kew Gardens, 1934
Gelatin silver print, ferrotyped; 28 x 24 cm (11 x 9½ in.). John L. Severance Fund 2007.76

INSCRIPTIONS
In red pencil on verso of print: *Kew Gardens*

Dora Maar estate stamp on verso of print: *DM/1999*

Purple stamp on verso of print: *KÉFER–DORA MAAR*

PROVENANCE
The artist's estate, Paris; PIASA, Paris, 19 November 1999, no. 87; David Raymond, New York

BIBLIOGRAPHY
Combalía, Victoria. *Dora Maar: Bataille, Picasso et les Surréalistes,* no. 76. Exh. cat. Marseille: Musées de Marseille, 2002.

Combalía, Victoria, and Hubertus Gassner. *Dora Maar,* no. 78. Exh. cat. Munich: Haus der Kunst, 2001.

60. Street Orchestra, Blind Musicians (Orchestre de rue, quatre musiciens aveugles), 1934
Gelatin silver print; 32 x 28.4 cm (12⅝ x 11¼ in.). John L. Severance Fund 2007.89

INSCRIPTIONS
Dora Maar estate stamp on verso of print: *DM/1998*

Sticker on verso of print, gummed label in upper left: *No 3017/H*

In pencil on verso of print: *NY DM 270* and *N1361*

PROVENANCE
The artist's estate, Paris; PIASA, Paris, 20 November 1998, no. 69; Edwynn Houk Gallery, New York; David Raymond, New York

BIBLIOGRAPHY
Combalía, Victoria. *Dora Maar: Bataille, Picasso et les Surréalistes,* no. 35. Exh. cat. Marseille: Musées de Marseille, 2002.

Combalía, Victoria, and Hubertus Gassner. *Dora Maar,* no. 36. Exh. cat. Munich: Haus der Kunst, 2001.

Johnson, Annabella, and Marcello Marvelli. *Dora Maar: Photographer.* Exh. cat. Long Island City, NY: Dorsky Gallery, 2004.

11. Fashion Study, c. 1934
Gelatin silver print; 27.7 x 22.2 cm (10⅞ x 8¾ in.). John L. Severance Fund 2007.84

INSCRIPTIONS
Dora Maar estate stamp on verso of print: *DM/1998*

PROVENANCE
The artist's estate, Paris; PIASA, Paris, 20 November 1998, no. 32; David Raymond, New York

[65] [60] [8]

BIBLIOGRAPHY
Johnson, Annabella, and Marcello Marvelli. *Dora Maar: Photographer.* Exh. cat. Long Island City, NY: Dorsky Gallery, 2004.

12. *Forbidden Games (Jeux Interdits),* 1935
Gelatin silver print, montage; 27.9 x 21.5 cm (11 x 8½ in.). John L. Severance Fund 2007.85

PROVENANCE
The artist, Paris; André Breton, Paris; Calmels Cohen, Paris, André Breton sale, 15–17 April 2003, no. 5055; David Raymond, New York

BIBLIOGRAPHY
Combalía Dexeus, Victoria. *Paris y los surrealistas,* 206. Exh cat. Bilbao: Fundacion Museo de Bellas Artes de Bilbao, 2005.

Combalía, Victoria, and Hubertus Gassner. *Dora Maar,* no. 88. Exh. cat. Munich: Haus der Kunst, 2001.

Johnson, Annabella, and Marcello Marvelli. *Dora Maar: Photographer.* Exh. cat. Long Island City, NY: Dorsky Gallery, 2004.

9. *Double Portrait with Hat,* c. 1936–37
Gelatin silver print, montage, from negatives with handwork; 29.7 x 23.8 cm (11¾ x 9⅜ in.). Gift of David Raymond 2008.172

INSCRIPTIONS
Dora Maar estate stamp on verso of print: *DM/1999*

PROVENANCE
The artist's estate, Paris; PIASA, Paris, 19 November 1999, no. 47 (cover illustration); Edwynn Houk Gallery, New York; David Raymond, New York

BIBLIOGRAPHY
Caws, Mary Ann. *Dora Maar with and without Picasso: A Biography,* 18. London: Thames and Hudson, 2000.

———. *Picasso's Weeping Woman: The Life and Art of Dora Maar,* 18. New York: Little, Brown/Bulfinch Press, 2000.

Combalía, Victoria. *Dora Maar: Bataille, Picasso et les Surréalistes,* no. 184. Exh. cat. Marseille: Musées de Marseille, 2002.

Combalía, Victoria, and Hubertus Gassner. *Dora Maar,* no. 176. Exh. cat. Munich: Haus der Kunst, 2001.

Johnson, Annabella, and Marcello Marvelli. *Dora Maar: Photographer.* Exh. cat. Long Island City, NY: Dorsky Gallery, 2004.

René Magritte
Belgian, 1898–1967

Born in the Hainaut region of Belgium, Magritte studied at the Academy of Fine Arts in Brussels in 1916 where he discovered Russian Constructivism through Victor Servranckx and Pierre-Louis Flouquet, joining their Antwerp-based circle. In 1920 he met E. L. T. Mesens who became a staunch supporter and soon exposed Magritte to avant-garde music and early surrealist ideas from Paris. Magritte had his first solo exhibition in Brussels that year, displaying Cubo-Futurist paintings. Beginning in 1922, he met Marcel Lecomte, Camille Goemans, and Paul Nougé, with whom he formed the nexus of the Belgian surrealist circle.

That same year he married Georgette Berger and worked as a graphic designer and decorator. He was active in publishing early Dada journals with Mesens, including *Marie* and *Oesophage.* Early in 1926 Paul-Gustave Van Hecke, publisher and owner of Galerie Le Centaure, agreed to support Magritte, marking his first surrealist period. Magritte expressed a unique style of imagery immersed in surrealist thought, conflating the function and setting of objects and places in ways that suggested a dream or fantasy world. In 1926 he created *The Lost Jockey,* a cornerstone work of the period that featured objects divorced from their expected contexts. The Belgian surrealist group was cemented that year, and Magritte was prolific during this period.

He and Georgette moved to the Paris suburbs late in 1927, where he joined André Breton's circle. He contributed the illustrated tract "Les Mots et les images" to *La Revolution surréaliste* in 1929. Thereafter he broke with Breton and the Paris surrealists, returned to Brussels, and opened an advertising agency with his brother Paul.

Photography maintained a constant place in Magritte's activity to document the role-playing silliness of his social circle. Magritte availed himself of the photo booth at the Jardin des Plantes in Paris in 1928 and also made a series of short films, directing his artist friends and family in outdoor surrealist antics. His photographs of Georgette moved beyond documentary note-taking to become incisive images of their own accord.

In the 1930s he exhibited at Julien Levy's gallery in New York (1936), in major surrealist exhibitions including E. L. T. Mesens's show at the London Gallery (1937), and at the Charles Ratton Gallery, Paris (1936). The relationship between objects and language, newly introduced into the paintings, played an increasingly important role in his work. By 1940 the couple was living in the south of France to escape the German occupation of Belgium. After World War II, Magritte continued to support an active surrealist culture in Brussels. His paintings and sculptures replayed much of the iconography of his earlier surrealist period.

8. *Georgette at the Table,* c. 1928–30
Gelatin silver print; 8 x 6 cm (3⅛ x 2⅜ in.). John L. Severance Fund 2007.90

INSCRIPTIONS
In pencil on verso: *Georgette/Magritte*

PROVENANCE
Paris art market; Ubu Gallery, New York; David Raymond, New York

BIBLIOGRAPHY
Combalía Dexeus, Victoria. *Paris y los surrealistas,* 116. Bilbao: Fundacion Museo de Bellas Artes de Bilbao, 2005.

Man Ray
American, 1890–1976

Born in Philadelphia as Emmanuel Radnitsky, Man Ray was raised in New York where he studied painting at the Art Students League and the Ferrer Center and also frequented Alfred Stieglitz's Gallery 291. By that time he was signing his work "Man Ray" and was intent on making radical art, having seen examples of Cubism, abstraction, and Precisionist painting. Discovering European modern art and seeing Marcel Duchamp's work at the Armory Show in 1913 were early turning points for Man Ray. He moved to an artist's colony in Ridgefield, New Jersey,

married Adon Lacroix in 1914, and was exposed to the French writers Stéphane Mallarmé and Guillaume Apollinaire, among others. Man Ray lived and painted in a free-thinking environment that he later said inspired him to move to Paris. Through collector Walter Arensberg, he met Duchamp and began a lifelong relationship with him. In 1915 Man Ray moved to New York. His first show of paintings that year at the Daniel Gallery was not commercially successful but made his name in avant-garde collecting circles. By 1917 he had begun making collages and assemblage sculptures as well as the aerograph images—paintings made with a commercial airbrush. At this time his experiments with form and material were all dedicated to subverting expectations of the fine art public and led directly to his immersion in Dada and a radical attitude toward the camera. In 1920 with Duchamp he created the personality of Rrose Sélavy, the cross-dressing matron, one of several collaborations with Duchamp that can be classified as a Dada production. Man Ray also began making straight photographs with artistic intent, such as the clothesline in *Moving Sculpture* and *Dust Breeding* (1920). Together with Duchamp and the American patron Katherine Dreier, he helped establish the Société Anonyme in 1920 to promote Dada and Constructivist artists in the U.S.

Man Ray moved to Paris in 1921 and quickly became a sought-after photographer for the fashionable and artistic social set. Soon, separately from others who were experimenting in a similar vein, he began making photograms (which he called rayographs) and published the portfolio of photograms titled *Champs délicieux* with Tristan Tzara. The fame of this project brought Man Ray into the orbit of André Breton and the burgeoning surrealist movement in Paris. By the end of the 1920s, Man Ray was central to the international art community in Paris, bolstered by photographers arriving from elsewhere in Europe. Lee Miller, an American model, became his assistant in 1929 and remained his muse until their relationship ended in 1932.

With the onset of World War II, Man Ray returned to America and settled in Hollywood, shooting fashion work and portraits of the film community. In 1950 he returned to Paris, but only in 1961 did he receive the gold medal at the Venice Photo Biennale and agree to an exhibition of his photographic work at the Bibliothéque Nationale in Paris. In the 1960s

and 1970s, Man Ray's reputation was resurrected through publications and exhibitions in America and throughout Europe.

46. *Untitled (Rayograph),* 1926–28
Gelatin silver print from a photogram; 16.5 x 12.3 cm (6½ x 4⅞ in.). John L. Severance Fund 2007.91

INSCRIPTIONS
Black stamp on verso of print: *MAN RAY/31 bis, Rue/Campagne/Première/PARIS*

In pencil on verso of print: *(1928)*

PROVENANCE
Zabriskie Gallery, New York; Edwynn Houk Gallery, New York; David Raymond, New York

10. *Lee Miller,* 1930
Gelatin silver print; 9 x 6.4 cm (3½ x 2½ in.). John L. Severance Fund 2007.92

INSCRIPTIONS
Black stamp on verso of print: *MAN RAY/31 bis, RUE/CAMPAGNE/PREMIÈRE/PARIS XIV*

In pencil on verso of print: *199.34*

PROVENANCE
Lucien Treillard, Paris; Edwynn Houk, New York; David Raymond, New York

BIBLIOGRAPHY
Combalía Dexeus, Victoria. *Paris y los surrealistas,* 116. Bilbao: Fundacion Museo de Bellas Artes de Bilbao, 2005.

Marcel Mariën
Belgian, 1920–1993

Born in Antwerp, Mariën discovered surrealism through the work of René Magritte. He soon was welcomed into the circle of Magritte, Paul Nougé, and Louis Scutenaire, and he contributed work to E. L. T. Mesens's 1937 London Gallery surrealist exhibition. Following a photographic apprenticeship during his teenage years, Mariën developed a lifelong interest in publishing. He made photographs and collages as well as written work.

Briefly imprisoned in Germany in 1940, Mariën returned to Paris and published work by Paul Eluard and his own monograph on Magritte in 1943. In

1946 he edited an issue of the New York magazine *View* for Charles-Henri Ford that focused on the Belgian surrealists. Mariën founded *Les Lèvres Nues,* a surrealist journal based in Brussels from 1954 to 1960, and then traveled in China from 1963 to 1965, working for a French magazine. He continued his writing on Belgian surrealism during this period and resumed artistic activity in collage and photography. His first solo exhibition was held at Galerie Defacqz in Brussels in 1967; many others followed. Mariën's only film, *L'Imitation du cinéma* (1959), was banned in France as pornography.

89. *The Spirit of the Staircase (L'Esprit de l'escalier),* 1949
Gelatin silver print; 12.6 x 8.8 cm (5 x 3½ in.). John L. Severance Fund 2007.93

INSCRIPTIONS
Blue stamps on verso of print: *MARCEL MARIEN/Rue André van Hasselt, 39/1030 Bruxelles (Belgique)* and *LES LÈVRES NUES/Revue trimestrielle/Jane Graverol, 35 rue Joseph II/BRUXELLES (Belgique)*

BIBLIOGRAPHY
Schneede, Uwe M., and Hamburger Kunsthalle. *Begierde im Blick: Surrealistiche Photographie,* no. 199. Exh. cat. Ostfildern: Hatje Cantz, 2005.

Herbert Matter
American, born Switzerland, 1907–1984

Born in the village of Engelberg, Matter studied art briefly in Geneva and then at the Académie Moderne in Paris with Fernand Léger and Amédée Ozenfant in 1928–29. His first job was as a graphic designer and photographer for the photographic studio of Deberny Peignot. Publishing often in Arts et Metiers Graphiques's annuals, he worked with graphic designer A. M. Cassandre and architect Le Corbusier. When Matter was forced to leave France in 1932 for not having appropriate identity papers, he returned to Zurich and established a career as a poster designer for the Swiss Tourist Office. His groundbreaking posters made his reputation in Europe and in the U.S. In 1936 he moved to New York at the invitation of a Swiss ballet troupe touring at that time. He stayed, working first for Alexey Brodovitch at *Harper's Bazaar* shooting design and fashion photographs. Eventually he established a photogra-

phy enterprise, Studio Associates, but also continued to develop his industrial design practice in the U.S.

In his fashion and advertising work as well as personal pictures, Matter explored many of the formal techniques adapted by the surrealists in the 1930s. His work for Knoll furniture was influential. He also taught graphic design at Yale University and worked with the Museum of Modern Art and the Guggenheim Museum on exhibition and graphic designs.

54. *Shirley Doll,* 1936
Gelatin silver print; 20.2 x 25.8 cm (8 x 10⅛ in.).
John L. Severance Fund 2007.94

INSCRIPTIONS
Purple stamp on verso of print: *photo/herbert matter* [inside grid]

In pencil on verso of print: *4825*

PROVENANCE
The artist's estate, New York; New York art market; Villa Grisebach, Berlin, 30 May 2003, no. 283; David Raymond, New York

Édouard Léon Théodore Mesens
Belgian, 1903–1971

Writer, composer, and art dealer E. L. T. Mesens was a central figure of the surrealist movement in Belgium and later in London. His interest in the avant-garde music of Erik Satie led him to visit Paris where he met Man Ray and saw his first exhibition of rayographs. These encounters prompted him to make his own experimental photographic works and to publish the images and writings of the French surrealist movement in Brussels. He met René Magritte in 1920; together they nurtured an anti-authoritarian movement in Brussels, first influenced by Dada actions and journals and later by André Breton's surrealism imported from Paris. Between 1921 and 1923, Mesens disseminated Satie's music and the Dada revolutionary spirit in gatherings, writings, and publications in Brussels. He worked at the Galerie Manteau in 1924 and then in 1927 with P-G Van Hecke at Galerie Le Centaure, relaunched as the Galerie L'Époque. When the business of Le Centaure failed, Mesens purchased the entire inventory of paintings by Magritte, which tied the two men together for years to come, sometimes with adverse results. Van Hecke published a surrealist

journal, *Variétés,* to which Mesens contributed from 1928 to 1930, soliciting writing and photography by the leading artists of the Paris circle. In 1929 Mesens edited a special issue of Van Hecke's journal, "Le Surréalisme en 1929," and in 1933 he produced his only extensive photographically illustrated work, *Alphabet of the Blind and Deaf (Alphabet Sourd Aveugle).* Three of his original photogram and photographic collages were included in the 1929 *Film und Foto* exhibition in Stuttgart. In the 1930s Mesens gave up photography to focus on collage.

An adept organizer, Mesens assumed directorship of the gallery at the Palais des Beaux-Arts in Brussels in 1931–36 and took the opportunity to organize ambitious international exhibitions on photography and cinema in 1931–32. He launched the Belgian section of the international surrealist exhibition in London in 1936 as well as Belgian contributions to the 1938 Paris and Amsterdam surrealist shows. In 1938 Mesens moved to London where he established the London Gallery and worked with Roland Penrose and Edward James to import French and Belgian surrealism to England before war broke out. He continued to support surrealist efforts in London throughout the war and returned to writing and gallery activities in the 1940s and 1950s.

47. *Untitled,* c. 1926
Collodion silver printing out paper, photogram; 17.9 x 23.8 cm (7 x 9⅜ in.). John L. Severance Fund 2007.95

PROVENANCE
The artist's family; Adrien Dubucq, Belgium; Paul Kasmin Gallery, New York; Ubu Gallery, New York; David Raymond, New York

László Moholy-Nagy
American, born Hungary, 1895–1946

Born in present-day Hungary, Lázsló Weisz lived with his uncle Dr. Nagy in Mohol. He studied law and, following military service, studied painting in Budapest. In 1919 he formed an avant-garde arts group around the journal *MA* but soon immigrated to Vienna and finally to Berlin in 1920.

Moholy-Nagy's work—painting, drawing, and sculpture—reflected the reductive form favored by the Russian Constructivists. Hannah Höch, Raoul

Hausmann, and Kurt Schwitters of the Berlin Dada circle were influential friends. In 1921 Moholy-Nagy met Lucia Schultz, who taught him the rudiments of photography and assisted in the darkroom.

Through his writing, Moholy-Nagy became influential in Berlin, a connecting force between the Constructivist artists and others. Before 1922 he was making photograms associated with the *Light-Space Modulator* sculpture that were exhibited in Hanover at the Kestnergesellschaft gallery. A joint publishing project with fellow Hungarian artist Ludwig Kassak, *Buch neuer Künstler* (1922), included Moholy-Nagy's first photographic essay combining photographs from advertising, the illustrated press, and art. In March 1923 Walter Gropius invited him to teach at the Bauhaus in Weimar where Moholy-Nagy introduced photography as a primary form of artistic expression and an applied art in essays such as "Photography Is Creating with Light" (1928). At the Bauhaus in 1924, he established the series Bauhaus Books with Gropius, publishing the first edition of his groundbreaking photographic book *Painting Photography Film* (1925) and *From Material to Architecture* (1929).

Moholy-Nagy's belief that the future of art was in technology was the basis for his experimentation with photography, film, and plastics throughout his life. He moved constantly among these media, seeking to increase the viewer's visual acuity through all his work, both personal and commercial. His photographic activity included photomontages, original photographs, experimental compositions, and photographic processes such as negative printing and superimposition.

In 1928 he resigned from the Bauhaus and returned to Berlin. A variety of commercial engagements with printing houses, theaters, and magazines supported his work in film and publishing. He also designed several important photography and media exhibitions, including the 1929 *Film und Foto* show in Stuttgart. His first U.S. exhibition of photography was held at the Delphic Studios in New York in 1932.

In 1937 Moholy-Nagy resettled in Chicago where he established the New Bauhaus School of Design and then in 1938 the School of Design within the Illinois Institute of Technology. He introduced a generation of artists, including scores of photographers, into the Bauhaus methodology. He was included in the Bauhaus exhibition at the Museum of Modern Art

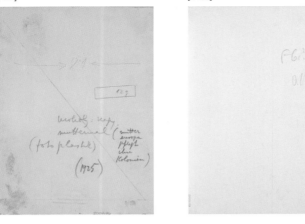

in 1938 and had a solo show at the Guggenheim Museum in 1947 as well as numerous retrospective exhibitions in the U.S. and abroad from 1969 onward.

40. *Mother Europe Cares for Her Colonies (Mutter Europa pflegt Ihre Kolonien),* 1925
Gelatin silver print of a collage; 16.1 x 12.3 cm (6⅜ x 4⅞ in.). John L. Severance Fund 2007.96

INSCRIPTIONS
In pencil on verso of print: *Moholy–nagy muttermal (fotoplastik)*

In pencil in a different hand on verso of print: *(mutter europa pflegt ihre Kolonien) (1925)*

Red rectangle and crop marks on verso of print, numbered in blue crayon: *129*

Artist's studio stamp on verso of print: *moholy/nagy/berlin . . . /freidenrichstr. 27 atelier*

PROVENANCE
Family of Otto Eisner, Brno, Czech Republic; Sotheby's, London, 4 May 2000, no. 161; David Raymond, New York

BIBLIOGRAPHY
Moholy-Nagy, László. "Fotografie, die objektive Sehform unsere Zeit." *telehor* 1–2 (February 1936): 54–55.

Monsieur X
French, 1900s

Known only by his erotic photographs of girls in a Parisian brothel, Monsieur X left a legacy of fine amateur views made for his own pleasure in the 1920s and 1930s, at the peak of the commercialization of erotica in Parisian society. Most were made in a brothel overlooking the Place Pigalle, near St. Denis, the heart of the vice district at the time. The photographer was probably a man of some means who did not sell his images.

The collection of 18-by-24-centimeter prints, stereoscope views, and two films were presented to an erotica dealer in the 1960s. Another lot of several thousand annotated contact prints surfaced separately, thus allowing his oeuvre to be reconstructed with names and notes of the models added.

140. *Three Graces,* 1925
Gelatin silver print; 17.9 x 23.9 cm (7 x 9⅜ in.). John L. Severance Fund 2007.97

INSCRIPTIONS
In pencil on verso of print: *III AA 26* and *F6.3/018*

PROVENANCE
Paris art market; David Raymond, New York

Oskar Nerlinger
German, 1893–1969

Nerlinger spent his youth in Strasbourg but moved to Berlin in 1911 where he studied at the Berlin School of Arts and Crafts under Emil Orlik until 1915. There he met his future wife, Alice Pfeffer (later known as Alice Lex-Nerlinger), and befriended George Grosz, who introduced him to Herwarth Walden's *Der Sturm* circle, a meeting point for the Expressionist movement in Germany. Nerlinger remained in Berlin until 1928 and, already a committed leftist, made Russian Constructivist–oriented art that reflected the principles upheld by the German New Objectivity. He was active in several artist groups, including the Abstract Ones (*Die Abstrakten*), which eventually became known as the Contemporaries (*Die Zeitgemaessen*). After 1928 he joined the German Communist Party and devoted much of his visual work to themes of the worker's plight in industrial society. He participated in the ASSO group of activist artists and also joined politically active groups outside Berlin, including the Cologne Progressives.

In 1925 Nerlinger was making abstract photograms in the style of his painting and graphic work. He was an early practitioner of photography in advertising and perfected the application of translucent tissue paper in photograms to create forms that appeared as light-infused silhouettes. His skilled advertising and book typography reveal the influence of other leaders in the field, including Piet Zwart and El Lissitzky. After political activity was banned in 1933, Nerlinger retreated into more benign personal work and remained in East Berlin after 1945.

49. *Arrival at Sea (Ankunft am Meer),* c. 1928
Gelatin silver print, photogram; 17.5 x 22.8 cm (6⅞ x 9 in.). John L. Severance Fund 2007.98

INSCRIPTIONS
Label on verso of print: *5 hauptbilder aus einem märchenfilm/bild 1:/ankunft am meere* and *fotogramm*

Black stamp on verso of print: *OSCAR NERLINGER/Berlin–Charlottenburg 6/Dernburgstr. 25/Tel.: Westend 918*

PROVENANCE
German art market; Villa Grisebach, Berlin, 4 June 1999, no. 1337; David Raymond, New York

Dorothy Norman
American, 1905–1997

Born in Philadelphia, Norman studied at Smith College and the University of Pennsylvania. She married and settled in New York where her relationship with Alfred Stieglitz inspired her interest in photography. Already drawn to social causes, Norman worked for the American Civil Liberties Union. After 1927 she began working for Stieglitz first at the Intimate Gallery and later at his last gallery, An American Place. Stieglitz taught her photography, and soon she began to make her own pictures, mostly in his straight style, of New York urban views and natural subjects on Cape Cod. She worked with the artists engaged at his galleries; her circle included artists, poets, and writers as well as photographers. In 1937 Norman established her own literary journal addressing the arts and civil liberties, *Twice A Year,* publishing Marcel Proust, Franz Kafka, Albert Camus, and Jean-Paul Sartre, among others. At the end of her life, Norman's photographic work was recognized in several major exhibitions.

155. *From 509 Madison Avenue,* 1946
Gelatin silver print; 9.9 x 6.5 cm (4 x 2⅝ in.). Gift of David Raymond 2009.476

INSCRIPTIONS
Signed in ink on verso of print: *Dorothy Norman*

In pencil on verso of print: *MOMA/From 509 Madison Avenue/after A.S.'s death/1946/1 NY*

[155]

[27]

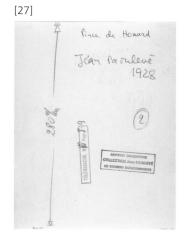

[57]

[142]

Black stamp on verso of print: *ORIGINAL BY DORO-THY NORMAN*

PROVENANCE
The artist, New York; Edwynn Houk Gallery, New York; David Raymond, New York

Jean Painlevé with Eli Lotar
French, 1902–1989

Son of mathematician and French Prime Minister Paul Painlevé, Jean was a student of biology at the Sorbonne who fused his interest in science with the emerging field of cinema. He subscribed to left-wing politics and liberal lifestyles and experimented with making underwater films and finding ways to import new film technology into laboratory research on oceanic life. Together with Ginette Hamon, he made over two hundred short films documenting the habits of undersea creatures, some more clinical, others more lighthearted in nature. Their operations base was the Hamon family home in Brittany. Painlevé worked simultaneously as a researcher and promoter of scientific cinema throughout the 1930s. He established the Institute of Scientific Cinema in 1930 and the Association of Scientific Documentation in Photography and Cinematography in 1932. His personal archive, Les Documents Cinématographiques, is located today in Paris.

Painlevé's art activity intersected with the surrealists as early as 1923, when André Breton was present at a screening of his films. In 1925 he contributed a text to the journal *Surréalisme* and soon after was acquainted with Luis Buñuel, Jacques André Boiffard, Georges Bataille, and Eli Lotar. Painlevé employed Lotar to shoot still photographs on the set of his films in 1929–30. Painlevé scored many of his films with jazz and avant-garde musical treatments, influenced by his friend the composer Edgar Varèse. Painlevé's photographic work was included in many exhibitions of the period and published in the popular and art press. In later years he continued to develop applications and partnerships in the realm of scientific filmmaking.

27. *Lobster Claw (Pince d'Homard),* c. 1929
Gelatin silver print; 22.9 x 17.2 cm (9 x 6¾ in.). John L. Severance Fund 2007.99

INSCRIPTIONS
In blue ink on verso of print: *Pince de Homard*

In pencil on verso of print: *Jean Painlevé/1928*

Black stamps on verso of print: *MENTION OBLIGA-TOIRE/COLLECTION Jean PAINLEVÉ/LES DOCU-MENTS CINÉMATOGRAPHIQUES* and *Télémagazine No. 168 page 8–9*

PROVENANCE
The artist's family, Paris; Alain Paviot, Paris; Jack Banning, New York; Ubu Gallery, New York; David Raymond, New York

BIBLIOGRAPHY
Heu, Bernard. "Pour le cinéaste Painlevé, les vedettes sont millimetrées." *Télémagazine* 168 (January 1959): 8–9.

Gaston Paris
French, 1905–1986

Paris was one of the most frequent contributors to *VU* magazine in the 1930s, concentrating on socially conscious documentary stories. He was the only salaried photographer on staff at the magazine, covering Spanish refugees, prostitute culture, life behind the scenes at the Opera and Folies Bergères—all subjects treated by many of his more well-known counterparts including Germaine Krull and Brassaï.

Aside from his classic reportage work, Paris photographed more lyrical, personal events and subjects in a more surrealist vein, including many commissions for detective magazines and gory scenarios from the Musée Dupuytren, a wax museum. Not much of a joiner, Paris eventually signed onto the Rectangle group of photographers formed in 1936 to support a French classical tradition in the medium. They disbanded during the German occupation. He was included in the 1936 Paris International Exposition of Photography. Later Paris joined the Roger-Viollet agency, which still holds many of his images.

57. *Mannequin (Dalí),* 1938
Gelatin silver print; 19.8 x 18 cm (7⅞ x 7 in.). John L. Severance Fund 2007.101

INSCRIPTIONS
In black ink on label on verso of print: *Mannequin décoré par/Salvadore DALi pour la/grande Exposition du Surrealism/de Paris 17.1.1938/collection Romi*

In black ink on label on verso of print: *cette exposition internationale fut/ouverte par Andre Breton à/la Galerie Beaux Arts, 140, rue/du Faubourg Saint Honoré*

Black stamp on verso of print: *PHOTO/GASTON PARIS/27, Boulevard des Italiens/RIC 70-47*

In red pencil on verso of print: printer's marks and *Marianne p. 4*

In black ink on verso of print: *Autour du Surrealisme/mannequin décoré par/Salvador DALi/[illegible] à Paris en 1938 par/Salvador DAlI*

PROVENANCE
Collection Romi, Paris; Yves de Fontbrune, Cahiers d'Art Archives, Paris; Paris art market; Ubu Gallery, New York; Barry Friedman Ltd., New York; David Raymond, New York

BIBLIOGRAPHY
Behind Closed Doors: The Art of Hans Bellmer. New York: International Center of Photography, 2001.

"La vie des arts." *Marianne,* no. 279 (26 January 1938): 11.

Puppen, Körper, Automaten: Phantasmen der Moderne, 432. Exh. cat. Düsseldorf: Kunstsammlung Nordrhein-Westfalen, 1999.

Schneede, Uwe M., and Hamburger Kunsthalle. *Begierde im Blick: Surrealistiche Photographie.* Exh. cat. Ostfildern: Hatje Cantz, 2005.

142. *Entertainers,* 1930s
Gelatin silver print; 23.9 x 17.5 cm (9⅜ x 6⅞ in.). John L. Severance Fund 2007.100

INSCRIPTIONS
Signed in pencil on verso of print: *G Paris*

Black stamp on verso of print: *PHOTO/GASTON PARIS*

PROVENANCE
Paris art market; David Raymond, New York

Roger Parry
French, 1905–1977

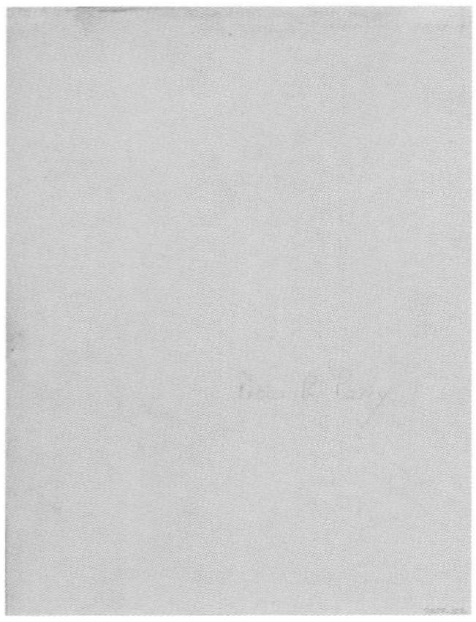

Raised in a Paris suburb, Parry pursued painting and applied arts at the École des Beaux-Arts, the École Germain Pilon, and the École des Arts Décoratifs before finding employment in design for the department store Le Printemps from 1925 to 1928. At that time he befriended a group of renegade young artists including Fabien Loris, Georges Pomiés, and René Zuber. Parry's introduction to photography came through a fortuitous meeting with Maurice Tabard, who in 1928 returned from the U.S. to Paris to live across the street from the Parry family home in Boulogne. Parry assisted Tabard in the studio, making his first pictures on a trip to the south of France later that year.

Parry's photography career took off in 1929 when Charles Peignot hired Tabard and Parry to work at his successful commercial photography studio, Deberny Peignot. The two photographers worked closely as a team in the studio and shared the editing of the inaugural annual published by Arts et Metiers Graphiques on photography in 1930. Parry published six images in that volume, superseding his photographic contributions to La Nouvelle Revue Française publication of *Banalit*é in 1929.

At that point, Parry's artistic career was confirmed and he became part of the new "School of Paris" of modernist photographers, appearing in shows of experimental photography in 1930. He traveled to Africa that year and to Tahiti in 1932. In between those trips, Parry established his own photographic studio in Paris, finding consistent work with illustrated magazines and book publishers including the La Pléiade press. His independent contract work continued throughout the decade and included feature stories for the commercial and left-wing press in France. He was exempted from military service but remained active in Paris under the German occupation. After the war Parry was attached to the Ministry of Interior, traveling through France and eventually to Algeria for photo stories. In the 1950s he resumed photographic projects for the publisher Gallimard and collaborated with André Malraux on his art and culture texts.

58. *Carousel Horse,* 1929
Gelatin silver print; 22.5 x 16.7 cm (8⅞ x 6⅝ in.). John L. Severance Fund 2007.151

INSCRIPTIONS
Black stamp on verso of print: *PHOTO R. PARRY/18. rue A, Gervais/ISSY–SEINE*

PROVENANCE
The artist, Paris; Julien Levy Gallery, New York; Witkin Gallery, New York; Mark Kelman, New York; Gilman collection, New York; Metropolitan Museum of Art, New York; Sotheby's, New York, 14–15 February 2006, no. 68; Paul Hertzmann, San Francisco; David Raymond, New York

131. *Hands with Crystal Ball, Variation (Mains avec Boule de Cristal, variante),* 1930
Gelatin silver print; 24 x 17.76 cm (9½ x 7 in.). John L. Severance Fund 2007.107

INSCRIPTIONS
In black ink on verso of print: *1930–Photo R. PARRY*

Signed in ink on verso of print: *M. R. Parry*

PROVENANCE
The artist's estate, Paris; Grob Gallery, London; Zabriskie Gallery, New York; David Raymond, New York

BIBLIOGRAPHY
Combalía Dexeus, Victoria. *Paris y los surrealistas,* 136. Exh. cat. Bilbao: Fundacion Museo de Bellas Artes de Bilbao, 2005.

143. *Nude,* 1930
Gelatin silver print; 23.7 x 17.6 cm (9⅜ x 6⅞ in.). John L. Severance Fund 2007.102

INSCRIPTIONS
In pencil on verso of mount: *Photo R. Parry*

PROVENANCE
Galerie Michèle Chomette, Paris; Paul Hertzmann, San Francisco; David Raymond, New York

BIBLIOGRAPHY
Bouqueret, Christian, and Christophe Berthoud. *Roger Parry le météore fabuleux,* 69. Paris: Mission du patrimoine photographique, 1995.

152. *Still Life (Nature morte),* 1930
Gelatin silver print; 23 x 17.4 cm (9 x 6⅞ in.). John L. Severance Fund 2007.105

INSCRIPTIONS
In ink on verso of mount: *1930 Photo R. PARRY/M.R. Parry* and *PAR 47* and *PR10237* and *RP43894*

PROVENANCE
The artist's estate, Paris; Grob Gallery, London; Zabriskie Gallery, New York; David Raymond, New York

BIBLIOGRAPHY
Schneede, Uwe M., and Hamburger Kunsthalle. *Begierde im Blick: Surrealistiche Photographie,* no. 212. Exh. cat. Ostfildern: Hatje Cantz, 2005.

154. *Still Life (Nature morte),* 1930
Gelatin silver print; 22.3 x 16.5 cm (8⅞ x 6½ in.). John L. Severance Fund 2007.103

INSCRIPTION
In pencil on verso of mount: *1930 M.R. Parry/53.*

PROVENANCE
The artist's estate, Paris; Grob Gallery, London; Michael Mattis, New York; Sotheby's, London, 9 May 2002, no. 145; David Raymond, New York

153. *Dirty Sink (Cuvette sale),* 1930–31
Gelatin silver print; 23.5 x 17.1 cm (9¼ x 6¾ in.). John L. Severance Fund 2007.104

INSCRIPTIONS
In ink on verso of mount: *Photo Roger PARRY*

In pencil on verso of mount: *1930.31 M.R. Parry*

Black stamp on verso of mount: *27bis, RUE SANTOS–DUMONT/PARIS XV–LEC.87–70*

PROVENANCE
The artist's estate, Paris; Grob Gallery, London; Zabriskie Gallery, New York; David Raymond, New York

BIBLIOGRAPHY
Schneede, Uwe M., and Hamburger Kunsthalle. *Begierde im Blick: Surrealistiche Photographie,* no. 211. Exh. cat. Ostfildern: Hatje Cantz, 2005.

[154]

[153]

[34]

[50]

37. Double Exposure, Robert Couturier (Surim-
pression, Robert Couturier), 1931
Gelatin silver print, montage; 17.3 x 22.9 cm (6⅞ x 9 in.). John L. Severance Fund 2007.106

INSCRIPTIONS
In black ink on recto of mount: *R Parry* [signed by Mme Parry]

PROVENANCE
The artist's estate, Paris; Grob Gallery, London; Zabriskie Gallery, New York; David Raymond, New York

BIBLIOGRAPHY
Schneede, Uwe M., and Hamburger Kunsthalle. *Begierde im Blick: Surrealistiche Photographie,* no. 215. Exh. cat. Ostfildern: Hatje Cantz, 2005.

34. Double Exposure, Woman on Bed (Surim-
pression femme sur lit), 1933
Gelatin silver print, montage; 18 x 23.4 cm (7 x 9¼ in.). John L. Severance Fund 2007.108

INSCRIPTIONS
In black ink on verso of mount: *Photo R. PARRY/18 rue A. Gervais/Issy–les Moulineaux/Seine–FRANCE* and *No. 114*

PROVENANCE
The artist's estate, Paris; Christian Bouqueret, Paris; Gitterman Gallery, New York; David Raymond, New York

BIBLIOGRAPHY
Schneede, Uwe M., and Hamburger Kunsthalle. *Begierde im Blick: Surrealistiche Photographie,* no. 215. Exh. cat. Ostfildern: Hatje Cantz, 2005.

Edward Quigley
American, 1898–1977

Quigley spent his entire career in his native Philadelphia. He was self-taught and employed as a local photographer's assistant in 1918. He opened his own studio in 1930, catering to advertising and corporate clientele. Quigley's first salon photograph was in 1930 at the Photographic Society of Philadelphia. He was also active in several other professional photographic societies and exhibited his work throughout the decade. In 1937–38 Quigley showed work in eighteen different photographic salons.

He published commercial work in trade and popular illustrated publications and penned numerous how-to articles for camera magazines and club journals, sometimes using his own photographs as illustrations. His work ranged from straight editorial work to Pictorialist prints in varied tones and techniques. He moved easily between the worlds of traditional and modernist art photographers and organized shows with Edward Weston and László Moholy-Nagy in the 1930s. Quigley was an avid experimenter; in 1931 he executed a series of light abstractions that brought him attention beyond the camera club circuit. The next year the Delphic Studios in New York exhibited the series, a selection of which was exhibited at the Cleveland Museum of Art in 1934 alongside work by other prominent photographers.

50. Photogram (Number 9), 1931
Gelatin silver print, photogram; 20.7 x 16.6 cm (8⅛ x 6½ in.). John L. Severance Fund 2007.110

INSCRIPTIONS
In pencil on verso of print: *5401c Edward Quigley*

PROVENANCE
New York art market; Sothebys.com, c. 2001; David Raymond, New York

Albert Renger-Patzsch
German, 1897–1966

Though Renger-Patzsch studied chemistry in Dresden in 1919–20, he taught himself photography and commenced a career as a press photographer. He was hired by Karl-Ernst Osthaus, arts patron and founder of the Folkwang Museum in Hagen, to direct the new photography archive there from 1920 to 1922. He worked under the direction of Ernst Fuhrmann, publisher of the newly formed publishing house Auriga-Verlag. Having begun to develop his distinctive sharp-focus style by documenting ethnographic objects for the photography archive, Renger-Patzsch expanded these ideas in close-up photographs of plant specimens for illustrated nature primers developed by Fuhrmann. In these early images of cacti and flowering plants, Renger-Patzsch moved popular photographic language away from Pictorialism toward the New Objectivity style championed by the German avant-garde after 1925. He left Fuhrmann's employ in 1923 and traveled to Berlin, Hamburg, and Kronstadt, Romania, before returning to the Auriga publishing house, relocated to Darmstadt.

In 1924 he published his first small photographic volumes of plant photographs, followed by his first major book, *The Choir Stall of Kappenberg (Die Chorgestühl von Kappenberg)* in 1925. It was the following photographic volume, *The World Is Beautiful (Die Welt ist schön),* published in 1928 by Kurt Wolff, that made his reputation as a pathfinder in photographic image and book design. The clean layout of one image per page and the high-quality reproductions made the volume a standard for the new market in photographic books. Moreover, the mix of close-up objects, industrial factories, and bucolic countryside, all rendered with ultimate fidelity to fine detail, provided a new context for the appreciation of straight photography.

Renger-Patzsch was included in several landmark photography exhibitions including *Film und Foto.* He continued accepting commissions for industry and advertising, though he lost most of his negatives in a 1944 bombing of the Folkwang Museum in Essen. In the later 1950s and 1960s, Renger-Patzsch received broad recognition and numerous exhibitions celebrating his excellence in photography.

159. *Annual Blooming of the Cactus Cereus Macrogonus (Jahres-Neutrieb bei Cereus macrogonus),* 1922–24
Gelatin silver print; 23 x 16.9 cm (9 x 6⅝ in.). John L. Severance Fund 2007.23

INSCRIPTIONS
In pencil and blue ink on verso of print: *Cact 37/ ~~Cereus~~ Fridercereus maßcrogonus*

Blue stamp on verso of print: *Folkwang-Auriga Verlag/G.m.b.H./Friedrichssegen/Lahn.* and *RENGER–FOTO D.W.B/ESSEN, GOETHESTR. 41*

PROVENANCE
Kicken Gallery, Berlin; Chester Dentan, Seattle; David Raymond, New York

158. *Cactus Leaves (Euphorbia),* 1922–24
Gelatin silver print; 23 x 16.9 cm (9 x 6¾ in.). John L. Severance Fund 2007.24

INSCRIPTIONS
Stamped in blue ink on verso of print: *Folkwang-Auriga Verlag/G.m.b.H/Friedrichssegen/Lahn.* and *RENGER–FOTO D.W.B/ESSEN, GOETHESTR. 41*

In pencil on verso of print: *Euph 23/Codiaeum* [illegible]

PROVENANCE
Kicken Gallery, Berlin; Chester Dentan, Seattle; David Raymond, New York

160. *Euphorbia (Codiaeum),* 1922–24
Gelatin silver print; 23 x 16.9 cm (9 x 6⅝ in.). John L. Severance Fund 2007.22

INSCRIPTIONS
In brown ink on verso of print: *Euphorbia bupleurifolia* and *abdrück nur gestaltet mit Naturschirft* [?] *Illus. . . . van Kakteen Haage Erfurt*

In pencil on verso of print: *II 3 b*

Blue stamp on verso of print: *Folkwang-Auriga Verlag/G.m.b.H./Friedrichssegen/Lahn.* and *RENGER–FOTO D.W.B/ESSEN, GOETHESTR. 41*

Purple stamp on verso of print: *oben* within a triangular border

Old gallery label on verso of print: *Galerie. . . . Dresden*

PROVENANCE
Kicken Gallery, Berlin; Chester Dentan, Seattle; David Raymond, New York

Alexander Rodchenko
Russian, 1891–1956

One of the most important figures of Russian Constructivism, Rodchenko was born in St. Petersburg, raised in Odessa, and studied art at the Kazan School of Art from 1910 to 1914. In 1915 he moved to the Stroganov School of Applied Art in Moscow. Upon meeting Vladimir Tatlin and Kazimir Malevich, Rodchenko became immersed in a new form of radical art. Born at the confluence of political, social, and industrial revolution, Constructivism valued material consideration above aesthetics and guided Rodchenko's early experiments with nonobjective art. Following a brief period of experimentation with Cubism and Futurism, in 1916 he exhibited abstract drawings made with a compass and rulers in response to Malevich's Suprematist canvases. There followed a series of monochrome black-and-white canvases (1918–20) that represented his philosophy of the form.

Soon Rodchenko was sustaining a two-pronged effort in visual experimentation and philosophical writing to serve as lesson plans for the new age. After the October Revolution in 1917, he was involved with the following: IZO-Narkompros, the government-sponsored arts and culture organization; VKhUTEMAS, the Higher State Artistic Technical Workshops; and the Proletkult school for designing goods for the proletariat. By 1921 the Constructivist movement emerged in opposition to the psychological approach favored by Wassily Kandinsky, then in Moscow. Rodchenko exhibited his hanging constructions at ObMoKhu, the society of young artists.

By 1922 Rodchenko was creating photomontages for advertising and magazine work tied to the burgeoning Russian film industry, specifically for directors Dziga Vertov and Sergei Eisenstein. His commercial graphic work, merging photographic images with bold typographical design, led to his original photography. In 1923 his photo collages for Vladimir Mayakovsky's poem *Pro Eto* appeared, but only in 1924 did Rodchenko begin making straight photographs. He helped establish the magazine *Novyi Lef* in 1927 and designed all of its covers. At this time,

Rodchenko's photography emphasized the formalist concerns of the still photograph and the possibilities of reshaping narrative space through oblique angles and roving viewpoints. His ideas were expressed in many articles in photography and film magazines as he defended his position. His important essay on the subject, "The Paths of Modern Photography," appeared in 1928. With the establishment of Stalin's First Five Year Plan that year, Rodchenko's work shifted to the social aspect expressed through the photographic essay. As his work was accepted into international exhibitions, including *Film und Foto* in 1929, Rodchenko played a greater role in the socialist journals in Russia, especially *USSR in Construction.* During the 1930s he mentored a generation of photographers who worked as journalists for the state news agencies, photographing the industrial achievements and working life of the Soviet Union.

116. *At the Telephone (U. telefona),* 1928
Gelatin silver print; 13.8 x 8.8 cm (5½ x 3½ in.). John L. Severance Fund 2007.146

INSCRIPTIONS
Postcard format printed in black on verso of print

In pencil on verso of print: *A. Rodchenko/At the Telephone 1928*

Black stamp on verso of print, rectangle with Russian text: *PHOTO RODCHENKO*

PROVENANCE
Rodchenko–Stepanova Archives, Moscow; Howard Schickler, New York; Private collection, New York; Sotheby's, New York, 7 October 1998, no. 351; Edwynn Houk Gallery, New York; David Raymond, New York

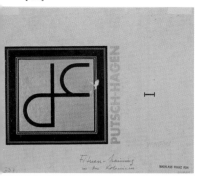   

Franz Roh
German, 1890–1965

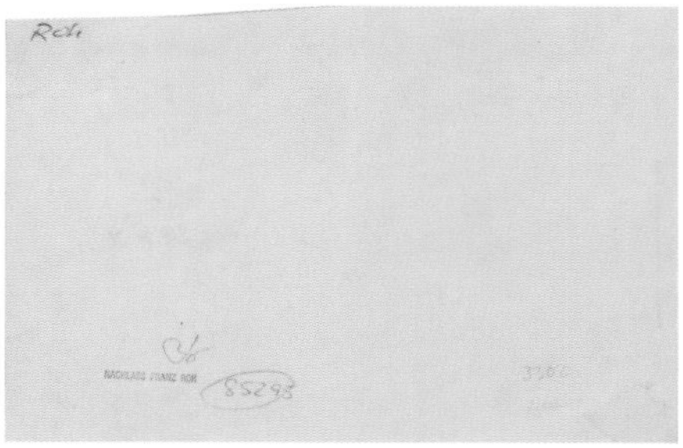

An art historian, critic, and photographer, Roh studied seventeenth-century Dutch painting with noted art historian Heinrich Wölfflin. However, Roh's most important intellectual contributions included essays on contemporary art, such as the influential *Post-Expressionism, Magic Realism (Nach Expressionismus, magischer Realismus)* in 1925, which outlined the sea change occurring in German painting during the Weimar Republic, the move from gestural expressionism to the cooler narrative style of the New Vision. Roh was in contact with several leading avant-garde European artists including Max Ernst, Lázsló Moholy-Nagy, George Grosz, Raoul Hausmann, and Kurt Schwitters, among others. In 1929 he assisted typographer Jan Tschichold in creating the book for the *Film und Foto* exhibition in Stuttgart. This publication, titled *Photo-eye (Fotoauge),* set a new standard for the photographically illustrated book as an art form. His "Mechanism and Expression" was one of many essays that considered photography an important aesthetic and technological aspect of contemporary society. Based on the success of this work, he planned a series of photography books under the rubric *Fototek.* He did publish two works, on Aenne Biermann and Moholy-Nagy, before the operation was suspended.

Roh was engaged in making photographs from 1922 to 1930, mostly involving experimental techniques of negative printing, superimposition, and photomontage. Often harassed for his support of artists unpopular with the Nazi regime, Roh stopped making and exhibiting photographs in the 1930s, turning to photo collage work in the spirit of Max Ernst. Roh was briefly imprisoned in 1933. After the war, he taught at the University of Munich, wrote avidly on photographic and contemporary art, and joined Otto Steinert's Subjective Photography movement in the 1950s.

45. *Fitness Training in the Colonies (Fitness Training in den Kolonien),* 1930s
Photomechanical reproduction, collage; 14.8 x 18.8 cm (5⅞ x 7⅜ in.). John L. Severance Fund 2007.114

INSCRIPTIONS
In pencil on verso of mount: *Fitness Training in Den Kolonien* and *337* and *Window*

Printed on verso of mount: *PUTSCH–HAGEN*

Purple stamp on verso of mount: *NACHLASS FRANZ ROH*

PROVENANCE
Juliane Roh, Munich; Marion Grčić-Ziersch, Munich; Mayor Gallery, London; David Raymond, New York

44. *The Isolation of Nazism (Der Einsamkeit des Nationalsozialismus),* 1930s
Photomechanical reproduction, collage; 9.2 x 15.8 cm (3¼ x 6¼ in.). John L. Severance Fund 2007.113

INSCRIPTIONS
On verso of mount: [illegible] *er gelaender*[?]

PROVENANCE
Juliane Roh, Munich; Marion Grčić-Ziersch, Munich; Mayor Gallery, London; David Raymond, New York

29. *Nude in Light,* 1925
Gelatin silver print, montage; 14.5 x 21.2 cm (5¾ x 8⅜ in.). John L. Severance Fund 2007.111

INSCRIPTIONS
Stamped on verso: *NACHLASS FRANZ ROH*

PROVENANCE
Schneider-Henn, Munich, July 2000; David Raymond, New York

BIBLIOGRAPHY
Schaffner, Ingrid, and Colin Westerbeck. *Accommodations of Desire: Surrealist Works on Paper Collected by Julien Levy,* no. 77. Exh. cat. Pasadena: Curatorial Assistance, 2004.

125. *Woman with a Comb,* c. 1930
Gelatin silver print from an internegative; 23.6 x 18.6 cm (9¼ x 7⅜ in.). John L. Severance Fund 2007.112

INSCRIPTIONS
In pencil on verso of mount: *Vanity Fair requested by Freeman Weist 141/VF 1316*

In lower left corner on verso of mount: *$1*

Blue stamp on verso of mount: *Dr. Franz Roh/ münchen 39/Pickelstrasse 11/Telefon 60277*

Typed label on verso of mount: *2) Woman (No. 67) with a comb, by Franz Roh*

PROVENANCE
Sotheby's, New York, 12 October 2000, no. 241; David Raymond, New York

BIBLIOGRAPHY
Schaffner, Ingrid, and Colin Westerbeck. *Accommodations of Desire: Surrealist Works on Paper Collected by Julien Levy,* no. 76. Exh. cat. Pasadena: Curatorial Assistance, 2004.

Werner Rohde
German, 1906–1990

Born to a successful artistic family in Bremen, Rohde was encouraged to pursue a career in the arts. In 1927 he studied film and photography with Hans Finsler at the Burg School for Arts and Crafts in Halle. The connection to Finsler probably resulted in the selection of Rohde's work for the important 1929 *Film und Foto* exhibition in Stuttgart. In 1928 he established a studio in his parents' home before leaving in 1929 to spend six months in Paris, where he met Paul Citroen and Umbo and Erwin Blumenfeld.

Rohde's first mature work reflected the pared-down aesthetic of the Bauhaus compositions. By 1929 he met Renate Bracksieck, a model he married in 1937. Together they created elaborate photographic scenarios using costumes, masks, and props focusing on archetypal figures from classical literature and film. Rohde built a portrait and modeling studio business and exhibited his photographs often throughout a productive period until 1933. At that time, the Nazis shut the school at Burg. As his photography career waned, Rohde renewed his interest in traditional crafts, such as painting on glass. In 1940 he joined the military, was eventually captured, and remained a prisoner of war until 1945. His parents' home and his archive were destroyed during the war, which led him to settle permanently in Worpswede, site of the prominent artists' colony in 1946.

[141]

[124]

[38]

[130]

141. *Renate, the Animal Tamer (Dompteuse Renate),* 1930
Gelatin silver print; 30 x 23.2 cm (11⅞ x 9 in.). John L. Severance Fund 2007.115

INSCRIPTIONS
In red grease pencil on verso of print: *155/9*

In pencil in lower left on verso of print: *Inv. #1258*

Purple stamp on verso of print: *FOTOGRAFIE/WERNER ROHDE/BREMEN/Tous droits réservés.*

PROVENANCE
Private collections, Cologne; Villa Grisebach, Berlin, 27 November 2003, no. 1363; David Raymond, New York

124. *Rule Britannia,* 1950s–early 1960s
Gelatin silver print of a collage; 39.5 x 29.1 cm (15½ x 11½ in.). John L. Severance Fund 2007.116

INSCRIPTION
In pencil on verso of print: *Werner Rohde/"Rule Britannia"*

PROVENANCE
Schneider-Henn, Munich, July 2000; David Raymond, New York

Thurman Rotan
American, 1903–1991

Born in Waco, Texas, and raised in San Antonio, Rotan was a self-taught photographer. Moving to New York in 1926, he joined the staff of the Frick Art Reference Library as assistant to the photographer Ira Martin. While traveling to photograph works of art for the library's research archive, he also made personal landscapes. Through Martin he joined the Pictorial Photographers of America and became one of the editors of the group's annual publication and newsletter, *Light and Shade,* founded in 1928. Together, Rotan and Martin sought to introduce more adventurous work to the amateur society, adding photographers such as Charles Sheeler and Anton Bruehl to the organization's board.

Rotan's dynamic images of skyscrapers began with a commission to photograph the *Daily News* building in 1930. In 1932 he had a solo show at the Art Center in New York. His *Photo-Patterns* were also enlarged and included as a mural-size installation in

the Museum of Modern Art's *Murals by American Photographers and Painters* exhibition that same year. Rotan exhibited his photography throughout the 1930s and used his images for fabric design in later years. His reputation was revived in the 1980s.

38. *New York Montage,* 1928
Gelatin silver print, montage; 11.5 x 8.2 cm (4½ x 3¼ in.). John L. Severance Fund 2007.117

INSCRIPTIONS
In pencil on verso of print: *New York Montage*

Signed in pencil on verso of print: *Thurman Rotan 1928*

Stamped twice on verso of print: *PHOTOGRAPH BY Rotan*

PROVENANCE
The artist, New York; Keith De Lellis, New York; Chester Dentan, Seattle; Christie's, New York, 6 October 1998, no. 277; David Raymond, New York

Ernst Schieron
German, active 1920s–1930s

Schieron was an amateur photographer working in the Schwabisch Gemund region. His father, Richard Schieron, was also an amateur photographer. Ernst took medals at several regional photography competitions in the late 1920s.

130. *Vertical: Stuttgart Central Station (Vertikale: Stuttgart Hauptbahnhof),* 1929
Gelatin silver print; 23.2 x 17.4 cm (9⅛ x 6¼ in.). John L. Severance Fund 2007.119

INSCRIPTIONS
In black ink on verso of print: *Titel: Vertikale/(Stuttgarten Hauptbanhof)* and *Foto: Ernst Schieron, Gmünd/Original ausgesttelt in/Berlin: "das Meisterphoto"/internationale Austellung/Göteborg (Schweden) Austellung/Silber Plaquette* and *No. 86*

PROVENANCE
Schneider-Henn, Munich, 18 June 1999, no. 507; Villa Grisebach, Berlin, 23 November 2000, no. 1410; David Raymond, New York

145. *In the Mirror (Im Spiegel),* c. 1930
Gelatin silver print; 37.8 x 28.2 cm (14⅞ x 11⅛ in.). John L. Severance Fund 2007.118

INSCRIPTIONS
In pencil on mount: *Schieron: "Im Spiegel"*

Signed in red pencil on verso of mount: *Ernst Schieron/Ernst Schieron/Schw.Gemünd/Zulp* [illegible] *6/* and *Essen* [upper left] in another hand

Exhibition labels affixed to verso of mount: *VDAV Verbands Ausstellung Nuermburg 1930* and *Die Kamera Ausstellung für Fotografie. Druck u Reproduktion Stuttgart. Abt. Amateurfoto* and *Photoausstellung . . . Gau Sud Westduetscheland . . . Karlsruhe . . . 1930*

PROVENANCE
Private collection, Berlin; Villa Grisebach, Berlin, 23 November 2000, no. 1409; David Raymond, New York

BIBLIOGRAPHY
Schieron, Ernst. "Zur Technik der Photomontage (Kopiermontage)." *Deutscher Kamera-Almanach* (1933): 80–88.

35. *Montage,* 1930s
Gelatin silver print, montage; 17.1 x 23.2 cm (6¾ x 9⅛ in.). John L. Severance Fund 2007.120

PROVENANCE
Galerie Bassenge, Berlin, 12 July 2005, no. 4337; David Raymond, New York

Emmanuel Sougez
French, 1889–1972

In 1904 Sougez began art studies in his native Bordeaux, committing to photography by the time he moved to Paris in 1911. He toured European cities to study contemporary photography in 1919, and by 1926 he was director of photography for *L'Illustration.* As such he had enormous influence over the careers of young photographers in France, supporting Ilse Bing, Dora Maar, and many others with assignments and published articles. He was the center of the Pure Photography movement in France (known as the Rectangle Group after 1936), which supported a Precisionist, detail-rich image for documentary 35 mm photography and thus allied

234

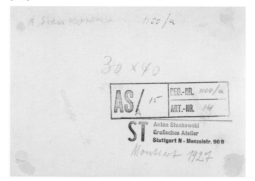

itself with the classicism pervading French culture beginning at this time.

Sougez excelled at shooting still-life arrangements for advertising, artistic exhibition, and publication. He often shot sculpture for reproduction; his nearly one-to-one prints made from large-format negatives captured formal detail and texture in print media. He was active in publishing Arts et Métiers Graphique's *Photographie* annuals from 1930 to 1939, and his work was widely exhibited in several important photographic shows during the 1930s, including *Advertising in Photography* at the Galerie de la Pléiade and *French Photography 1839–1936*. Sougez published *Nude Forms* in 1936, a collection of nudes by well-regarded photographers of the era. A large donation of his prints and negatives to the Bibliothéque Nationale in 1971 led to the revival of his artistic reputation.

48. *Film Negative (Film-négatif),* 1928
Gelatin silver print, photogram; 28.7 x 22.4 cm (11¼ x 8⅞ in.). John L. Severance Fund 2007.121

INSCRIPTIONS
Signed in red ink in lower right corner of recto of mount: *Sougez*

Stamped on verso of mount: *SOUGEZ*

PROVENANCE
The artist, Paris; Charles Peignot, Paris; André Jammes, Paris; Serge Plantureux, Paris; David Raymond, New York

BIBLIOGRAPHY
Schaffner, Ingrid, and Colin Westerbeck. *Accommodations of Desire: Surrealist Works on Paper Collected by Julien Levy,* 33. Exh. cat. Pasadena: Curatorial Assistance, 2004.

Anton Stankowski
German, 1906–1998

Born in Westphalia, Stankowski trained as a decorator but studied photography at the Folkwang Museum School in Essen in 1923. A job painting churches in Düsseldorf led to meeting gallerist Johanna Ey and her circle of artists that included Otto Dix. Stankowski returned to the Folkwang school in 1927–28 to study with Max Burchartz, a photographer and graphic designer involved with the Bauhaus and De Stijl circles. In 1929 Stankowski was hired by the Max Dalong advertising studio in Zurich and established rich connections there with the Russian Constructivists.

Noted for his emphasis on photography and radical composition, Stankowski developed a successful career in commercial graphic design. He brought photography to the forefront of graphic design in Switzerland, laying the groundwork for a model known as "Constructivist graphics." In 1934 Stankowski's residence permit in Switzerland was revoked, forcing his move to the German side of the border where he worked as a freelancer. In 1940 he was inducted into the German army and became a prisoner of war until 1948. He then settled in Stuttgart where his career as a typographic and graphic designer and photographer blossomed. He designed many corporate logos and identity campaigns of the postwar era and was design chair for the 1972 Munich Olympics.

30. *Photo Eye (Foto-Auge),* 1927, printed 1938–40
Gelatin silver print, montage, from negatives with handwork; 10.9 x 14.5 cm (4¼ x 5¾ in.). John L. Severance Fund 2007.122

INSCRIPTIONS
In pencil on verso of print: *A. Stankowski*

In pencil on verso of print: *Montiert 1927*

Two studio stamps on verso of print: *ST/Anton Stankowski/Graphische Atelier/Stuttgart N Menzlerstr. 90 B* and *AS/REG-NR 1100/a ART-NR 14*

In red grease pencil on verso of print: *30 x 40*

PROVENANCE
Prakapas Gallery, New York; Thomas Walther, Berlin; Barry Friedman Ltd., New York; Chester Dentan, Seattle; David Raymond, New York

146. *The Questioner (Der Frager),* 1930
Gelatin silver print; 16.9 x 11.9 cm (6⅝ x 4¾ in.). John L. Severance Fund 2007.152

INSCRIPTION
In pencil on verso of print (artist's hand?): *Der Frager 1930/18 x 24/"17"/6* [circled]/*"A"*

PROVENANCE
Edwynn Houk Gallery, New York; David Raymond, New York

André Steiner
Hungarian, 1901–1978

Steiner was born in Hungary and studied engineering in Vienna (1918–28) where he worked with Josef Maria Eder, the scientist who published a groundbreaking history of photography in 1932. Steiner's primary focus, however, was electrical engineering and x-ray technology. In 1924 he began to experiment with one of the earliest Leica cameras before it appeared on the market. He moved to Paris in 1927, working as a cinema sound engineer at Alsthom, Paramount, and Phototone studios.

By 1934 Steiner had become a professional photographer, making his name with sports photography as well as studio nudes. He contributed regularly to *Art et Médecine, Photographie,* and similar publications that featured other noteworthy New Vision photographers. He practiced all forms of experimental photography and printing—photomontage, photogram, solarization—and his technical skill brought him success as an advertising photographer, a job highly valued in 1930s Paris. He showed in several important exhibitions on advertising, including *La Publicité par la Photographie* at the Galerie de la Pléiade in 1935, Emmanuel Sougez's *Formes Nus* of the same year, and George Besson's exhibition of international contemporary photography in 1936. Steiner had an active commercial career and a respected fine art exhibition record. He joined the French Resistance during World War II and later, when he resumed his work, concentrated on scientific and medical photography.

147. *Advertising Image,* 1940s
Gelatin silver print; 18.9 x 17.8 cm (7½ x 7 in.). John
L. Severance Fund 2007.123

INSCRIPTIONS

Black stamp on verso of print: *COPYRIGHT BY/
STUDIO/ANDRÉ STEINER/18, Rue Louis-le-Grand.
Paris-2e/Tel.: Opéra 66-30/Nr_____/Mention
Obligatoire*

In blue pencil on verso of print: *[illegible] VUE/
2 [circled]/6/208 x 190*

In pencil on verso of print: *2912/PV32*

PROVENANCE

Paris art market; David Raymond, New York

Carl Strüwe
German, 1898–1988

Strüwe was raised in Bielefeld, Germany, where he
attended the School of Arts and Crafts and studied
under Karl Muggly. He found work as a graphic
designer for the publishing and advertising industries in the region and taught lithography before
beginning his photographic career in the 1920s. An
interest in botanical forms led Strüwe to photograph
microscopic organisms in a practice he perfected
as "photomicrography." Besides his scientific work,
Strüwe traveled throughout Italy, France, and North
Africa photographing landscape and street scenes.
In 1955 he published *Formen des Mikrocosmos,* a
compendium of microscopic photographs dating
from the mid-1920s to the 1950s. The volume appeared at the height of the Subjective Photography
movement in Germany and was well received by
Otto Steinert's group. The City of Bielefeld awarded
Strüwe the 1986 Cultural Prize, the town being the
site of his archive.

**169. *Construction of Chain Algae in Chlorophyll
(Bau einer Kettenalge als Chlorophyll-Fabrik),***
1928, printed 1950s
Gelatin silver print, micrograph; 36 x 29 cm (14⅛ x
11½ in.). John L. Severance Fund 2007.124

INSCRIPTIONS

In pencil on verso of print: *38. Schöne reine Form:
Keffen Algae/120x*

Black stamp on verso of print: *CARL STRÜWE/For-
men des Mikrokosmos*

Black stamp on verso of print: *URHEBERRECHTLICH/
GESCHÜTZ.COPYRIGTH* [sic] *BY*

Two different studio stamps on verso of print: *CARL
STRÜWE/BIELEFELD/DITFURTHSTR. 89* and [crossed
out] *CARL STRÜWE/BIELEFELD/AM SCHILDHOF 12/
ALLE RECHTE BEI/COPYRIGHT BY*

PROVENANCE

Gottfried Jäger, Bielefeld, Germany; Schneider-Henn,
Munich; David Raymond, New York

BIBLIOGRAPHY

Strüwe, Carl. *Formen des Mikrokosmos Gestalt und
Gestaltung einer Bilderwelt,* no. 38. Munich: Prestel
Verlag, 1955.

**168. *Structure of a Bath Sponge (Struktur des
Badeschwammes),* 1933**
Gelatin silver print, micrograph; 22.7 x 18 cm (9 x
7⅛ in.). John L. Severance Fund 2007.125

INSCRIPTIONS

In pencil on verso of print: *WV2 1–98, 1933*

In pencil on verso of print: *Konstruktionsform./* [illeg-
ible] *200x*

Black copyright stamp: *URHEBERRECHTLICH/GE-
SCHÜTZT. COPYRIGTH* [sic] *BY CARL STRÜWE/BIELE-
FELD, AM LOTHBERG 3* [crossed out, with *am* (illeg-
ible) *12* in pencil]/*NACHDRUCK NUR MIT VERMERK:
FOT. STRÜWE/BIELEFELD*

Printed on verso of print: *AgfaBrovira*

PROVENANCE

Private collection, Germany; Villa Grisebach, Berlin,
26 November 1999, no. 1463; David Raymond, New
York

167. *The Spiral (Die Spirale),* 1935
Gelatin silver print, ferrotyped; 23.4 x 17.9 cm (9¼ x
7 in.). John L. Severance Fund 2007.126

INSCRIPTION

In pencil on verso of print: *WV2 1–100, 1935*

PROVENANCE

Private collection, Germany; Villa Grisebach, Berlin,
25 May 2000, no. 1438; David Raymond, New York

Maurice Tabard
French, 1897–1984

Tabard worked in the family silk business in Lyon before leaving for New York in 1914 to study photography. In 1922 he joined the Bachrach photography
studio, working between Washington, DC, Cincinnati, and Baltimore. Several personalities, including
President Calvin Coolidge, sat for him. In 1928 he
returned to France.

Already very skilled at darkroom and printing techniques, Tabard gave up portrait photography for
more personal interpretive endeavors. In 1929 he
received work from Lucien Vogel for *VU* magazine,
joining André Kertész, Germaine Krull, Eli Lotar, and
others as a regular photojournalist. That year his
photographs were chosen for the Stuttgart *Film und
Foto* exhibition, assuring his reputation as a leading experimental photographer in Europe. He also
expanded his relationships with the Parisian surrealist
crowd, affiliating with Man Ray and René Magritte,
among others. At the same time, he was receiving
commercial work from agencies as a freelance studio
photographer for all the big brands in Paris. Around
1929 Tabard also began collaborating with Roger
Parry, a colleague at the Deberny Peignot agency.
They worked on commercial assignments and for
film companies, posed for each other, and photographed at the same avant-garde dance evenings in
Paris.

Tabard's experimental techniques, including solarization, double printing, and masking, were described
in several articles published in professional art and
photographic journals. In 1932 Julien Levy showed
his work in New York. In the mid-1930s, the French
government employed Tabard as a photographer
and filmmaker while he did fashion work for

Harper's Bazaar in Paris. He continued fashion photography in England and Scotland in 1946–48, spent 1950 in Indiana teaching, and eventually retired in Paris after 1965.

33. *Dancer Georges Pomiès,* 1929
Gelatin silver print, montage; 23.7 x 17.5 cm (9⅜ x 6⅞ in.). John L. Severance Fund 2007.127

INSCRIPTIONS
Signed and dated by artist in pencil on recto of mount: *Tabard Paris 31*

Embossed on lower right of recto of mount: *BRISTOL* above shield with logo and *C F.*

Black stamp on verso of mount: *MAURICE/TAB-ARD/38, RUE/FALGUIÈRE/PARIS XVe*

PROVENANCE
Robert Shapazian, Los Angeles; Museum of Modern Art, New York; Sotheby's, New York, 22–23 October 2002, no. 86; David Raymond, New York

BIBLIOGRAPHY
Schaffner, Ingrid, and Colin Westerbeck. *Accommodations of Desire: Surrealist Works on Paper Collected by Julien Levy,* no. 71. Exh. cat. Pasadena: Curatorial Assistance, 2004.

129. *Portrait of Roger Parry,* c. 1930
Gelatin silver print; 22.5 x 17 cm (8⅞ x 6¾ in.). John L. Severance Fund 2007.153

INSCRIPTIONS
Black ink stamp on recto of mount: *tabard*

Black stamp on verso of mount: *MAURICE/ TAB-ARD/38, RUE/FALGUIÈRE/PARIS XVe*

In pencil on verso of mount: *Photo. M. Tabard.*

Embossed on lower right of verso of mount: *BRISTOL* above shield with logo and *C F.*

PROVENANCE
Maurice Verneuil, Paris; Phillips, New York, 6 April 1998, no. 79; David Raymond, New York

Richard Tepe
Dutch, 1864–1952

A photographer born in Amsterdam and dedicated to preserving the natural environment, Tepe cofounded the Netherlandish Ornithological Association and belonged to several civic groups invested in conserving natural habitats. He was a self-taught photographer but an active member of Dutch photographic societies.

For forty years Tepe photographed birds in natural surroundings using plate cameras, a tripod, and a long cable release. He published his photographs privately, producing albums and books, and exhibited prints throughout the Netherlands. In 1915 he presented a large-format album to the royal family. His archives are kept in the National Archives of the Netherlands with some material housed at the University of Leiden and the Rijksmuseum.

114. *Eggs of a Stone-curlew or Plover (Eier der Triels oder Dickfussel),* 1900s
Gelatin silver print on printing out paper; 11.7 x 16.8 cm (4⅝ x 6⅝ in.). John L. Severance Fund 2007.128

INSCRIPTIONS
In pencil on verso of print: *Eier der Triels/oder Dickfussel/2250 10*

Gallery stamp on verso of print: *Max Lörich/ Kunstanstalt/Innsbruck/Fischergasse Nr. 18*

Artist stamp on verso of print: *foto/R. Tepe* [circled]

PROVENANCE
Simon Lowinsky, New York; David Raymond, New York

115. *Yellowhammer Nest with Eggs (Nest und Eier der Goldammer),* 1900s
Gelatin silver print on printing out paper; 11.7 x 16.6 cm (4⅝ x 6½ in.). John L. Severance Fund 2007.129

INSCRIPTIONS
In pencil on verso of print: *Nest und Eier der Goldammer/Foto R. Tepe A.C.* [signed]

PROVENANCE
Simon Lowinsky, New York; David Raymond, New York

Alfred Tritschler
German, 1905–1970

Tritschler studied photography and cinema in Munich and worked at Universum Film AG's Babelsberg studio as a technician. In 1927 he apprenticed with Dr. Paul Wolff, the successful photojournalist and Leica enthusiast with whom he established the Wolff and Tritschler studio, producing editorial, advertising, and industrial photographic projects throughout the 1920s and 1930s. They published successful photographically illustrated books on topics ranging from the 1936 Olympics to the natural features of the Rhine Valley. After Wolff died in 1951, Tritschler continued the studio work until 1970. The studio's negative archive remains intact in Germany. Tritschler was a member of the Society of German Photographers.

2. *Airship Hindenburg: View Inside the Engine (Hindenburg: Blick in die Motorengondel),* c. 1936
Gelatin silver print; 23.4 x 17.4 cm (9¼ x 6⅞ in.). John L. Severance Fund 2007.134

INSCRIPTIONS
In pencil on verso of print: *"Hindenburg"*

In pencil on verso of print: *Holland Press Service/ Amsterdam*

Printed on verso of print: *Agfa/Brovira*

Pink paper label on verso of mount: *87/Blick in die motorengondel*

Blue paper label on verso of mount: *AG Schostal*

PROVENANCE
Villa Grisebach, Berlin, 23 November 2000, no. 1498; David Raymond, New York

[127] [56] [94]

127. *Wire Strainers (Drahtsiebe),* 1938
Gelatin silver print, ferrotyped; 23.7 x 17.9 cm (9³⁄₈ x 7 in.). John L. Severance Fund 2007.133

INSCRIPTIONS
Purple copyright stamp on verso of print: *Veröffentlichung nur unter Angabe/W. & Tr. (Tristchler)*

Purple stamp on verso of mount: *Bestellnummer B/260/Dr. Wolff & Tritschler OHG/Frankfurt am Main*

PROVENANCE
Villa Grisebach, Berlin, 25 May 2000, no. 83; David Raymond, New York

Raoul Ubac
Belgian, 1910–1985

Born in German-occupied Belgium, Ubac traveled between Belgium, France, and Germany, eventually adopting a French name. He studied literature and art in Paris and Cologne (1928–29) but also made extensive camping trips into the wilderness. In Paris Otto Freundlich drew Ubac into the radical artists' group the Cologne Progressives. In 1932 he studied at the School of Applied Arts in Cologne, learning basic advertising photography, but began adding photo collage, photomontage, and superimposition of negatives to an increasingly experimental body of imagery.

In 1933 Ubac met Man Ray, who encouraged his photography and a permanent move to Paris, where he joined André Breton's surrealist circle and collaborated with Raoul Hausmann and Erwin Blumenfeld. In the mid-1930s, he made photographic work that combined several experimental techniques that evoked the surrealist spirit, including photomontage, solarization, and unique operations he developed and named, such as *paraglyphe,* a low relief created by using the negative image to mask the positive one. This led to the *brûlages,* in which Ubac melted the negative and then printed it. His *Penthesilea* series of collaged nude photographs (1937–39) was published by Breton in *Minotaure* as a commensurate surrealist undertaking.

During World War II, Ubac and his wife, Agui, returned to Brussels. There he collaborated with René Magritte and his Belgian group on the journal *L'Invention Collective,* becoming an important fixture in that distinct artistic circle.

91. *The Battle of the Penthesilea (Le Combat des Penthésiliées),* 1937
Gelatin silver print; 16.9 x 22.8 cm (6⁵⁄₈ x 9 in.). John L. Severance Fund 2007.154

INSCRIPTION
In blue ink on recto of print: *à Victor Brauner, mon ami/Raoul Ubac* [signed]

PROVENANCE
The artist, Paris; Victor Brauner, Paris; Christie's, New York, 6 October 1998, no. 296; David Tunkl, Los Angeles; G. Ray Hawkins Gallery, Los Angeles; David Raymond, New York

BIBLIOGRAPHY
Combalía Dexeus, Victoria. *Paris y los surrealistas,* 252. Bilbao: Fundacion Museo de Bellas Artes de Bilbao, 2005.

56. *Mannequin (André Masson),* 1938
Gelatin silver print; 22.8 x 9.3 cm (9 x 3⁵⁄₈ in.). John L. Severance Fund 2007.130

INSCRIPTIONS
In black ink on verso of print: *Mannequin 1937*

In red ink on verso of print: *André Masson (Exposition international du surréalisme à la Galerie Beaux Arts)*

Exhibition stamp on verso of print: *Surréaliste La Revolution/Bureau des Recherches*

Artist stamp on verso of print: *RAOUL UBAC/46, rue Hippolyte Maindron/Paris XVe*

PROVENANCE
Ubu Gallery, New York; Barry Friedman Ltd., New York; David Raymond, New York

BIBLIOGRAPHY
Lichtenstein, Therese. *Behind Closed Doors: The Art of Hans Bellmer,* no. 252. Exh. cat. Berkeley: University of California Press, 2001.

Schneede, Uwe M., and Hamburger Kunsthalle. *Begierde im Blick: Surrealistiche Photographie,* no. 233. Exh. cat. Ostfildern: Hatje Cantz, 2005.

Willem van de Poll
Dutch, 1895–1970

Van de Poll was raised in Amsterdam and joined the police force after completing his schooling. In 1919 he left the force to study at the Graphic Arts Academy in Vienna, documenting crime scenes for the Viennese police. Once back in the Netherlands, he dedicated himself to photojournalism, beginning with the traditional plate camera but later using smaller handheld cameras.

He began working in the early 1920s with the Associated Press in Berlin, submitting pictures from extensive travels around Europe in the later 1920s and early 1930s. He spent longer trips documenting life in Berlin and Warsaw, including reports on the military build-up along the Russian border in 1934. In addition to work for Dutch and German picture agencies, van de Poll joined the roster of the Black Star and Associated Press agencies. He spent a year in Paris (1936–37) and added fashion shoots to his hard-news reportage. He continued work for Black Star throughout the Nazi era and directed the photographic services for Philips after 1939. In 1944 he was attached to the Allied Command during the liberation of Europe, photographing internment camps.

In 1946, in a new chapter of his career, van de Poll became photographer to the Dutch royal family, visiting the Dutch East Indies, Surinam, and Malaysia. He traveled to Palestine with Jewish refugees from Europe, photographing their settlement. A long tour of the Middle East in the early 1950s resulted in more books. In the mid-1960s he retired in Switzerland. In 1998 his complete archive was acquired by the National Archives of the Netherlands.

94. *Paris, Double Exposure of the City of Light (Paris, Surimpression Ville Lumière),* 1935
Gelatin silver print, ferrotyped, montage; 17.3 x 23.5 cm (6³⁄₄ x 9¹⁄₄ in.). John L. Severance Fund 2007.131

INSCRIPTIONS
In pencil on verso of print: *Paris surimpression de la Ville lumière*

Purple stamp on verso of print: *Made in Austria*

Black stamp on verso of print: *This is/A GLOBE PHOTO/Credit line must be observed/must not be syndicated, loaned or used for/publishing purposes*

[21]

[55]

without permission/GLOBE PHOTOS/33 WEST 42nd STREET/NEW YORK CITY

Black stamp on verso of print: *COPYRIGHT/[in triangle] PHOTO/WILLEM/VAN DE/POLL*

Black stamp on verso of print: *Not to be reproduced/without permission of/Willem van de Poll/Nr. 35/5975*

Black stamp on verso of print: *reproduction interdite/sauf autorisation spéciale/la mention est/obligatoire*

PROVENANCE
Phillips, New York, 5 October 1999, no. 81; David Raymond, New York

Emiel van Moerkerken
(Dutch, 1916–1995)

Born in Haarlem near Amsterdam, van Moerkerken was raised in an intellectual household and began photographing at an early age with a Kodak, and later a Leica, exhibiting a surrealist mood in his early work.

In 1934 he discovered an issue of the Belgian periodical *Documents* produced by E. L. T. Mesens. That, along with André Breton's writings, guided him deeply into the literary and political aspects of the movement. His friendships at home with writers such as Jef Last encouraged his radical political views.

Van Moerkerken traveled to Paris in 1935, met Man Ray and Brassaï, and established connections to Parisian surrealism that blossomed later in the decade. He photographed in desolate urban areas, sometimes at night. He found steady work as a still photographer and film director in France and the Netherlands, making avant-garde experimental films such as *Sonate* (1934), inspired by Luis Buñuel's *L'Age d'Or*. In Holland he was associated with photographers Eva Besnyö, Cas Oorthys, and Emmy Andriesse who created documentary work for BKVK, an agency promoting social change. Van Moerkerken also worked with noted Dutch film director Joris Ivens.

Van Moerkerken's association with sculptor Chris van Geel in 1938 produced a series of significant surrealist collaborative performance photographs, a notable highlight of his work. Using medium-format cameras, van Moerkerken began shooting advertising as well as experimental studio photography in the New Photography style imported from Germany.

During the war he continued his writing and photographic work, publishing his first collection of images, *Reportage in Light and Shadow,* in 1947, followed by *Amsterdam* in 1959. He was included in Otto Steinert's landmark *Subjektiv Fotografie (Subjective Photography)* exhibition in 1954. In addition to photographic assignments that took him throughout Europe, North America, and North Africa, van Moerkerken continued writing essays and poetry under a pseudonym. He became involved with *Barbarer* (1958–71) and *De Schoen Zakdoek (The Lovely Handkerchief),* two of several literary journals supporting the surrealist impulse in the Netherlands.

21. *Surrealist Act with Chris van Geel,* fall 1938, printed later
Gelatin silver print; 22.8 x 17.5 cm (9 x 6⅞ in.). John L. Severance Fund 2007.132

INSCRIPTIONS
In pencil on verso of print: *1938*

Purple stamp on verso of print: *COPYRIGHT © E. VAN MOERKERKEN/AMSTERDAM*

In pencil in lower left on verso of print: [Zabriskie Gallery numbers] *EVM 9575 EVM*

PROVENANCE
European auction market, May 1985; Zabriskie Gallery, New York; David Raymond, New York

Wols (Alfred Otto Wolfgang Schulze)
German, 1913–1951

Wols spent time in Dresden in his youth, but he studied photography in Berlin with Genja Jonas and moved on to the Berlin Bauhaus briefly in 1932. At Lázsló Moholy-Nagy's suggestion, Wols moved to Paris in 1932 where he photographed the streets, the city's periphery, and its down-and-out population. In style and mood Wols was sensitive to the New Objectivity movement in France and friendly with the surrealist community there. In the later 1930s, he began a series of surrealist-inspired still-life images, often including food in various states of decomposition. His major photographic commission came in 1937 when he was invited to photograph the Pavilion of Elegance at the Paris Exposition Universelle. The dramatically lit images of sumptuously dressed mannequins were reproduced in illustrated periodicals. Wols was given a solo show at the Galerie de la Pléiade.

As a German residing in Paris, Wols was interned at the beginning of World War II near Aix-en-Provence. He escaped and remained in southern France until the war's end. At this time he adopted the pseudonym Wols. His photographic activity slowed dramatically, and he began making watercolors and paintings in an abstract style that were later included as part of the postwar Tachism art movement. Wols was championed by Jean-Paul Sartre and Simone de Beauvoir during his final years in Paris.

161. *Posts,* 1933
Gelatin silver print; left side 29.2, right side 29.6 x 24.2 cm (left side 11½, right side 11¾ x 9½ in.). John L. Severance Fund 2007.135

INSCRIPTION
In pencil on mount: *1933*

PROVENANCE
The artist's estate, Paris; Baron Ribeyre (Drouot Richelieu), Paris, 17 November 2000, no. 25; David Raymond, New York

55. *Antique Seller, Paris,* c. 1937
Gelatin silver print; 22.7 x 17.2 cm (9 x 6¾ in.). John L. Severance Fund 2007.136

INSCRIPTION
Red stamp on verso of mount: *WOLS* [in a circle]/*5, rue de Varenne, Paris*

PROVENANCE
The artist's estate, Paris; Baron Ribeyre (Drouot Richelieu), Paris, 17 November 2000, no. 31; David Raymond, New York

BIBLIOGRAPHY
Schneede, Uwe M., and Hamburger Kunsthalle. *Begierde im Blick: Surrealistiche Photographie,* no. 66. Exh. cat. Ostfildern: Hatje Cantz, 2005.

239

[123] [121] [95]

123. *Portrait of a Woman,* 1938
Gelatin silver print; 22 x 15.6 cm (8¾ x 6⅛ in.). John L. Severance Fund 2007.137

INSCRIPTION
Red stamp on verso of print: *WOLS* [in a circle]

PROVENANCE
The artist's estate, Paris; Baron Ribeyre (Drouot Richelieu), Paris, 17 November 2000, no. 111; David Raymond, New York

René Zuber
French, 1902–1979

Zuber completed an engineering degree at the School for Arts and Manufacturing and in 1927 left for Leipzig to study the book trade at the Graphic Design Institute. There he discovered photographic New Objectivity in Albert Renger-Patzsch's landmark photo book *The World Is Beautiful* (1928). Zuber returned to Paris and joined the technical staff of Emmanuel Sougez's magazine *L'Illustration.* Soon thereafter he was employed at the advertising studio of Etienne Damour, founder of the magazine *Vendre,* shooting photo campaigns for luxury goods makers. In 1932 Zuber opened his own studio with Pierre Boucher, specializing in advertising campaigns. They were joined by Emeric Feher and Maria Eisner, who initiated the Alliance Photo Agency. Besides publishing his photographs as advertisements, Zuber also made work that was widely shown in artistic photography annuals. He became a leader in fine art advertising photography and published technical articles on photographic printing in the early 1930s. Fine art exhibitions featuring his work included *Film und Foto* in Stuttgart (1929), two international photography exhibitions in Brussels (1931–32), and several shows in Paris at the Galerie de la Pléiade (1933–34).

After World War II, Zuber turned to other work, including a small press under which he published an album on the liberation of Paris in 1945. In the 1950s he also delved into the cinema and worked for television in his later years.

121. *Grate over Coins (Quadrillage sur Pièces),* 1932
Gelatin silver print; 22.8 x 17.3 cm (9 x 6⅞ in.). John L. Severance Fund 2007.138

INSCRIPTIONS
Purple copyright stamp on verso of print: *AUCUNE REPRODUCTION NE SERA/AUTORISÉE SANS LA MENTION/PHOTO RENÉ ZUBER/TOUS LES DROITS DE REPRODUCTION/SONT RÉSERVÉS*

In pencil on verso of print: *no. 298*

PROVENANCE
Étude Tajan, Paris, 27 November 1998, no. 298; David Raymond, New York

Piet Zwart
Dutch, 1885–1977

Zwart studied architecture from 1902 to 1907 and in Delft in 1913 before joining Jan Wils's architectural studio as a draftsman in 1919–21. He later worked for Dutch Arts and Crafts architectural firm HP Berlage as chief draftsman. In 1919 Zwart was exposed to the De Stijl movement of art and design led by Wils and Vilmos Huszár and thereafter concentrated his design work along the lines of the pared-down Russian Constructivist aesthetic. In the early 1920s, he received commissions for typography and corporate design and developed radical designs that merged letters, abstract forms, and photography into dynamic, decentralized motifs. He was one of the major figures in the field of modern typography, calling himself a "typotect."

In 1923 Zwart received a large commission from the Nederlandsche Kabelfabriek in Delft, which produced steel cables for industry. In ten years he created more than 275 typographic designs for the firm's corporate identity and advertising campaigns. His photographic work was called "photo typography." That year Zwart met El Lissitzky and forged a rich, ongoing interchange with him. From Lissitzky Zwart learned photogram and photomontage techniques that from 1926 onward found their way into his graphic design projects. As in Lissitzky's *Proun* spaces, Zwart combined his architectural and graphic training into images that aggressively defined the spaces for advertising information and products.

Zwart became a leader in Dutch avant-garde photography, publishing images and opinion pieces. His work was in landmark exhibitions of the period including *Film und Foto* (1929). In 1933 he returned to interior design in the Bauhaus mode. His radical reformist spirit suffered when he was arrested in 1942 in Nazi-occupied Holland. After the war, he returned to industrial design.

95. *Typographic Composition,* 1931
Gelatin silver print, montage; 12.3 x 17.3 cm (4¼ x 6¼ in.). John L. Severance Fund 2007.139

INSCRIPTION
Green copyright stamp on verso of print: *piet zwart rijksstraatweg* #[illegible]/*wassenaar holland*

PROVENANCE
Private collection, Berlin; Kunsthaus Lempertz, Cologne, 2 November 2002, no. 120; David Raymond, New York